bloomingdale's®

bloomingdale's

by Maxine Brady

Harcourt Brace Jovanovich
New York and London

Requests for permission to make copies of
any part of the work should be mailed to:
Permissions, Harcourt Brace Jovanovich,
Inc., 757 Third Avenue, New York, NY 10017

Library of Congress Cataloging in Publication
Data
Brady, Maxine.
    Bloomingdale's.
    1. Bloomingdale Brothers, inc., New York—
History.   I. Title.
HF5465.U6B582   381'.45'00097471
80-15867
ISBN 0-15-113219-4

Printed in the United States of America

First edition
B C D E
Design: Robert Aulicino

For Frank, with love
And for Jane, with respect

Acknowledgments

Books of nonfiction are rarely written in splendid isolation. This one certainly was not. Researching Bloomingdale's long, sometimes obscure, sometimes manifest history led me to numerous people who extended their assistance and goodwill. Some provided advice. Some provided facts. Some directed me toward further sources of information. Some supplied me with illustrations. Some gave encouragement and support. It was all indispensable, and each of them has my gratitude. But for some there must be a special thanks, for the very special roles they played in helping this book come to fruition.

Marvin Traub and Jim Schoff have my deepest appreciation for encouraging me with this project, granting me their time, advice, and support, and giving me access to the entity that is Bloomingdale's. To Richard and Sue Ernst, my thanks for their trust in allowing me to search among the yellowing papers of the family's archives. To Joan Glynn, Gordon Cooke, John Jay, Mary Liska, Margot Rogoff, and Debby Weber, my grateful appreciation for the time they took with me, and the things they did, and the things they made possible.

Betty Rothbart, Ellen O'Neill, Bill Shannon, Drew Lynch, James Seligmann, and the entire staff of the Fairchild library (but especially Barbara Shaw, who's still smiling at the end of an eye-weary day) deserve special mention. So does Siegfried Liebmann, for his memories and his kindness.

There were many others, but this book is quite long enough. Let me just list those I must not forget: Frank Asaro, Charles Banuchi, Ann Bertsch, Jayne Binzer, Mike Blumenfeld, Frank Boehm, Gerri Bowman, Vincent Brennan, Brian Burdine, Fred Burmester, Joan Cuomo, Barbara D'Arcy, Cindy Davidson, Frank De Vito, Dorothy Devlin, Allen Docal, Gillian Freshwater, Barbara Gottlieb, Lester Gribetz, Will Hellemeyer, Margaret Hofbeck, Richard Knapple, Eleanor Koslofsky, Robert Krissel, Sol Leibowitz, Carl Levine, John Manos, Elaine McAllister, Howard Meadows, Ruth Straus Neisser, Fred Palatinus, Hugh Paulk, Sybil Piccone, Noel Rubinton, Kal Ruttenstein, Jeanne Sacklow, Pat Schaum, Jack Schultz, Julian Tomchin, Joyce Tuers, Richard Udell, Amy Wall, Janina Willner, and everyone else who helped.

And most of all, for his advice, assistance, good judgment, and abiding sense of humor, I would like to thank Fred Grumman.

May your lives be filled with elegant bargains.

Contents

Prologue
Welcome to Bloomingdale's, Your Majesty

"Pussycat, pussycat, where have you been?"
"I've been to Bloomingdale's to visit the Queen."

Nineteen seventy-six. The two-hundredth birthday of the United States of America. The celebration of our independence from Great Britain. What does Bloomingdale's do to celebrate this historic occasion? It invites the Queen of England to come visit the store.

That's merely audacity. What makes it remarkable is the fact that she accepted. It started in January of '76. Marvin Traub, then president of Bloomingdale's, issued an invitation to Queen Elizabeth II, *by the grace of God of the United Kingdom of Great Britain and Northern Ireland and of Her other Realms and Territories Queen, Head of the Commonwealth, Defender of the Faith, Sovereign of the British Orders of Knighthood,* descendant of William the Conqueror and of King Arthur, and sixty-second sovereign of the British empire. Since one doesn't simply drop a friendly note to such a personage, Traub contacted both the office of the British consul-general in New York and the British Embassy in Washington, extending an invitation to the Queen and Prince Philip to attend a special fashion show at Bloomingdale's when the royal couple came to the United States later that year.

British officials had begun planning for the Visit, as the embassy staff called the U.S. trip, in late 1974, when Great Britain decided, albeit belatedly, to congratulate her former colony on gaining its status as an independent nation and an ally. The planning for such a state occasion is as detailed and comprehensive as that required to launch a manned rocket into space.

After the initial preparations were made with the State Department and the White House, setting the stage for the Queen to attend the Bicentennial celebrations, officials on both sides of the Atlantic set to work arranging, coordinating, and seeing to the endless details, great and trivial, of the occasion. Early in 1975, more than a year before her arrival, British diplomats David Walker and Edward Glover came to America to devote themselves full time to the specific arrangements. To assist them, they assembled two press experts and two dozen other embassy staff members.

One of the most difficult and delicate of tasks involved deciding which of the innumerable invitations, from officials and private individuals, should be accepted. Although the British Embassy attempted to choose those with the greatest relevance to the Bicentennial, given the strict time schedule allotted to the trip, the Queen herself insisted, as she often does, that she make the final decisions about whom and what to see on her six-day visit to the States.

And so, one day late in the month of April, Bloomingdale's received official acceptance of its invitation: the Queen of England was coming to Bloomie's. And that's when organized bedlam began.

Nothing, absolutely nothing, about a royal visit is left to chance. As the chief of White House protocol commented, for such a state occasion to be successful, there must be no surprises.

On April 22, Jack Morrison, consul commercial of the British Trade Development Office, met with Peggy Healy, then Bloomingdale's public relations director. He announced that several people would visit the store on May 5, to discuss the Queen's visit. Then he handed Healy a list of the entourage.

VISIT OF HER MAJESTY THE QUEEN RECONNAISSANCE PARTY, 5 MAY 1976

1 *Buckingham Palace and British Embassy*

Sir Peter Ramsbotham	Ambassador
Mr Philip Moore	Deputy Private Secretary to The Queen
Mr John Moreton	Minister, British Embassy
Mr Ronald Allison	The Queen's Press Secretary
Mr Richard Fyjis-Walker	Information Counsellor, British Embassy
Air Commodore Archie Winskill	Captain of the Queen's Flight
Mr E C Glover	2nd Secretary, British Embassy
Captain C K K Brown	British Navy Staff
Commander W Corrigan	British Navy Staff
Chief Superintendent Trestrail	The Queen's Chief Police Officer
Miss Christine Bailey	Personal Assistant to Mr Moore
Mr Frank Holland	Travelling Yeoman

2 *State Department*

Mr William Codus	Assistant Chief of Protocol
Miss MaryLou Sheils	Assistant to Mr. Codus
Miss Mary Masserini	Press Liaison Officer
Secret Service Representative	(Washington)

3 *New York*

Mr Gordon Booth	Consul-General
Mr C A Lovitt	Deputy Consul-General
Mr M Shea	Acting Director General, British Information Services
Ambassador Angier Biddle Duke	New York City Commissioner for Civic Affairs and Public Events
Mr L Olshan	Department of Civic Affairs and Public Events
Mr F Shaw	Assistant Manager, Special Service Division, Port Authority of New York and New Jersey
Lt J Grimes	New York Police Department Traffic
Secret Service Representative	(New York)
New York Police Department Intelligence Division Representative	

During the ensuing week, Bloomingdale's devised a detailed memorandum on exactly what would occur during the visit: who would be presented to the Queen, where she would go, what exhibits she would see.

O n May 5 the British reconnaissance party invaded the store. They were taken, en masse, on a walk along the same route that the Queen would later take, entering through the Lexington Avenue doors, riding in elevators up to the fifth floor, glancing at the model room settings Richard Knapple had designed to commemorate the Bicentennial, riding down the escalators, nodding politely as they were led through the china, glass, and silver exhibition area, and considering the display in the men's department on the Third Avenue side of the main floor, from which the Queen would make her exit.

Then everyone assembled in the board room for a question-and-answer session with Bloomingdale's executives. For the next half-hour, they discussed whether it would be proper to present a plaque to the Queen, exactly how many people may be presented to her, and whether or not it is proper to give a gift to the Queen.

It is proper, but not just any gift will do. The group narrowed the possibilities down to three categories: an American Indian artifact, a piece of Early American silver, or a handmade Early American quilt (the Queen collects quilts).

After the meeting, Bloomingdale's intensified its preparations for its portion of the Visit. The royal gift had to be selected, according to the limitations that had been established. Special displays had to be created, specific merchandise made available, the store and its personnel made ready.

Rigid requirements were established for press accreditation, and the applications from myriad reporters and photographers seeking permission to cover the event inside the store were scrutinized in coordination with the U.S. State Department and British Information Services. Ultimately, news pools were formed—CBS's television crew, for example, was stationed on the third floor, NBC's on the fourth, and ABC's on the fifth floor. No TV cameras were permitted on the ground floor, for security reasons. Reporters and photographers from the news services and from key newspapers and magazines were also divided among the floors the Queen was scheduled to visit. This limited the numbers of newspeople necessary to cover the story adequately, and low numbers had been stipulated by the security personnel orchestrating their end of the visit. Commissioner Angier Biddle Duke, then New York City's chief of protocol, called a special meeting on July 1 at the New York City Department of Civil Affairs and Public Events, to iron out the logistics of the pooled news coverage for the New York City segment of the Queen's trip.

Bloomingdale's prepared groups of identification badges. Some were for the press; others were for staff members who would be permitted to remain in their department during the Queen's tour, but who would be separated from her by stanchions and velvet ropes; and still other badges were for the elite who would be permitted within the secured areas.

Candy Pratts, often called Bloomingdale's *enfant terrible* of window display, started doing a special set of windows that "opened" at the end of June and through the first week of July, highlighting special merchandise as well as items relating directly to the Bicentennial. The window featuring Stanley Blacker sportswear also contained a flag bearing the Bicentennial logo, and another window presented "Workwear of America."

New carpeting was installed in elevators 1, 2, and 3, which would carry the Queen and her party. Elevator 4 was assigned to the press, who had to make do with the existing carpet, only slightly scuffed by the shoes of less extraordinary customers. Arrangements were made to borrow antique pieces of Early American silver and Wedgwood, and new Wedgwood pieces were designed expressly for the Bicentennial.

Data on everyone who was to meet the royalty, as well as on those who would be permitted to stand near them, had to be sent to the State Department in advance for security clearance. The Office of Protocol sent the store information detailing proper dress and decorum for those who would actually be presented to the Queen and Prince:

Ladies who will be presented to the Queen and Duke (Prince Philip also bears the title Duke of Edinburgh) should wear street dresses or suits, hats and gloves. When presented to the Queen, they should say only "Your Majesty," and nod their head. If the Queen extends her hand, they can extend their gloved hand. When presented to Prince Philip, they nod and say, "Your Royal Highness," and extend hand if the Duke extends his first.

Gentlemen who will be presented to the Queen and Duke should wear suits and ties. On being presented to the Queen, they should say, "Your Majesty." Thereafter, if they address the Queen, they should say "Ma'am." When presented to the Duke, they nod and say, "Your Royal Highness," and extend hand if the Duke extends his first.

Then the ladies and gentlemen are to "fall *behind* into the entourage, if you are touring with the Queen and/or Duke."

From May through the beginning of July, Bloomingdale's held fifteen dress rehearsals, each one with a minimum of twenty people, who walked through the tour precisely as would the royal party. Key personnel from the British Embassy in Washington, the consulate in New York, Her Majesty's Secret Service, and officials of the royal palace joined members of the U.S. State Department, security agents, top Bloomingdale's executives, and the American fashion designers who were to be introduced to Her Majesty, in rehearsals designed to ferret out every possible mishap before it occurred. Repetitious though they were, the very formality of the rehearsals imbued them with an air of authenticity. In the last one, on July 7, just two days before the real Visit, Mr. and Mrs. Gordon Booth— he was the consul-general—stood in for the Queen and Prince Philip. Designer Donna Karan recalled: "When I stood there waiting for Mrs. Booth, my heart was pounding. You do sort of feel like plain folk. When you've spoken a line like 'It's nice to meet you, Your Majesty,' what else can you say? Believe me, nobody was laughing. This is *the* Queen."

By that time, of course, the real Queen Elizabeth and Prince Philip were already in the United States. They had crossed the Atlantic on the 5,769-ton 412-foot royal yacht *Britannia,* accompanied by fifty-two people. Fourteen were part of the royal "party," and went with the Queen on her tour of seven of the thirteen original colonies. The other thirty-eight members of the entourage were domestic and state staff.

The *Britannia* serves as a base to entertain dignitaries whenever the Queen is in a foreign port, it provides privacy and respite for the traveling monarch, and on this trip it enabled the British to engage in several highly symbolic gestures. The first was the choice of landing site: the royal yacht docked at Penn's Landing in Philadelphia on the morning of Tuesday, July 6. (As David Walker of the British Embassy remarked, "July Fourth was really pushing it." In this visit to a wayward colony, "Forgiveness can go so far.")

The next morning the royal party went on to Washington, D.C., to be welcomed by President Gerald Ford (and Betty), lay a wreath at Arlington National Cemetery, and attend a State Department dinner at the White House. They spent Thursday touring embassies, the Capitol, and the Smithsonian Institution, held a banquet of their own at the British Embassy, and finally set off for New York early Friday morning, July 9, via a rather circuitous route. For the sake of yet more symbolism, they flew to Newark, drove to the naval base at Bayonne, boarded the waiting *Britannia,* and finally arrived in New York by steaming across the Hudson River into New York Harbor, past the Statue of Liberty and a twenty-one-gun salute, and a

fireboat sending five jets of water high into the air in a watery tribute.

The *Britannia* docked at the Battery for the start of a whirlwind one-day visit to New York City: eight stops in six hectic hours. Outside historic Federal Hall in lower Manhattan, where George Washington was sworn in as the first president in 1789, and standing on the site where an Englishman had turned over the colonies to Washington more than two hundred years ago, Queen Elizabeth II was given an honorary citizenship to New York City by then-mayor Abraham Beame, who was born in London. As crowds cheered, she walked the short distance to Trinity Church, stopping to shake hands and, occasionally, chat with people lining the police barricades.

Then on to the Waldorf Astoria to be the guest of the Pilgrims Society of the United States and the English Speaking Union, where Governor Hugh Carey spent most of the luncheon deep in conversation with Prince Philip.

After lunch, freshly bedecked in a different hat, the Queen and her party were taken to the historic Morris-Jumel Mansion in Harlem, which Washington had used as his headquarters in 1776.

Finally, running about forty minutes behind schedule, the Queen came to Bloomingdale's, where she managed to tie up traffic outside and in.

The entourage of sixteen limousines drove south on Fifth Avenue to Fifty-ninth Street, turned east to Lexington Avenue, and then, although the one-way signs clearly pointed in the opposite direction, turned *north* onto normally southbound Lexington. It wasn't a surprise, of course, not on a trip as minutely planned as this one. Police had blocked off Lexington Avenue for several blocks above the store to allow the Queen's limousine to arrive heading north. That way, she could alight from the right side of the car, the side always used by royalty when emerging from a vehicle, be it boat, barge, carriage, or whatever.

The appearance of the cavalcade of limousines was the starting signal for a carefully planned chain of events in and around Bloomingdale's (planning was so precise that a twenty-five-page confidential memo had been prepared by store officials, detailing a minute-by-minute countdown of activities).

Early that morning, according to plan, Bloomingdale's had laid a red carpet from the curb to and up the right side of the stairs to the store entrance. The section of carpet on the street had been covered with canvas to protect it, and the "royal" section of the staircase had been cordoned off. Now, when the royal cavalcade came into sight, the canvas covering and ropes was whisked away: the Queen's foot would be the first to trod the royal pathway.

The vestibule—the "sunken" area just inside the Lexington Avenue entrance—had been cleared of customers since 3:45, and a portrait of the Queen and Prince Philip had been hung in the window. The revolving doors had been collapsed, to permit the Queen to walk through without having to push a pane of glass before her.

Stanchions had been placed on the sidewalk outside the store to keep back the crowd. By 3:00 P.M. so many curious bystanders had gathered to catch a glimpse of real royalty that the New York City police department had added a human barrier: a line of cops frantically calling "Get back! Stay back!" Other officers sat in cars parked all around the building, keeping watch on the crowds, but also craning for a view of the arriving limousines.

When the Queen and Prince Philip stepped out of the first car, Henry Catto, chief of protocol of the United States, stepped up to them to formally present Bloomingdale's chairman of the board, Lawrence Lachman, the store's president, Marvin Traub, and their wives. Then, according to the established protocol, Lachman escorted the Queen through the collapsed revolving doors; behind them, Traub escorted Prince Philip, who in public must always walk behind the Queen. Mrs. Lachman accompanied the Mistress of the Robes—the Duchess of Grafton—and Mrs. Traub accompanied Lady Ramsbotham, wife of the British ambassador to the United States. After more presentations in the vestibule, the party walked up the short staircase to the elevators, which awaited them on the main floor. The automatic mechanism had been disconnected for security purposes, and each elevator now contained a decidedly nervous operator.

The Queen and Prince and their escorts, accompanied by Mr. Catto and his assistant, William Codus, and the inevitable Security Guard, rode in elevator 1, along with the huge planter of red roses that designated this as the royal car.

The rest of the Queen's party rode up in elevators 2 and 3, and the press pool was relegated to number 4. The cars went directly to the fifth floor, the first stop on the Queen's guided tour of Bloomingdale's.

Many customers had heard that Queen Elizabeth was scheduled to visit the store, but no one knew precisely when, or which parts of the store she would see. By the time they found out, it was too late to do much rushing about in an attempt to gain a better view. For security reasons, the moment the Queen entered the store the escalators were stopped, the air conditioning was shut off, and well-guarded velvet ropes blocked off the route of her tour. But many of those inside the store, while considerably crowded and growing increasingly warm, did have excellent vantage points from which to see Her Majesty and the royal party. The Queen had recognized this tour as an opportunity to visit briefly with the American public, so she had requested Bloomingdale's to temporarily remove some merchandise, to provide a bit more room for people to see her. The craning audience waited expectantly for the first glimpse. But they had to look quickly; this was not a casual browsing trip, but a precision journey, timed to the last second. From entrance to exit, it was to take *precisely* twenty-five minutes.

Fifth floor: The Queen and her party were led from the elevator banks along the aisle between "the traditional environment" and the antique shop into the "Red, White, and Bloomingdale's" display area that had been created for the Bicentennial. They were escorted past Model Room 3, complete with blue-denim-covered furniture. An antique English military chest had been borrowed for the occasion and placed outside the model room. It bore a legend card explaining the relationship between the antique and the reproduction leather military chest in the room. To the smiling Queen, the card must have been a blur; she had a total of three minutes to view that model room and the two beside it, both featuring furnishings and accessories from colonial times.

Queen Elizabeth discusses a model room with Senior Vice-President Carl Levine (right) as Bloomingdale's Chairman Lawrence Lachman (left) looks on.

Then the group was led to the escalator (thirty seconds), and rode down to the fourth floor (forty seconds). Here, the crowd already had a hunch about which direction the Queen would enter from.

Stanchions extended from the china department all the way to the shoe department at the other side of the store, and people were lined up ten deep behind them while the staff stood by, glancing about to be sure every display was perfect, occasionally adjusting the drape of a tablecloth, the crease of their own clothing. All of the Bloomingdale's executives seemed to be wearing Bicentennial colors: navy suits, white shirts and, often, red or red-striped ties. They stood, watching the empty escalator, and waited. And the crowd waited. And fidgeted. At 4:45, a uniformed repairman came down the escalator, and the crowd cheered and whistled.

Finally a contingent of Bloomingdale's staff came down, followed by a crew of television cameramen, some precariously turned backward, shooting up the moving stairway as they rode down.

Prince Philip listens as President Marvin Traub describes the merchandise.

Then a crowd of security people came down: about twenty policemen followed by a group of Secret Service men, most with the telltale "hearing aids" (miniature radio receivers) plugged into their ears. Finally, in a gap behind the miniature army, came the Queen. A small woman, standing about five feet four, she seemed even more diminutive and frail as she rode down, smiling softly, her white-gloved hand moving only from the wrist as she made small waving motions to the spellbound crowd below. Behind her, a safe but respectful distance away, came still more police and Secret Service, surrounding Prince Philip.

With the royal couple on the escalator, the crowd burst into spontaneous cheering, oohing, aahing, and conversation, and one tired little girl who had waited patiently to see the Queen turned to her mother and asked, "But where's her crown?"

The royal visitors were shown a collection of Wedgwood designed expressly for the Bicentennial, including a five-color trophy plate of jasper bearing a cameo of Queen Elizabeth II, made in honor of her visit to New York, along with some antique pieces; then she was shown several Early American silver pieces, on loan to the store from the New-York Historical Society. And then it was time to receive her gift from Bloomingdale's.

The store had worked hard to come up with something unique and memorable that would fit within the criteria stipulated by royal protocol. It had located an Indian peace pipe. Its wooden stem was ringed with brass tacks, and its head inlaid with pewter. According to the American Museum of Natural History, which authenticated the pipe, the pewter probably came from the tea packages which were frequently traded to the Indians by the British. The inscription on the pipe reads: "Sioux Peace Pipe from the American Plains 1850–1870. Presented to Her Majesty Queen Elizabeth II on the occasion of her visit to Bloomingdale's New York July 9th, 1976."

Lachman formally presented the peace offering to the British monarch, who graciously accepted it and handed it to Mary Morrison, her lady-in-waiting, who stands conveniently nearby at all such occasions.

Then the group split in two. The Queen, accompanied by Marvin Traub and half the entourage, went down to the third floor to visit a specially prepared fashion boutique called American Classics. To give Her Majesty a feeling for American apparel, partic-

Bloomingdale's Chairman Lachman presented a peace pipe to Britain's Queen Elizabeth. To her right are store President Marvin Traub and Prince Philip.

ularly sportswear, Bloomingdale's had asked designers Ralph Lauren, Calvin Klein, and Donna Karan and Louis Del 'Olio, both of whom design for Anne Klein, to create a special group of fashions for the occasion. Each of these designers was presented to the Queen, who was then, by royal request, shown a mini-fashion show of children's back-to-school clothes, worn by ten very excited young models.

Meanwhile Prince Philip, accompanied by Mr. Lachman and the rest of the group, was shown a series of "Bloomingdale's Best Bets," a specially arranged collection of such notables as the "Talking Calculator," the Pet Rock (which had long since sold out for ordinary customers), and Famous Amos Chocolate Chip Cookies, which the store sold at the rate of two tons per week.

Then Prince Philip, who has expressed interest in the workings of American business, was shown how Bloomingdale's computerized Regitel machines handle transactions, detailing the purchases made, the amounts and taxes, and all other relevant data, which are simultaneously recorded on the purchaser's receipt and charged to the customer's charge account. The Prince listened carefully to an explanation of the system's efficiency and virtues. Afterward he was asked his opinion of this complex facet of American know-how. He nodded politely, said it was all fascinating, and quietly clipped: "But wouldn't it be easier to use cash?"

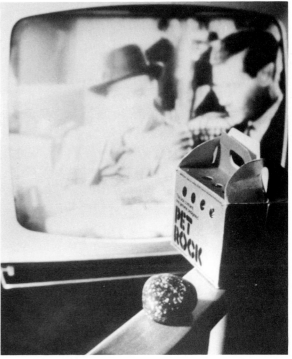

Bloomingdale's started the Pet Rock craze by treating a rock just as you would any other friendly creature. This fellow had a television set to entertain him, and, in case he got hungry, there was a bowl of pretzels nearby.

The royal pair were reunited on the main floor, in the newly erected Aquascutum Shop (the Queen had arrived there via the Third Avenue escalator, which had been reversed for the occasion, according to the incredibly involved plan which, even more incredibly, proceeded without a flaw). As farewells were exchanged at the Third Avenue doors, the large digital clock indicated that the royal tour had taken precisely twenty-five minutes, as scheduled.

The Queen and Lachman consider a display of Wedgwood pointed out by Doug Bertsch.

When the Queen emerged onto the street (no red carpet required), she looked at the people jamming the sidewalks, and the traffic jam caused by the police cordon across Third Avenue, and said, softly: "Now things can get back to normal."

For Third Avenue, perhaps. For Bloomingdale's, it was just another day. The Queen of Spain had been in only two weeks before. And even before this royal visit was over, the store was preparing itself to host 160 wives of senators, governors, and the official diplomatic corps. They were all coming to New York for the next week's Democratic convention, and would be given a special breakfast at the store.

Carrie Donovan, then operating vice-president of communications, watched the Queen and her cavalcade drive off (in the right direction this time), smiled with relief that everything had worked, then turned to go back to her office above the store, to prepare for Bloomingdale's next special event. "It really never stops," she said.

Part 1

From Small Beginnings: The Origin of Bloomingdale's

BLOOMINGDALE'S

Corsets & Millinery.

Suits & Underwear.

938 Third Avenue.

On April 17, 1872, a cool but sunny day, Lyman Bloomingdale and his brother, Joseph, hung bright streamers outside their new retail dry goods store to announce that it was open to the public. A rainbow of pennants fluttered in the breeze, attracting pedestrians to peer into the two large, well-stocked windows. Signs proclaimed: "Great East Side Bazaar" and "Skirts, Corsets, Hosiery, Millinery, Gloves, Fancy Goods." Their curiosity aroused, many people wandered into the store, but few bought anything. At the end of the day, receipts totaled $3.68.

Thus began what ultimately grew into perhaps the world's most elegant and provocative chain of department stores: Bloomingdale's. It was born in the Victorian era, into a New York City that was far different from the one we know today. Bloomingdale's founders had a unique sense of their times, and a talent for predicting both what their countrymen might do and what their customers might want, which enabled them to set trends rather than follow them.

The chain's large flagship store is located only three blocks from the site of the original shop, a continuity of location that has given Bloomingdale's a close relationship with its home community. The history of Bloomingdale's parallels the story of New York from the post–Civil War period to today, and to some extent, to relate one story is to reveal the other.

When Napoleon III reigned over France, from 1853 to 1870, his beautiful and charming consort was the Empress Eugénie, an elegant woman renowned throughout the world for her style and in-novative sense of fashion. When she became pregnant, she vowed not to hide from society for nine tiresome months, as was the custom. Instead, she invented the hoopskirt as a graceful look that would conceal her changing shape. Soon every woman—pregnant or not—craved this new silhouette, and across the ocean in New York, Benjamin Bloomingdale and his elder son, Lyman, opened Bloomingdale's Hoopskirt and Ladies' Notions Shop to enable New York women to keep up with their European counterparts.

It was a demonstration of the Bloomingdale sense of timing: getting in on the first wave of something new, taking the lead in satisfying public demand, and recognizing that nebulous moment when a new style rolls in to nudge out the old. The hoopskirt factory was a huge success until the hoopskirt itself began to go the way of many styles, first into the dim, crowded corners of the fashionable woman's closet, then discarded altogether for history to mention years later in a fashion footnote.

By 1872, Lyman was eager to try something new. Thirty-one years old, he had merchandising experience that dated back to his early youth. At eleven, he'd begun working in retail stores between school sessions—everything from a crockery store to a watchmaker's supply house—starting with odd jobs as a stock boy and delivery boy, and working up to salesman and buyer. He had operated a store in Leavenworth, Kansas, and gained organizational and managerial skills from his experience in the Civil War when he served as an orderly sergeant in the First Regiment of the Kansas State Militia.

Working with his father in their hoopskirt

Lyman G. Bloomingdale, 1841–1905

Joseph B. Bloomingdale, 1842–1904

business, Lyman had encouraged and put into effect the idea not only of selling from their small shop in Manhattan, but of carrying their goods to individuals and other retailers outside the local market.

Lyman was confident in his finely honed perception of what people wanted to buy and of how best to attract customers. But his merchandising theories were sometimes radical, and working for other people, he'd not been free to apply them fully to see how effective they might really be. So he decided to open his own store.

His brother, Joseph, was equally energetic and also widely experienced in the merchandising field. A successful traveling salesman, he had sold the Bloomingdale hoopskirts throughout the eastern states and had even carried them west to Califor-

nia. Joseph had fine sales techniques himself, but he recognized that his brother's retailing instincts were unusually keen. So when Lyman began to discuss opening his own business, Joseph agreed to join him. In March of 1872, the two brothers began to look for a good location for a store.

The heart of New York City's shopping center at that time was Union Square—the junction of Fourteenth Street and Broadway. Fine shops, some of them still in existence, were situated in or near the area: F.A.O. Schwarz had its children's wonderland of toys and games at 42 East Fourteenth Street; Gorman & Company and W. & J. Sloan were at opposite corners of Broadway and Nineteenth Street. A. T. Stewart, who had opened New York's (and very probably the world's) first department store in 1846, moved his emporium "uptown" to Broadway and Ninth Street in 1859, and Lord & Taylor, which had opened in the 1850s, moved in 1871 to an elegant new site at the corner of Broadway and Twentieth Street, in the vanguard of the northward move that was beginning to change the face of the island of Manhattan. Nonetheless, Union Square remained the merchandising center of fashionable New York. Elegant theaters and concert halls had opened there after the end of the Civil War. In 1866, Steinway Hall had opened at 109 East Fourteenth Street, and it remained the focal point of classical music in the United States for the next twenty-five years.

New York City as a whole was, then as now, a mixture of great wealth and abject poverty. The contrast between the two classes showed in what people wore and where they lived. The stately homes of the wealthy and successful either faced the spacious expanse of Fourteenth Street, framed Union Square, or were situated on Fifth Avenue between Fourteenth and Thirty-fourth streets. Elegant residential New York moved no further east than Fifth Avenue.

Manhattan's East Side, however, was home to the working class and the poor. Slums covered much of the southeastern tip of the island up to and past Fourteenth Street, which was far less elegant there than it was farther west. People of the middle class, able to choose where they might live, avoided the area north of Fourteenth Street and east of Third Avenue, and there the real estate speculators built tenements extending north into Harlem.

Yet it was in this area, in what was then

the uptown East Side, that Lyman Bloomingdale sought a site for his new store. He sensed a change coming: the city had, twelve years before, purchased a huge tract of land (for $5.5 million) and was busily creating a green haven of lakes, trees, hills, and footpaths to be called Central Park.

The Metropolitan Museum of Art had just opened on Fifth Avenue and Fifty-third Street, with the valuable collection of John Taylor Johnston, one of the founders of the museum, as its first exhibit. This was hardly a location in the heart of town, and visitors to the museum designed their trips there as a sort of expedition; many combined a trip to the Metropolitan with a picnic on the as yet unmanicured lawns of Central Park.

Lyman Bloomingdale suspected that the park would be a constant lure for visitors and would also lead to a considerable increase in the value of the surrounding property. In 1872, when Ulysses S. Grant was president, the newly reunited nation was emerging from the strain and hardship of the Civil War into a time of vigorous growth. New York City, with a population of nearly one million people, was a key manufacturing center, with imports and exports valued at $569,337,000. It was an era of invention, of emerging urban amenities and style (indoor plumbing, electricity), and the city promised to grow and prosper as never before, expanding almost monthly into the rural areas to the north, filling in more and more open fields and vacant lots each year.

Appraising these changes, Lyman decided that the East Side, especially the neighborhood nearest the southern tip of

Central Park, was going to become an increasingly valuable location. Against the
better judgment of fellow businessmen,
who suggested he and Joseph try to acquire a space near Union Square, the
Bloomingdale brothers followed their instincts and negotiated to rent a store at
938 Third Avenue, near Fifty-sixth Street,
just a few blocks east of a popular skating
rink at Fifty-ninth Street and Fifth Avenue. The store was narrow but deep,
twenty feet by seventy-five feet, and the
rent was, for that day, exorbitant: $2,400
for the first year, increasing to $3,600 for
the second. But the store had a feature
that, to Lyman, justified the rent: two
large, perfect plate-glass windows—the
best on the Avenue—which would provide
exciting showcases for the hundreds of
items the store would sell. The brothers
checked through the neighborhood once
more, and concluded that, rent notwithstanding, this was the best location. Hoping they
were right, they signed the lease.

Their original stock consisted of a wide
variety of clothing, accessories, and inci-
dentals. In total, it cost between $7,000
and $8,000, which was financed partly by
their own capital and partly by loans from
relatives.

While Joseph organized the stock and
made careful records of their inventory,
Lyman went to work decorating the two
windows. He had devised a theory, radical
for that time, that a shop window should
not attempt to display one of each kind of
merchandise the store carried, but rather
that the windows should be a silent stage, a
panorama designed to catch the attention
of even the casual passerby. Once interest
had been sufficiently aroused, he believed,

1872	
April	897 18
May	3 119 05
June	3 429 83
July	3 276 85
August	2 597 40
September	216 9 67
October	264 4 38
November	3 415 81
December	3 816 89
	25 367 04

Handwritten entries in the store's ledger list
sales figures for the first year of business.

that individual would probably take a moment to step inside to see the rest of the show. At that point, a passerby would be likely to become a customer.

It was all hypothetical, however, still to be proven—or disproven. The first day's sales figures hardly represented a triumphant beginning, but the little store attracted attention, and quickly gained a steady clientele of local customers. The first week's gross was $242.92, and within just one month, sales had improved so dramatically that the storeroom partition had to be knocked down to give the sales area space to grow. Slowly but surely, the store began to gain a reputation as the place to find decent—even very good—products at reasonable prices.

The young business progressed fairly smoothly until economic calamity struck the country. Just as New York was finally breathing free of the Civil War, a depression began to brew. Around the world, a general decrease in prices had prompted a rash of stock speculation and overdevelopment in the West, resulting in a financial panic which built rapidly to the point of crisis. In September 1873, just eighteen months after Bloomingdale Brothers opened its doors, the crash came. Hundreds of millions of dollars were lost in one brutal day, and a depression began that eventually took a three-year toll on the city.

In an effort to minimize the effects of the depression on their own enterprise, Lyman and Joseph carefully analyzed the financial prospects of their existing or potential customers. They realized that most of their regular clients were not speculators who had been wiped out in the stock

Business card, 1873

market crash, but were from the conservative middle class, whose jobs were fairly secure. Most of their customers worked at trades so linked with basic needs that their jobs were virtually indispensable; they wouldn't starve, but their purchasing power was decidedly curtailed.

So Bloomingdale Brothers revised its merchandising policy: they would now carry only goods that provided the best possible value for the lowest possible price. And they decided to announce their new policy openly, to demonstrate their sensitivity to their customers' financial predicaments—and to promote some goodwill for their store.

To achieve this dual end, Lyman came up with the innovative *19th Ward Gazette,* a free newspaper that supplemented the store's regular advertising. Focusing on local news, particularly the humorous anecdotes and human-interest stories of neighborhood happenings, it was a combination advertising bulletin and goodwill ambassador, and it was something no other store had. It provided light news to counteract the pain of the depression, it identified

Bloomingdale Brothers even more strongly with the community, and it effectively attracted more customers to the shop that featured high value and low prices.

The effects of the depression were severe; many businesses lagged or closed over the next seventeen years. But Bloomingdale's continued to prosper. Customers appreciated the opportunity to buy good-quality items without incurring financial hardship, and developed a loyalty to the store. Decades later, in the Great Depression that began in 1929, Bloomingdale's returned to this successful policy of adapting itself to customers' pocketbooks; it became the only department store in the country whose sales actually surpassed those of previous "boom" years.

Lyman and his wife, the former Hattie Collenberger, lived above the store. It was there that their oldest son, Samuel, who later became president and chairman of the board of Bloomingdale's, was born. As residents of the community, they were in tune with the concerns and tastes of their neighbors, whom they would greet on leisurely strolls.

When Lyman and Joseph had opened their shop in 1872, Fifty-ninth Street on the East Side was almost at the outskirts of the city proper. A horse-drawn trolley ran up Second Avenue as far north as 122nd Street, carrying New Yorkers to the frame houses and occasional groups of row houses that had been built there in what was then an inexpensive suburbia. But those who lived there had to spend long hours commuting to jobs in lower Manhattan.

Anything east of Madison Avenue and south of Fifty-ninth Street was a working-class or middle-class neighborhood. Brick row houses, interspersed with occasional four- or five-story tenement buildings, lined most of the crosstown streets from Third Avenue to the East River, while more tenements lined First, Second, and Third avenues. But the city was far from densely developed even here. Occasional shanties, garbage dumps, stockyards, and quarries dotted the unpaved streets near Fifth Avenue. Park Avenue was even more unsavory. Stockyards, garbage dumps, and factories lined the sidewalks above Fortieth Street, culminating in the F. & M. Schaefer brewery, which occupied the block between Fiftieth and Fifty-first streets (the site now occupied by St. Bartholomew's Church). North of Forty-second Street, railroad tracks and switching yards ran down the middle of the wide dirt avenue. Where the Waldorf-Astoria Hotel now stands, there was originally a potter's field.

ess than a decade later, radical changes were revitalizing the city as a whole and this area in particular. Lower Fifth Avenue, once the residential bastion of enormous wealth, had suffered an influx of businesses, which, desirable though they were to the residents, nonetheless robbed the neighborhood of its exclusivity. The fine shops, hotels, and restaurants had spread upward from Fourteenth Street and Union Square and now extended along Fifth Avenue up into the forties. So New York's elite moved even farther north, toward the beckoning green of Central Park. Elegant brownstones were built along the side streets from the upper forties to the park, and the accoutrements of the rich followed their patrons. On Fifth

Avenue between Fiftieth and Fifty-first streets the regal St. Patrick's Cathedral, begun in 1858, was completed in 1879 (except for the twin spires, which weren't finished until 1888). The Fifth Avenue Presbyterian Church had moved up Fifth Avenue from Nineteenth Street to its present location at Fifty-fifth Street. Exclusive clubs and expensive hotels opened in elegant decorum.

Not everyone rushed to move to such a distant section of the city, yet. A. T. Stewart, who had shown great foresight in creating the first store to sell a variety of merchandise, misjudged the speed of the city's northward rush when, in 1864, he began construction of a white marble mansion at the corner of Fifth Avenue and Thirty-fourth Street. By the time it was completed, ten years and $3 million later, opulent New York had passed him by.

It wasn't only the lure of Central Park; there was another, more ominous reason to move north. The increasing density of lower Manhattan now threatened to cover much of the sky, as well as the streets. In 1872, construction of the Western Union building had begun. With a mixture of awe and horror, New Yorkers watched it rise to the unheard-of height of ten stories. The Tribune building, only a few blocks away, went it one better. Several stories higher than any other building in New York at the time, these were the portents of building changes that would ultimately transform the business section of the city. And as they rose, the middle and upper classes fled north to the sanctuary of the relatively open lands near the park.

There was one more factor: the railroads. In 1875, construction began on what would become the Third Avenue Elevated Railroad, which would run all the way up to East 129th Street. By 1877, one year before the completion of the "El," this combination of factors caused property values between Fortieth and Sixtieth streets to skyrocket. Business and home sites changed hands at fantastic rates, sometimes as often as sixteen times a day, as real estate profits went wild. The influx of new homes could only bring more and more customers to the area, and the Bloomingdale brothers once more reassessed their store. They'd already begun to stock a greater variety of merchandise in the waning years of the depression, as their customers, with more available money to spend, had shown a growing willingness to buy more diversified items. And if their predictions were correct and many potential customers would be moving into the area, the once-comfortable shop suddenly seemed too small.

On July 5, 1877, Bloomingdale Broth-

In 1880 the brothers expanded into a five-story building on the corner of 56th Street and Third Avenue.

ers moved a few doors south, to 924, 926, and 928 Third Avenue. The additional space enabled them to increase their lines of merchandise, which further increased their business so much that the new, larger store was soon too small. Three years later, the brothers acquired a five-story building on the southwest corner of Fifty-sixth Street and Third Avenue. It had plenty of the good window space that Lyman now considered a necessity. The move was only a short distance from the original location, but it put them into a new category: all at once, Bloomingdale's had become a department store.

While Joseph supervised the day-to-day operation of the store, Lyman devoted an increasing amount of his energy to promotion. He began to place full-page advertise-

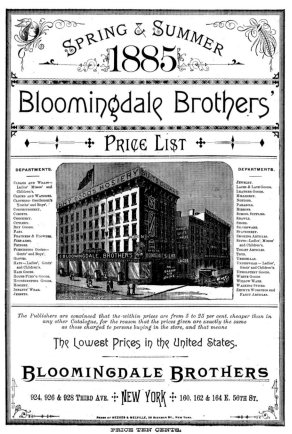

ments in the daily newspapers; at the time, it was an extremely expensive experiment. The ads emphasized high value for low cost, which was the trademark of the store, but with the end of the depression they also included mention of higher-priced items to tantalize customers.

In-store promotions were also devised to tempt passersby into the store. In the book department, for instance, a young woman read aloud from current popular books, while in one of the store windows an employee demonstrated the making of stockings on a tubular form with a newly invented machine.

A woman shopping at Bloomingdale's in the early 1880s could find a genuine mink neckpiece and muff for $10—or an extra fancy one for $20. If she preferred a chinchilla collar, five inches deep, it would cost her $18. A hoopskirt was 50 cents, with perky six-ruffle bustles priced from $1.25 and cambric corset covers with lace trimming just $1. And if she wanted the utmost in fashion, she might splurge on a pair of kid shoes for $1.25, to go with a 78-cent tea gown.

Her husband could pick up a nice selection of shirts priced at 48 cents. Suits and overcoats, however, were more costly items at $9.98 apiece.

With the additional floor space available in the new building, Bloomingdale's expanded its line of merchandise to include furniture. During the Christmas sale, a piano could be bought for $225, including cabinet chair with rubber cover. When an extended payment plan was inaugurated, the piano was available for $5 down and $1 per week.

If neither the husband nor the wife had

ever learned how to play the piano with finesse, they might prefer Bloomingdale's new Victor Talking Machine: wind it up and hear one of three selections, such as "Little Annie Rooney," "Hush, Don't Wake the Baby," or "I Love You As the Roses Love the Dew." They could hum along while reclining on silk plush suites bought for $45 to $100, or overstuffed ones from $150 to $250, and they could rest their sherry glasses on pillar extension tables bought for $11.50 to $25.

Bloomingdale's was doing very well. By 1879, the Third Avenue El raced along New York's East Side from 67th to 129th Streets, making the store extremely accessible to the people living in the northern suburbs, and the sales records of the period showed incredible increases. In 1877, sales totaled $184,184. By 1883 they had swelled to $851,156. But it wasn't only because of the El. Lyman's inventiveness and showmanship were gaining a steadily growing audience of customers. It all worked—the newspaper advertisements, which stood out in part because there were few or no other ads in the daily newspapers; the "special events" in the store which entertained or instructed people even as they drew them in to buy; the *19th Ward Gazette;* the good value and good prices and the larger-than-ever selection of merchandise.

New York's neon started at Bloomingdale's. Less than a year after electric arc lights began to be manufactured, Lyman had them installed outside the store. Mesmerized crowds gathered to stare as two carbon pencils attached to the wall played Ping-Pong with an electric spark which shot back and forth between them.

Lyman's interest in new inventions extended to the practical, as well as the promotional. In 1883, seven years after the telephone was invented, only 4,500 phones existed in New York City. One of them was at Bloomingdale's.

In only a few years, the flourishing business had outgrown its third store. Again, it was time to seek more space, and with this fourth and final move Bloomingdale's reaffirmed its commitment to the Upper East Side.

This time, there was never even a question of whether a downtown location would be wiser. With each year, it became more evident that Lyman's original hunch had been correct: The residential section of New York was moving uptown. Upper Fifth Avenue had become a showplace for some of the greatest and grandest palatial mansions this side of the Atlantic. The Vanderbilt family dominated the crown of the Avenue with their four fabulous homes which cost, in total, $15 million to build and furnish. The Huntingtons had commissioned an Italian palazzo, and the Fricks' eighteenth-century manor house was adorned with Italianate embellishments. Bloomingdale's did not then cater to the very wealthy, but the rich brought with them hosts of tradespeople and servants, and those who serviced the rich were in turn serviced by Bloomingdale's.

The Brooklyn Bridge, connecting lower Manhattan with the huge borough of Brooklyn, had opened in 1883 as the world's first steel-wire suspension bridge. An armada of schooners, their sails open full, celebrated the opening with an exuberant display of fireworks. With a span of 1,595 feet, the bridge was then the longest

82　　　**BLOOMINGDALE BROS.' PRICE LIST FOR FALL AND WINTER, 1882-3.**

Nos. 924, 926 and 928 Third Ave., and 160 and 162 East 56th St., New York.

HAIR GOODS.

Grecian Scallop.

2832　Grecian Scallop, 8 rows......69c, 10 rows 79c

Crown Scallop.

2833　Crown Scallop, 8 rows, 69c; 10 rows......79c

Patent Front Wave.

2834　Patent Front Wave, with movable parting
....$1.19

Ring Scallop.

2835　Ring Scallop.....................95c

Perfection.

2836　Small.................................39c
2837　Large.................................59c

HAIR GOODS.

Our hair goods counters are in charge of the most practical hair dressers, who understand hair work in all its branches. Every article necessary for the dressing of the hair in the fashionable style furnished to match all shades of hair at the most reasonable rates.

Montague Coquet.

2838　Montague Coquet.......................42

Ultimatum.

2839　Ultimatum...........................59c

Seaside Coquette.

2840　Seaside Coquette.......................69c

ADVICE.

In ordering Hair Goods do not fail to enclose a sample of your hair.

Ventilated Star Wave.

2841　Ventilated Star Wave for covering head and ornamenting the forehead, price..............$2 39

Le Bon Ton.

2842　Le Bon Ton patent movable parting, with fine wave....................................$1.19

Patent Ventilated Scallop.

2843　Patent Ventilated Scallop...............$1.39

Patent Ventilated Wave Scallop.

2814　Patent Ventilated Wave Scallop.........$1.50

Ventilated Coquet.

2845　Ventilated Coquet.....................$1.49

195. Imported Cashmere Jersey, handsomely braided in front and on sleeves, black, blue and garnet, $4 25

196. Elegant Black Cashmere Jersey, trimmed with gilt braid (imported).................$6 75

197. Neat Cashmere Jersey (imported), with vest insertion; trimmed with braid, black only, $4 50

198. Black Cashmere Jersey (imported), trimmed with gilt braid, Grecian style..............$7 00

199. Very richly-braided Jersey, made of stockinette cloth, fan back and bow, black only, $2 75, 3 25 and 4 00
200. Same, without fan back, $1 75

201. Very rich Cashmere Jersey (imported), with vest insertion; embroidered and scalloped, various colors.....................$5 25

202. Black French Cashmere Jersey (imported), trimmed with gilt braid.........$4 25

203. Black Cashmere Jersey, richly braided all over; up to size 46 bust measure.......... ....$4 75

204. Elegant Jersey, richly beaded (our own importation), made of fine French Jersey Cloth, black only..............$4 75 and 5 50

205. Imported Cashmere Jersey, coat back, colors black, garnet, blue, brown and cream, $2 65, 2 85, 3 25 and 3 75
206. Same, of Domestic Cashmere, black only, $1 50, 1 75 and 2 25

207. Elegant black all-wool Cashmere Jersey (imported), scalloped and trimmed with gilt braid, $4 25

208. Very rich black Jersey, made of Jersey Cloth, trimmed with gilt and mohair braid............$4 25

209. Misses' Jersey of Jersey Cloth, trimmed with black and gilt braid, colors blue, brown and garnet, $2 15

210. Misses' Jersey of fine Jersey Cloth, with trimming of same; color braid outside and Hercules braid at bottom inside between scallops; colors garnet, blue and brown.....................$2 15

211. Lisle Thread Jerseys, plain black only............. 65c 95c
212. Worsted Jerseys, all colors, 98c, $1 25, 1 50
213. Misses' and Children's Jerseys, all colors...........85c and $1 25
214. Fine Imported Cashmere Jerseys..........................$1 85

215. Misses' Jersey of Jersey Cloth, trimmed with gilt braid, garnet, blue and brown.............$2 15

341. Handsome Dress of Cashmere; skirt with two tucks, and plaid fold between; body of plain goods; Mother Hubbard yoke and sash, both of plaid; sleeves trimmed to match; all colors.
Years,   2   4   6   8   10
Price, $1 95, 2 10, 2 25, 2 40, 2 60

342. Child's all-lace Dress, with two deep ruffles on bottom.
Sizes,   4, 6   8, 10   12 years.
Price, $3 25,   2 60   2 95

343. Misses' Pique Dress, trimmed with Hamburg embroidery,
Sizes,   8,   10,   12 years.
Price $2 00

344. Child's Dress of all wool plain and plaid goods; Fedora front; deep box-plaiting at bottom; handsome drapery; deep rolling collar, trimmed with ribbon; all colors.
Years,   4   6   8   10
Price, $3 35, 3 50, 3 65, 3 80

Children's Spring Cloaks.

345. Neat Mother Hubbard Walking Coat of basket flannel, collar and cuffs trimmed with lace; all colors.
Sizes, 1 to 5 years,..........$2 50

346. Child's Coat of Basket Cloth; double collar bound with satin cord and satin ribbon sash; colors, cream, light blue, pink and garnet. Sizes, 2 to 6 years of age.... $4 25
347. Same, of Gilbert all-wool Plaid, Striped Flannel or Jersey Cloth.
Age,   2   4   6   8 years.
Price, $3 75, 4 25, 4 75, 5 25

348. Very pretty Child's Suit, made of all-wool Ladies' Cloth; yoke, and side plaited back and front; ribbon belt.
Sizes,   2   3   4   6   8 yrs.
Price, $4 25, 4 55, 4 87, 5 52, 6 17

349. Misses' Spring Newmarket, in fine French diagonal or Ladies' cloth, double breasted, trimmed with heavy silk cord.
Sizes,   2   4   6   8 yrs.
Price, $2 60, 2 95, 3 25, 3 60
350. Sizes, 10   12   14   16 yrs.
Price, $4 00, 4 50, 4 95, 5 40

351. Child's Suit, made of Tricot, with colored ribbon bow.
Age,   4,   6,   8,   10,   12 yrs.
Price, $4 25, 4 75, 5 25, 5 75, 6 25

352. Neat Mother Hubbard Child's Walking Coat, of all-wool plaid goods, in all colors.
Sizes, 2 to 4 years...........$2 98

ENTIRELY NEW.
353. Very handsome Child's Walking Coat, of all-wool Cashmere, richly embroidered all over with fine embroidery silk, and trimmed with elegant bows of ribbon; sleeves and bottom made to lengthen without extra work; colors, cream, light blue and cardinal.
Sizes, from 1 to 3 years.....$11 98

354. Child's Mother Hubbard Cloak, basket flannel; colors, light blue, cream, cardinal, garnet and navy, sizes, 6 months to 4 years.... $3 75

Shawls, Etc.

1. Elegant all-wool Cashmere Scarf, can be had plain or with embroidery, all colors; price, plain, $2 75 and $3 50; embroidered, $3 75, 4 50, 6 00 and 8 50

2. Hand-knitted Shetland Wool Shawl, in shell or basket stitch, in blue, black, white or cardinal, $1 50, 1 75, 2 00 and 2 50

3. Machine made, fancy stitch, 75c, $1 00, 1 25, 1 50, 1 75, 2 00 and 2 50

4. Hand made......$1 50, 1 85, 2 50, 3 00, 3 50 and 4 00

5. Hand made Zephyr Breakfast Scarfs............$1 75

6. Embroidered Cashmere Fichu, all-wool, black only. $1 75, 2 25, 3 00, 3 50, 4 00, 4 50 and 5 00

7. Imported Jacquard Shawl, plaid center and broché border......................$7 50 and 9 00

8. Camel's Hair, felled centers..$65 00 to 75 00

9. Imitation, $9 00, 10 50, 12 50, 15 00, 18 00, 22 50, 25 00 to.....................$30 00

10. Square Persian Shawls, various colors and designs......$2 00, 3 50, 5 00, 6 00, 8 00 and 10 00

11. Checked all-wool Shawl, Watervliet make, $3 85

12. Waterloo make.....................$4 15

13. Rochester make.....................$4 00

14. Sterling make............. ......$3 65

15. Blanket Shawl, plain centers, with checked borders, extra heavy.....$7 00, 8 50 and 10 00

16. French Silk Broche Shawls, $10 50, 12 00 aud 15 00

suspension bridge in the world.

Lower Manhattan had become the province of the export-import trade; the rest of the island was experiencing an even faster northward flow of residences and businesses. The entertainment center, too, now shifted; while the majority of theaters had been located on or near Fourteenth Street, the Theatre Comique and others made their new home on or around Forty-fifth Street and Broadway.

There was no looking back; it seemed impossible that lower Manhattan would ever again be a merchandising center. Would the center move *above* Fifty-ninth Street? Lyman and Joseph thought not: Central Park, museums, and other municipal and private establishments had laid down a structure that would make this part of the city fairly stable. Watching stores hustle to move uptown, the brothers could only think that other merchants were trying to catch up with them. Whether by luck or by perspicacity, they'd chosen the right location in the first place. Now, with this latest relocation, they determined to solidify their claim and reaffirm their faith in the Upper East Side.

By the beginning of 1886, plans were underway to build a six-story store at 990–998 Third Avenue. It would have 100 feet of frontage on Third Avenue, and 145 feet on Fifty-ninth Street. Lyman knew that the emerging residential neighborhood meant that more and more people would be strolling by the new store, so he arranged with the architects to construct an unbroken line of windows at street level. This theaterlike showcase for merchandise anticipated the concept of "window shopping" even though the term had

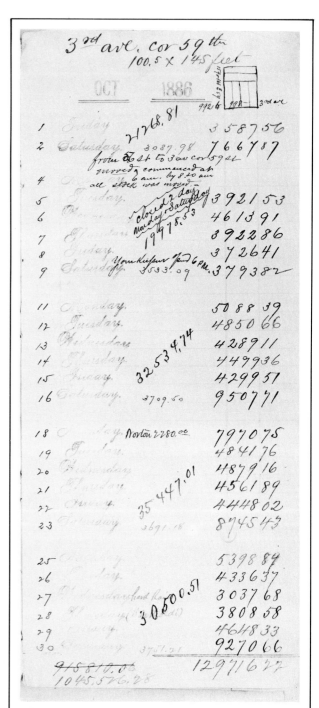

The next move was to a small building on the corner of 59th Street and Third Avenue, which is now only a fraction of the present store. Note the ledger entry for October 2: "Commenced move at 6 AM. By 8:30 AM all stock was moved."

not yet become a part of the language.

The first story of the new building was an awesome eighteen feet high, creating an impressive main floor that would lend itself to ever-changing, eye-catching displays. The second story was fifteen feet high, and the top four floors were each twelve feet high. The floors were so solidly designed and built that they did not need any strengthening when later years brought additions and remodeling to the store.

Lest some customers avoid the top floors because they wouldn't or couldn't climb so high, two cable-operated elevators were installed. Although steam-powered hoists had been introduced in New York in the 1830s, they were only used for merchandise. Passenger elevators were virtually unknown until 1870, and by 1886 were still a fascinating and terrifying rarity. Ever the master promoter, Lyman termed his elevators "sky carriages," announced them with great fanfare, and thus attracted people into the store to try out the wondrous conveyances. Outfitted with plate-glass mirrors, mahogany walls, and little upholstered seats, each "sky carriage" was a miniature parlor which carried customers from floor to floor in inimitable grandeur.

Before the elevators could be approved for public use, of course, they had to be tested. A glass of water and an egg were placed on the floor of each car to test the automatic stop mechanism. The car was sent down; to the surprise of many of the onlookers, the water didn't spill and the egg didn't break. Next, each car made a second trip during which the glass of water and the egg were accompanied by a nervous operator. Only after that trip was the conveyance pronounced safe.

A few weeks before the new store opened, the Statue of Liberty was unveiled. Lyman was invited to attend the ceremony, but he was too busy taking care of the myriad details involved in the completion of the new building. Instead, the precocious Samuel represented the family aboard the cutter which carried the official party of dignitaries to the celebration. New Yorkers who read about the event and who followed the *Evening World*'s day-to-day campaign to raise money for the statue also saw Bloomingdale's advertisements on adjoining pages. The ads announcing the opening of the new store took the form of a poem, pharaphrasing "Excelsior":

The shades of night were falling fast
When thro' Third Avenue I passed
And saw great crowds throng round a store,
The windows this brief legend bore: LOWER.

High quality, low cost, soaring sales: this continued to be Bloomingdale's focus, for while customers numbered more than in the past, socioeconomically they were still the same: lower middle class, tradespeople, blue-collar workers who liked nice things but couldn't buy them at most other stores because of high costs. For them, Bloomingdale's was the only place to shop.

The new store finally opened on October 5, 1886. Samuel Bloomingdale said that he "was at school at the time, but I remember the day it opened there, and the commotion that was caused by the fact that it had two elevators."

The store opened early and closed late. Except, of course, for March 12, 1888. On that day, two years after the opening of the

MARCH 1888

Date	Day	Weather	Remarks	Sales
	Mon.		over	1 4 4 8 0 5 1
	Tues.			
	Wed.			
1	Thurs.	cloudy		4 8 2 1 74
2	Fri.	cloudy, rain	Adv. for week 162.80	4 5 7 3 85
3	Sat.	clear, windy		10 3 9 1 27
			Sal. 4972.37	3 4 2 6 7 37
5	Mon.	cloudy, gold	Special Sale of Boys Clothing	7 1 7 1 31
6	Tues.	clear & cold	from the fire of Stern, Folk & Co	6 5 5 6 95
7	Wed.	" "	40 m circulars	6 5 7 9 05
8	Thurs.	" windy		6 0 3 9 19
9	Fri.	" "	Adv for week 397.—	5 0 1 7 01
10	Sat.	" fine		8 7 6 7 63
			Sal. 5035.61	4 0 1 3 1 14
12	Mon.	Blizzard	closed at 4.45 P.M.	1 4 0 1 36
13	Tues.	snow, stormy	cars stopped, most of stores closed	1 7 7 6 17
14	Wed.	snow forenoon	melting in the afternoon	3 5 0 9 04
15	Thurs.	clear, melting		6 2 2 2 73
16	Fri.	" "	Adv. for week 382.35	5 5 8 3 79
17	Sat.	" "		9 2 3 5 77
			Sal. 4747.08	2 7 7 2 8 86
19	Mon.	clear, mild	Furniture Opening	7 0 1 6 41
20	Tues.	rain, cloudy	Millinery Opening	4 6 2 2 17
21	Wed.	rain, all day	" Spring "	4 4 4 8 41
22	Thurs.	snowing	" Goods "	5 6 8 9 57
23	Fri.	cold & clear		5 2 1 0 83
24	Sat.	" "	Adv. for week 656.35	9 6 3 1 40
			Sal. 4992.15	3 6 6 1 8 79
26	Mon.	rain all day	Sale of 9¢ Sateens	4 7 5 5 24
27	Tues.	Drizzling "	Isaach	5 4 2 4 64
28	Wed.	rain		5 5 5 7 04
29	Thurs.	clear in the afternoon only		5 2 0 9 98
30	Fri.	clear, mild	Good - Friday	6 0 9 0 78
31	Sat.	fine		1 1 5 0 1 29
			Sal. 5097.14	3 8 5 3 8 97
			20½% over last year	1 6 2.8 0 4 1

For most of its existence, Bloomingdale's has recorded daily weather reports. It still does. Weather conditions both influence and explain sales figures.

new store, came the great blizzard. The storm was so severe that it virtually paralyzed the East Coast; into Bloomingdale's daily ledger someone conscientiously penned a single word: "Blizzard." Even more remarkably, the store was closed at the unheard-of time of 4:45 P.M. The next day, although the ledger noted "snow, stormy, cars stopped, most of the stores closed down," Bloomingdale's was open and recorded modest sales.

Americans in the 1880s craved imported merchandise, for Europe was viewed as the style leader for the rest of the world. Americans were intrigued by French fashions, which were regularly illustrated in *Godey's Lady's Book,* and ornate English and French antiques were decidedly favored over traditional American furniture. Lyman decided to make European merchandise regularly available at Bloomingdale's. In 1886, he appointed Sam Mayers as the store's foreign trade representative. Mayers and Edward C. Blum, a trimmings importer, crossed the ocean to establish the first of Bloomingdale's foreign contacts. (Blum, who later worked with Abraham Abraham, founder of Abraham and Straus, eventually became president of both A&S and Federated Department Stores, the management corporation founded in 1929 which now oversees Bloomingdale's and other major department stores.)

Soon Mayers, Blum, and other representatives made trips three times a year to Europe. The first European Bloomingdale's office was in Paris; later, Berlin, Vienna and other key cities became part of the Bloomingdale network. The aggressive

Business card of the Paris branch

American store was the talk of German, French, Italian, and Spanish merchants, and European goods not readily available at most New York stores were easy to find at Bloomingdale's.

Sales soared. At the end of the first year of business at the new location, the sales figures jumped $500,000, and at a time when the population of New York City was 2.5 million, Bloomingdale's annual gross was $2 million.

The sparkle of Bloomingdale's was now international, and its available merchandise, both domestic and imported, was unusually diversified. On March 5, 1880, for example, the *New York Times* reported that at "Bloomingdale Brothers' special preliminary opening of trimmed and untrimmed millinery . . . ladies . . . found a large and varied stock to examine and admire."

The array of fashionable items at Bloomingdale's was dazzling. For the many women who made their own clothing, the store's sewing center became famous for its large assortment of fabrics and notions, all reasonably priced. One could buy silks and satins in a dozen different hues—as many as twenty yards of which might be used for a single afternoon gown. Many types of trim were available, along with lace sashes. Bustles were still in fashion, but the newly emerging softer look, plus the increased popularity of the bicycle, made them so impractical that they soon became obsolete.

Bicycles themselves were a hot item at Bloomingdale's. In New York City nearly $20 million was invested in the manufacture of bicycles; while most of these were exported to other areas of the country, almost 200,-000 New Yorkers were so "addicted to wheeling," according to *Publishers Weekly,* that literacy itself was threatened. The publication exhorted bookstores to join the trend rather than try to beat it, and to offer bicycles for sale as well as books.

Bloomingdale's could always be counted on for something new or for amazing bargains. In 1894, the store made headlines with what the *New York Times* called "one of the most remarkable sales ever known in the dry goods trade." Hecht and Morris, which for thirty years had been one of the most popular shopping places on the West Side, went bankrupt. Bloomingdale's bought out their entire stock for about one-quarter of its original cost, and offered it to the public at about half the usual retail prices. Unexpected sales bonanzas like this one, coupled with the constant influx of European merchandise and basic domestic goods, all at reasonable prices, plus the dividend of Lyman's constant showmanship in promoting the store and its products, resulted in ever-increasing sales figures.

As sales rose, the store—again—outgrew its size. By this time Lyman and Joseph were unwilling to change their location. Instead, they embarked on an active program to acquire property adjoining their store, or at least on the same block. On December 4, 1887, they had opened an addition at 166–170 East Sixtieth Street, not quite next door to the existing store. In 1890 they filled in the missing gap, acquiring the property at 162–164 East Sixtieth. Over the next twelve years, Bloomingdale's expanded along Third Avenue and then onto Lexington Avenue, tear-

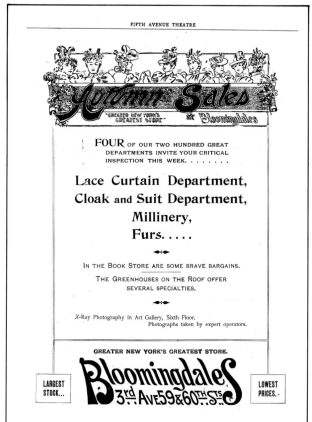

An early advocate of the power of advertising, Lyman Bloomingdale even placed store ads in theatrical playbills. This one appeared in the weekly program of the Fifth Avenue Theater in October 1896.

As Bloomingdale's expanded, it acquired other buildings on the same block. Some of them adjoined the main store. Others were separated by various businesses, creating a fragmented series of entrances and shops.

ing down existing buildings when necessary and preserving exterior frames when possible, but completely renovating the interiors of the newly acquired buildings to serve the needs of the rapidly growing store. By 1902, fully 80 percent of the city block extending from Third Avenue to Lexington, and from Fifty-ninth to Sixtieth streets, had been incorporated.

Much of the detail work of the real estate negotiations was handled by Samuel, who showed a keen head for the family business. After graduating from Dr. Sack's Collegiate Institute, a private school, he had attended Columbia College, where he studied architecture. But when he got his degree in 1895, he decided to join the staff of Bloomingdale's. "I asked Professor Ware, the dean of the school, what he considered my chances to become an architect," Samuel recalled years later. "He told me that success in the field could be won if you possessed all the great qualities of mind and heart, architectural proficiency, as well as personal charm. So I went to work at the store." It wasn't surprising; the store had preoccupied his life as a boy, and both his father and his uncle Joseph had encouraged his interest and fostered his merchandising ideas.

On January 1, 1896, Joseph Bloomingdale retired, leaving Lyman and Samuel to carry on the business. Together, they continued what had by then become an unspoken policy: utilize constantly changing features to attract people into the store, and then aggressively promote sales. The latest wonder was a moving staircase—an escalator—installed between the first and second floor. Naturally, Lyman found his own name for it, dubbing it the Inclined Eleva-

tor. The contraption drew droves of customers; they came to ride, and lingered to buy.

Lyman was so pleased with the success of the escalator that he helped finance the inventor's company, simultaneously foreseeing and promoting a successful future for the moving, cleated platforms. He appreciated their transportation value, but saw two other important features that the inventor had not anticipated: the escalator was a fantastic attention-getter, and it permitted the slowly descending customer to have a dramatic panoramic view of the merchandise on the floor below.

Samuel began to carve his own niche in the business. He promoted badly needed changes in the day-to-day operations, including budgeting and schedules. He instituted a system of advertisement money allocations, insuring that each department got a fair chance to publicize its wares. Up until that time, the department manager who yelled the loudest received the most advertising.

Samuel also hired employees to do some comparison shopping, to keep the store informed of prices set by downtown competitors. He forbade the use of superlatives in advertising, relying on product descriptions and excellent prices to attract customers.

Samuel revised the scheduling of sales, as well. Most large stores at that time were constantly marking down some item or another, so that sales became commonplace events. Sam Bloomingdale had the idea of promoting sales as celebrations—of the store's anniversary, or changing seasons, or holidays—and as annual traditions, such as furniture sales in February and August,

Samuel J. Bloomingdale

Manhattan's web of mass transit routes. It sat at the foot of the steam-driven Third Avenue El and was a popular stop of both electric and horse-drawn cars. Few stores could boast of such a lucky location, and Lyman decided to celebrate it with the slogan "All cars transfer to Bloomingdale's." It was a phrase which was to become familiar not only in New York, but internationally.

The first step in the new Bloomingdale publicity campaign was to place ad placards in the Fifty-ninth Street trolleys. Lyman and Samuel commissioned the famous *Evening Journal* cartoonist Richard F. Outcault to illustrate these placards with whimsical, cheerful drawings. Outcault created a fanciful driver for the trolley, an odd but endearing little creature named the Yellow Kid.

The Yellow Kid drove the BB—for Bloomingdale Brothers—trolley, but eventually Outcault retired him and put a new character in the driver's seat. Buster Brown, whose initials just happened to be the same as those of the store he publicized, became one of the most popular cartoon characters of the day. The beginning of his career was spent driving the BB trolley, with his pet boxer dog, Tige, by his side. Underneath the Buster Brown cartoon was a quatrain that always ended with the line "All cars transfer to Bloomingdale's."

Buster Brown had wide innocent eyes, bright yellow chin-length hair styled in the famous haircut that bears his name, and round cheeks, and was always dressed in a gentlemanly though rumpled sailor suit decorated with a big bow. When Buster Brown eventually diversified to become the

and white sales in snowy January. The practice became standard at Bloomingdale's and widely used in many other stores as well.

Samuel proved to have his father's sense of dash and savvy; Lyman had always been an innovator. His advertising and publicity techniques were groundbreakers, and served as models for other merchants to imitate. Now he was ready to launch the grandest campaign of all. Spurred into even greater exuberance by the increasing success of their business, Lyman sought to establish Bloomingdale's as not just a store, but a landmark.

Bloomingdale's marked the epicenter of

Buster Brown drove the Bloomingdale Brothers' trolley and rhymed his way from an advertising campaign into his own comic strip.

hero of his own comic strip, he became such a beloved character that thousands of little boys across the country nicknamed themselves Buster and called their dogs Tige.

The Buster Brown trolley placards were just the beginning of the Bloomingdale campaign. Lyman, well known in the art world for his collection of fine paintings, decided to bring color to public spaces by emblazoning the name of his store on every available wall. "All Cars Transfer to Bloomingdale's" decorated walls to the north, south, east, and west of the store. Passengers awaiting the El at 138th Street and Third Avenue could not glance in any direction without seeing the name of the store, and began to refer to that stop as Bloomingdale Alley.

When Bloomingdale's had opened its newly constructed quarters at the corner of Third Avenue and Fifty-ninth Street, Lyman had been keenly aware of the proximity of the Third Avenue El that ran alongside the store. The new railroad was considered quite grand, and its passengers were rich and poor alike. With a station right on "their" corner, the El was an excellent source of customers. At least it would be, if passengers happened to think about going shopping as they were being carried swiftly alongside the rooftops. Lyman had decided to encourage them to think about his store, so he had purchased perpetual advertising rights at the Fifty-ninth Street station. "All cars transfer to Bloomingdale's" thus became imprinted on the public mind—as well as on walls, streetcar transfers, newspaper ads, and Bloomingdale's own horse-drawn delivery cars.

Samuel, in appreciation of his father's sense of theater, came up with a promotional idea of his own. He suggested that the store give free red-and-white umbrellas to the vendors who drove throughout the city in their open horse-drawn wagons, to shield them from both sun and rain. Emblazoned across each large umbrella was the store's new motto. Within a year more than 5,000 were dispensed.

No store had ever carried out such a publicity campaign before. It was upbeat, startling, imaginative, and highly successful. Gimmicky, maybe, and certainly immodest, but it worked: Bloomingdale's was at the crossroads, available to every shopper, a fun and special place to shop.

Bloomingdale's was at the forefront of everything new, the reflector of what was current and the harbinger of change. Lyman and Samuel were keen observers of the shifting values of their time. They noted that the workday was shortening, creating more opportunities for leisure activities. Bloomingdale's customers now had more time for reading, sports, and music, so the store increased its stock in related items. Dickens, with his lengthy novels, was the best-selling author; tennis racquets and shoes, croquet sets, and baseball bats were lugged to the country for sporting weekends. The store sold more large trunks and valises than ever before as people traveled more, especially abroad. When the Kodak Brownie camera became available in 1900, Bloomingdale's urged its customers to immortalize those "special moments" with a camera of their own; the price was only one dollar.

Other customers, however, chose a

Lyman signed a contract with the company that ran the elevated railroad, to hang the store's posters in every station. This was the El station at Third Avenue and 59th Street.

The Bloomingdale's fleet of horse-drawn delivery cars

The umbrellas became collector's items, and could be seen on the beaches of New York and the lawns of European health spas.

more domestic bliss, and flocked to the store's music section to try out the pianos, both regular and player. The latter became one of the store's biggest hits, and Bloomingdale's became the largest distributor of player pianos in the world, selling more than 7,000 a year, adding $2.5 million to the store volume. Only the invention of radio dashed Samuel's hopes of placing a player piano in every New York parlor.

Popular songs of the day reflected pride in the new technology with such tunes as "In My Merry Oldsmobile" and "Come, Josephine, in My Flying Machine." The economy was booming, jobs were plentiful, and the spirit was patriotic as people sang George M. Cohan's "You're a Grand Old Flag" (at first irreverently titled "You're a Grand Old Rag"). Composer Harry Von Tilzer wanted to write the most romantic ballad of his time, and tested out the heart-wringing "A Bird in a Gilded Cage" in a brothel to see if it would make the ladies cry.

On Twenty-eighth Street, the block called Tin Pan Alley rang with music all day long as composers struggled to come up with hit songs. Music publishers almost turned down "In the Good Old Summertime" because they thought it would only have audience appeal in June, July, and August. To their astonishment, it sold a million copies in the first twelve months.

Romances blossomed to the tunes of "Sweet Adeline," "Shine On, Harvest Moon," "Hello Central, Give Me Heaven," and "Meet Me in St. Louis, Louis." Children walked home from school whistling "School Days," and men poked each other in the ribs upon hearing "My Wife's Gone to the Country, Hurrah! Hurrah!"

On January 22, 1901, Queen Victoria died. The end of her reign ushered out an era of conservatism and restraint. The incoming twentieth century was ready and willing to be exuberant. Women's clothes were changing silhouette again. The Gibson Girl, drawn by Charles Dana Gibson, became the ideal: no bustles for her. She was tall, slender, even regal, with upswept hair maneuvered into a pompadour, and loose, filmy, pleated dresses.

Skirts still reached to the floor, except for walking skirts which nearly bared an ankle. The latest innovation in ready-to-wear was the shirtwaist, a blouse designed to be tucked into a matching skirt, usually embellished with pleats, tucks, lace, braid, bows, buttons and/or other trim.

Men wore silk hats and sleek shirts with detachable collar and cuffs, and chose with great care their array of essential accessories, such as silver-topped cane, pocket watch, and cigar case.

Teddy Roosevelt's teenage daughter Alice was the darling of the country. Alice

Shortly before his death, Lyman Bloomingdale conceived the idea of having an immense oil painting made on the west wall of the newest addition to the store. During a trip to Europe, he had been much impressed by the quaintness and architectural beauty of the houses in old Nuremberg, and decided to have a scene of the town portrayed on the brick wall. After his death, Samuel had the idea carried out, and the 7,000-square-foot painting was finished in 1904. The lower red-tiled roof, immediately above the house's windows, is part of the painting; the topmost is the roof of the store's immense greenhouse, in which Bloomingdale's grew thousands of plants and flowers, all available for purchase.

was ebullient, irrepressible, and as pretty as a Gibson girl. She flouted convention by smoking cigarettes, playing poker, and dancing the hula in Hawaii. She was the life of one party when she jumped into a swimming pool fully dressed, pulling a congressman in with her. Most of all, though, she enjoyed dancing, and the Paris *Journal des Débats* reported that in fifteen months Alice had attended 407 dinners, 350 balls, and 300 parties. She exemplified the carefree tone of the times.

In this era of ease, Lyman Bloomingdale, who had always believed that his commitment to his community went further than providing a fine place to shop, became increasingly involved in various projects for improved community services. He had contributed a great deal of money and time to help build the country sanitorium of the Montefiore Home and Hospital for Chronic Diseases. At the sanitorium dedication on May 30, 1901, Theodore Roosevelt, then vice-president, said to Lyman and other community leaders, "I have come to express to you the debt of obligation that the people of the United States are under to you, not only for the deed itself, but for the example of the deed." Four months later, Roosevelt was president.

uring the Spanish-American War in 1898, Lyman contributed most of the space in the men's furnishings department to the federal government. He had a recruitment center erected in the store, and granted leaves of absence with full pay to any employee who enlisted in the armed forces. An avid collector of American art, Lyman served as a patron in perpetuity at the Metropolitan Museum of Art (to which he also donated several important works) and was known among young artists as a man who would give unknowns a chance.

Lyman Bloomingdale died on October 13, 1905, at his country home in Elberon, New Jersey. Those who mourned him remembered not only his keen business sense, genius in advertising, and extracurricular activities for the public good, but also his indomitable spirit and ebullience of energy. His funeral took place at Temple Beth-El. In his will, he left $100,000 to charity.

Lyman's three sons, Samuel, Hiram, and Irving, had all joined the family business, but while Hiram and Irving eventually moved on to other pursuits, Samuel stayed with the store to continue and expand his father's vision of a landmark enterprise which, by its very existence, encouraged further settlement of the Upper East Side.

One of Lyman's pet projects had been lobbying for a bridge to cross the East River, linking Queens with Manhattan. Samuel now joined the lobby, along with other business and civic leaders. After years of work, their efforts were finally rewarded when the Queensborough Bridge, also called the Fifty-ninth Street Bridge, opened in 1909.

Lyman G. Bloomingdale

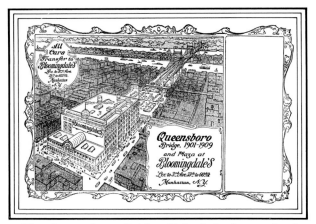

The Queensboro Bridge linked the borough of Queens to Manhattan only a few blocks east of the 59th Street station of the Third Avenue El—and Bloomingdale's.

In 1905, the year Lyman died, the annual business was in excess of $5 million. With the opening of the bridge, even more cars could "transfer to Bloomingdale's." Samuel anticipated a surge of new customers, and the store spruced up for the occasion. Bloomingdale's spent $100,000 for alterations, installing a forty-ton-capacity icemaking machine to replace the old ten-ton machine, and increasing sales space. About 3,000 square feet of space were added to the cut flower department, and the rug department was enlarged to three times its previous size.

The year 1910 was an exhilarating one for Bloomingdale's, and on the day before Independence Day, the store proclaimed its appreciation for the "full confidence and liberal patronage of the public" in an ad in the *New York Times.* The ad went on to state:

Many years ago, when we entered the arena to fight the fight for right merchandising principles, we had but one goal— one prize—in view, and that was the confi-dence, endorsement and approval of our public.

We won, as fighters of strenuosity will when on their banner is inscribed: "Justice, Equity and Fair Dealing." Time has but served to make that Bloomingdale motto grow brighter, larger, more luminous and vastly more meaningful. . . .

At the outstart we adopted our DECLARATION OF INDEPENDENCE—to be absolutely free and impartial buyers in the markets of the world at all times; to exercise our great spot cash buying ability in a free and untrammeled manner; to be positively fearless of all competition.

To that end we have established many workrooms of our own for the production of wearing apparel,—we buy entire products of mills and factories—we maintain an extensive, permanent Paris organization— we send numbers of our own buyers throughout the length and breadth of Europe and the Orient as well as America.

The ad concluded with an invitation to the public to look over 10,000 bargains the day after Independence Day.

In 1904, the first subway had opened under Broadway, turning west at Forty-second Street and diverting traffic from Bloomingdale's. But now, construction was under way on the Lexington Avenue subway, and major changes were already raising the status of the neighborhood. Real estate developers were busily buying land, clearing away existing structures, and constructing whole blocks of expensive residences.

On December 14, 1913, the *New York Times* reported that for the first time "New York's social center is moving eastward . . . away from Fifth Avenue and under the magnetizing force of Park Avenue."

Christmas, 1905

Park Avenue had been known as one of the ugliest streets in the city. Scarred by uneven metal railroad tracks, dingy with tenements, and shadowed by hulks of factories, the Avenue badly needed the resuscitation the Queensborough Bridge and new subway afforded. Into Queens fled the factories; the budget for Grand Central Station, just being completed, included money for covering Park Avenue's tracks. The tenements abdicated to pretty new apartment buildings that attracted a different class of people. Fifth Avenue was still the reigning queen of the East Side, but Park Avenue became the fairest thoroughfare of the urban court. Green islands parted its wide space, flanked by new buildings the colors of eggshell and kid. The new Plaza Hotel was being built at Fifty-ninth and Fifth, and became a lavish place to hold tea dances and luncheons.

Bloomingdale's was now without question in the right place at the right time. Maids and matrons alike shopped there for groceries, wines, and spirits, and Bloomingdale's butchers were declared to be the best. Women who met at Bloomingdale's delicatessen were constantly discovering that yet another friend had just moved into the neighborhood, most likely into one of the houses rising almost weekly on the

A picture postcard. Notice the store's name on the packages.

streets to the north. It seemed as though the neighborhood grew up around the nucleus of Bloomingdale's, and the store showed its appreciation to new and old customers alike. "We assure invariable courtesy and promptness of service," one ad read, plus ". . . the widest range of seasonable, serviceable merchandise and the lowest prices compatible with quality." More than that: Bloomingdale's not only provided home delivery, but also maintained a "Free Delivery Service to all Summer Resorts."

Lexington Avenue had always been a fairly empty back street, not comparable to Third Avenue, whose El brought it traffic. But the opening of the Lexington Avenue subway in 1915 was to give the street above it a new importance. Pedestrians would surface in droves, and stores already located on Lexington Avenue eagerly anticipated the business they would bring.

Bloomingdale's main entrance was on Third Avenue, however, and Samuel realized that a new Lexington Avenue entrance must be created to accommodate the subway travelers and new neighbors who lived in the houses springing up above the subway route. He also felt that the new entrance would heighten Bloomingdale's position as the hub of the community. Bloomingdale's already faced east to Queens; now it had to face west as well, toward the burgeoning neighborhood of Lexington Avenue. And the store's design had to be modernized, to keep Bloomingdale's abreast of the modern structures going up daily around it.

The import counter, 1915

In June 1916, the same year he was married, Samuel filed plans for expansion of the store. The *New York Times* hailed the filing as the "most striking evidence of the confidence of the merchants in that vicinity in future improvement and business progress."

With his architectural knowledge, Samuel closely oversaw the redesigning of this store. Subway trains rumbled beneath Lexington; above it hammers and riveters rang out with a staccato beat. The street level was laid with stylish travertine flooring, and new escalators were installed on three floors. The new Lexington Avenue section of the store was connected with the Third Avenue buildings by an ingenious network of open corridors which matched the disparate levels of the various buildings. And the store's new facade and entrance on Lexington commemorated the avenue's new status as a main artery of the city.

Within a year, construction was completed, and except for three houses which together measured only 60 feet by 60.5 feet, the store covered the entire block from Fifty-ninth to Sixtieth Streets and Third to Lexington avenues. Upon incorporation of the store in 1917, Samuel became its first president.

He figured that the success of the store should benefit its employees even beyond their salaries. So every week during the summer, beginning in 1913, Samuel sent from forty to fifty employees to the seashore for a week, or sometimes two weeks, as guests of the store. They continued to receive full salary, and all transportation was paid; in addition, a full program of free entertainment was provided. Near the cottages in Far Rockaway, employees enjoyed tally-ho rides, corn roasts, surf bathing, and other activities. Invigorated by the sea air and tanned by the summer sun, they returned to work with energetic spirits—and, one would assume, considerable goodwill toward their employer.

Another unusual opportunity for employees was a vocational school, the first such program in the city. Employees took

The main floor and balconies, 1915

courses in salesmanship and other job-related skills, and often gained valuable promotions as a result.

One employee, however, availed himself of a rather unique fringe benefit. One night, in the course of his normal prebedtime walk, Samuel Bloomingdale visited his store and asked the watchman to take him to the top floor so that he could walk down through the various departments. He did this occasionally, as a way to keep tabs on new merchandise and to get ideas for new promotions. This time, however, the watchman looked slightly apprehensive; he made no comment, though, as the two rode up in the elevator. When they reached the third floor, Samuel heard the melody of a wedding march coming from the piano department. He demanded that the watchman let him out of the elevator, and to his amazement, there was a wedding procession in the piano department, complete with preacher, bride, groom, parents, and a few guests.

Samuel waited silently as the ceremony continued. Scrutinizing the faces of the wedding party, he recognized the father of the bride. He was the assistant watchman of the store. Suddenly, just as the couple were pronounced man and wife, the bride's father looked up and noticed Samuel standing there.

"Oh, Mr. Bloomingdale," he exclaimed, "please forgive me. I've been a loyal worker for forty years and never missed a night. My daughter was to be married and I didn't have the courage to ask you for the time off. That's why we held the wedding here. Please forgive me. . . ."

Samuel was touched, and quickly reassured the watchman that his job was safe. Then he called out to the gathering, "Congratulations, everyone! Now I want you all to come down to the kitchen of the second-floor restaurant. I'll unlock the refrigerator so we can have a wedding celebration!"

Samuel continued to use his father's

The grocery department, 1915

technique of placing full-page advertisements in the New York papers, but, he said, "since you can't advertise your full copy in every New York paper, I had a theory that you use one or two papers for your full copy, and be represented in all papers with some attractive card." The January 17, 1914, edition of the *New York World,* for example, had this small ad.

SARAH BERNHARDT'S BEAT
over Father Time is as remarkable
as our Winter Sale of Toilet Articles
now in progress.

"These were annoying to the ad department" said Samuel with a chuckle. "It was only by my sheer strength of determination that they were kept up as long as they were—five or six years."

The Queensborough Bridge and the Lexington Avenue subway weren't the only transportation news in New York. All across the country, Henry Ford's Model T was changing the way America traveled. The car was first introduced in 1908, advertised as "The Universal Car." It could go through mud and over rocky trails. With attachments, it could also pump water, plow fields, and generate electricity.

In 1911, Ford began to make the body out of metal instead of wood, and sales zoomed. The vehicle still had a few problems that had to be smoothed out; despite its mechanical flaws, however, the Model T sped up the pace of the nation. Farmers didn't feel so isolated, and for the rural dweller a jaunt from Long Island to, say, Bloomingdale's, became easier and more fun. And Bloomingdale's, store of so many innovations, became the first in the city to use the automobile to make deliveries.

There was light, humorous conflict about whether the automobile was a worthwhile gadget to tamper with, but the conflict over women's suffrage notably lacked humor. Cartoons in popular magazines projected that if women got the vote, it would spell the death of femininity itself.

Women's fight for the vote coincided with their new role in the economy. Although the traditional place of the woman was still the home, by 1910 about 7.5 million women were employed as secretaries, salesclerks, and telephone operators. During the next ten years another million women joined the work force. Their dress reflected their new liberation. More and more women were discarding the tight corsets which prevented them from breathing easily. Instead, they copied the more relaxed approach of dance star Irene Castle, whose gowns hung in loose folds and whose hair was styled in a carefree bob. Supporting the new fashion trend, Bloomingdale's stocked more casual, comfortable styles, adapting its own fashion outlook to the changing times.

During that same decade, movies became a major industry. By 1914, fifty-two film companies in Hollywood spent $5.72 million to churn out flicks, and new companies opened in New York and Chicago. Mary Pickford was every woman's idol and every man's dream. Charles Chaplin became so popular he commanded a salary nearly seven times that of the president of the United States. People eagerly dropped anywhere from a nickel to a quarter at the box office to shiver at *The Perils of Pauline,* howl at the antics of Mack Sennett's Keystone Kops, or stare in awe at the grandeur of D. W. Griffith's *Intolerance.* Thus, when Samuel Bloomingdale married in 1916, he and his bride took the most popular honeymoon trip of the day: going out to California to tour Hollywood.

On April 2, 1917, President Woodrow Wilson declared war against Germany. "You're in the Army Now" became the song on everyone's lips, and all hearts were in the war effort. It needed all the help it could get. The United States hadn't fought a major war in more than fifty years, and was ill-prepared to do so now. The Army had only 208,034 men; the Air Force had 130 pilots and 55 decrepit planes.

The rug department, 1915

The country rallied, however; men were drafted or volunteered for service. Their families back home organized war bond rallies, saved peach pits for gas masks, and "Hooverized" in response to Food Administrator Herbert Hoover's call for planting backyard gardens and voluntarily rationing food. The grocery department at Bloomingdale's reminded customers when it was wheatless Monday or Wednesday, meatless Tuesday, or porkless Thursday or Saturday. Samuel Bloomingdale donated an en-

The grocery department, 1915

The tea department, 1915

tire floor for Red Cross Headquarters, run by actress Eleanor Robson Belmont, and joined the drive to sell "Liberty Bonds."

The first radio broadcast, in 1920, announced the returns of the Harding-Cox presidential election. Bloomingdale's, the largest distributor of player pianos in the world, had to shift gears quickly as the radio pushed out the player piano as the preferred source of music and entertainment in the home. But the store had already begun to stock the new invention, buying sets almost as quickly as they could be manufactured. Nationally, sales of radios rose from less than $2 million in 1920 to $609 million in 1929. Families sat around the radio to listen to baseball scores, "Amos and Andy," and the Paul Whiteman Orchestra.

Bloomingdale's was crowded with shoppers buying everything from radios to silk stockings (39 cents a pair) to Hudson Seal (dyed muskrat) coats for $295. There was also a new market for memorabilia celebrating the New York visits of the Prince of Wales in 1924 and Queen Marie of Romania in 1926, and of Charles Lindbergh's solo flight to Paris in 1927.

By the mid-twenties, the East Side had become one of the city's most fashionable sections. Lovely brownstones housed the wealthy and upper middle class, while Sutton Place, Turtle Bay, and other areas around Bloomingdale's were now home to some extraordinarily wealthy families, many of whom had moved there from the once-preferred West Side. Brass nameplates affixed to carved wooden doors bore such names as Vanderbilt, Morgan, and De Wolfe. Samuel Bloomingdale, a member of the Yorkville Chamber of Commerce, felt that residents and businesses on the East Side—especially those close to the East River—would be well served by a subway on First Avenue. Along with other merchants, Samuel launched a letter-writing campaign to the Transit Commission and to the editors of major New York papers to try to rally support for this idea.

"Can there be anything wrong in the building of a subway on First Avenue?" he wrote to the *New York Times*. "First Avenue is free from encumbrances that delay and hinder the building of a subway . . . [it] is wide and extends through the heart of the city, north and south, and to those portions of the city which are most congested and in need of transit facilities."

The idea was excellent, but the subway was never built, disappointing both Samuel and the residents—then and now—of the East River area who must hike or take a bus to the Lexington Avenue subway.

As the East Side continued to grow, Bloomingdale's, still essentially the only department store in the neighborhood, became crowded. Samuel again decided to remodel, enlarging the store and enabling it to meet new needs. The grocery department was eliminated in favor of expanding the bar-gain basement, which contained departments for silk, muslin, and flannel underwear, boys' and men's clothing, and women's ready-to-wear and shoes. A new system was added for transporting merchandise from stock rooms to the various departments, and a conveyor belt was installed to carry merchandise from sales departments to the delivery section. Two new elevators were added for a total of nine in the store.

At the Bloomingdale warehouses at Fifty-second and Fifty-fifth streets, a new fur storage plant, a garage for electric cars, a machine repair shop, a paint shop, and other additions were built to ensure as comprehensive and efficient an operation as possible.

But the most impressive addition to Bloomingdale's was an elaborate stairway, built of pale travertine stone and inlaid with panels of Italian mosaic. It was an adaptation of the main staircase in the Bargello, the famous palace of the podestas in Florence, Italy. Samuel had visited Europe while a student at the Columbia School of Architecture and had greatly admired the staircase, long considered a significant landmark in Florentine architecture. In

The northeast corner of 59th Street and Lexington Avenue during the 1920s. The corner building and the third from the corner were the last two "holdouts." Other than these, Bloomingdale's occupied the whole block, from 59th to 60th Street and from Lexington to Third Avenue.

MEMORIAL STAIRWAY IN HONOR OF LYMAN G BLOOMINGDALE TO COMMEMORATE THE FIFTIETH ANNIVERSARY OF HIS FOUNDING OF BLOOMINGDALE BROS APRIL 17 1872

1923, with architect Elisha Harris Janes, Samuel designed a replica of the staircase as a memorial to his father, to commemorate the store's fiftieth anniversary.

The *New York Times* editorial of July 14 warmly commended this addition to the store: "No assiduous shopper, one must hope, can see repeatedly a masterpiece of architectural design without gaining some inkling of the dignity and beauty which can be combined with usefulness. Too much building today is so streaked and weakened with shoddy that no reminder of its best estate is negligible. . . . Let the Bargello staircase at least quicken the desire to preserve a threatened ideal."

In 1927, Samuel announced the purchase of the last of the sixty-two parcels which comprise the block on which Bloomingdale's stands. These were rapidly incorporated into the store, bringing the total ground area to 84,000 square feet, with 1,240 linear feet of window display frontage on the four sides. The new space was all to be used for selling area, though, and almost immediately, additional storage space was needed. Bloomingdale's leased out its six-story-plus-basement cement garage on East Fifty-fourth Street, and built a new seven-story combination warehouse, delivery station, garage, and manufacturing plant in Long Island City, on the Queens side of the nearby Fifty-ninth Street Bridge. The new building was a mammoth two city blocks long and one block wide. It sat on a high, rolling, 120,000-square-foot plot of land served by a twelve-car railroad siding from the adjoining tracks of the Long Island Railroad. The steep hill had the advantage of providing trucking entrances on both the first- and second-floor levels. The building became the point of origin for all deliveries; it also housed a complete factory to manufacture the Walters piano.

The *Times* reported that "every modern device to expedite service, every piece of equipment to insure speed and eliminate as far as humanly possible chances of error in shipment, has been utilized to make this structure one of the finest of its kind."

Like his father before him, Samuel Bloomingdale was greatly interested in new inventions and procedures. He saw wide implication for Henry Ford's principles of standardization and mass production, and suggested to manufacturers of major household appliances—washing machines, ironers, refrigerators, and stoves—that they adopt these techniques.

He further suggested that there was a marked need for simplification of many of these household items. "Some of the differences between products are meaningless and unnecessary," he noted. "Variety of design, except for a few basic models, is obviously unnecessary. Sometimes meaningless accessories are added to provide a new selling angle. All this is done at the expense of the consumer, who would otherwise be satisfied with a simpler design."

Interesting sentiments from a merchant, especially in view of the multitudinous choices of the modern Bloomingdale's, in keeping with the desires of today's customers. But the statement does more than reveal Samuel's sense of responsibility to his own "consumer"; it also sets a precedent for a highly unusual practice which became standard procedure for Bloomingdale's during the 1950s, '60s, and '70s: suggesting to manufacturers that they produce a particular item, and sometimes even providing precise design specifications, as we shall see.

Samuel also had a deep interest in the welfare of his employees, and instituted programs to give them a sense of participation in the store. He offered prizes to the employees who came up with the best sales slogans, mottos, or essays on retailing. To fourteen chauffeurs of delivery trucks he awarded prizes for driving a full year without an accident. Bloomingdale's employees had their own Victory Chorus, and their

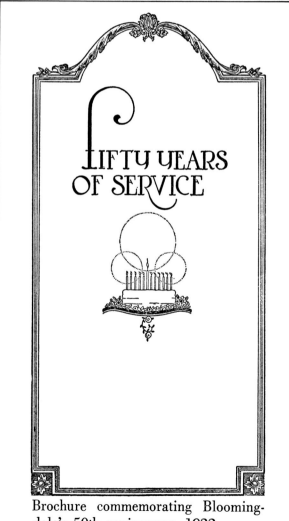

Brochure commemorating Bloomingdale's 50th anniversary, 1922

annual entertainment and ball featured a musical revue written and acted entirely by co-workers.

Bloomingdale's had incorporated in 1917, but first offered securities to the public on March 19, 1926, following the then-current trend of opening family-owned businesses to the public. The store made application to list both preferred and common stocks of the company on the New York Stock Exchange. The *New York Times* reported on its financial pages that the Bloomingdale corporation "has no funded debt and no bank loans and has not been a borrower for many years. . . . The balance sheet as of January 31, 1926 . . . shows net tangible assets of $8,211,117, or more than $205 for each share of preferred stock." The report also stated that from 1909 to 1926, ". . . growth in volume of business has averaged more than $1,000,000 a year."

The next day, March 20, the stock was completely sold by 10:00 A.M.

As the twenties drew to a close, rumors of financial disaster began to spread, but merchants, like other citizens, refused to believe them and issued public statements to refute them. Samuel was quoted by the *Times* in January 1928 as saying that the "old idea of the inevitable recurrence of business depression in Presidential years is a theory which the best economists of today have branded as fallacious. I think the continued development of high standards of living, a sound banking system and the good favor with which eminent economists . . . look upon installment buying, will all be potent factors in producing favorable retail conditions."

Disclaimers notwithstanding, he took some radical steps to protect the financial stability of the store. In February 1929, Lehman Brothers, the investment-banking firm that had handled the sales of Bloomingdale's stock, began to promote a merger of certain highly successful department stores. Paul Mazur, who had worked for Filene's in Boston but who was now a partner in Lehman Brothers, quietly approached Samuel to discuss the idea of Bloomingdale's joining in such a merger. Within months, the heads of three other stores were ready to seriously consider the proposal, and they all met to discuss the details: Samuel Bloomingdale, Louis Kirstein, general manager of Filene's, and Fred Lazarus, Jr., head of the Ohio family that owned the Lazarus and Shillito department stores in Columbus and Cincinnati. They gathered on the yacht of Simon F. Rothschild, president of Abraham & Straus, a large family-owned department store in Brooklyn, and as they sailed the cool waters of Long Island Sound, Paul Mazur elaborated on his suggestion that they set up a holding company to share the risks of their businesses.

In September, Bloomingdale's announced that all issues of common stock (the majority of which were owned by Samuel and his two brothers) would be transferred to its own newly formed holding company, which would then negotiate directly with the company to be formed from the merger. That November, Federated Department Stores, Inc., was incorporated, bringing together Abraham & Straus, Inc., whose annual net sales were $25 million; William Filene's Sons Company of Boston, controlling R. H. White

Company, with combined annual sales of $46 million; and F. & R. Lazarus & Company of Columbus, Ohio, with annual sales of $12 million. When Bloomingdale's joined Federated the following February 1930, with its sales record of $24 million, the new organization's annual sales totaled $107 million. Each department store exchanged a majority of its stock for the newly created Federated shares.

Samuel stepped out of the office of president to become chairman of the board and invited Michael Schaap, who had been vice-president of Bamberger's in Newark and, before that, a political protégé of Theodore Roosevelt, to become president of Bloomingdale's.

The merger came at the best possible time, for it strengthened all four stores against the ravages of the Great Depression. The stock market crashed in 1929, precipitating a slide which lasted until mid-1932, when there was no farther down to go. Bitterness spread through the land like a hot wind. Twenty thousand people committed suicide in 1931 alone, a number much higher than the more widely and sensationally publicized suicides following the crash in 1929.

Herbert Hoover, unable to lead the country out of the Depression, went down in defeat. When Franklin Delano Roosevelt became president in 1933, he faced the incredible task of pulling the nation out of the worst economic disaster in its history. Roosevelt promised the country a "New Deal," and the programs he instituted were staggering in scope. The National Recovery Administration (NRA) regulated wages, working hours, and, to some extent, prices. The Civilian Conservation Corps

In 1931, Bloomingdale's completed construction of a totally new Lexington Avenue store. The $3 million building replaced the small, disconnected shops. Architects Starrett and Van Vleck followed Samuel Bloomingdale's concept and retained the "modern, useful buildings" already standing along Third Avenue and extending down the block; they were merely reconditioned, refurbished, and ingeniously joined to their modern addition. During the two years of construction, the store was open for business as usual, but when the hammering stopped, Bloomingdale's had a new face. Lexington became the new front of the store.

Because Bloomingdale's is on a hill—the Third Avenue side is nine feet higher than the Lexington Avenue side, and the 60th Street side is two feet higher than the 59th Street side—an arcade was built on the new Lexington Avenue side. It not only solved the problems of different levels, but also had a merchandising advantage: customers who want to go to upper floors are first led through much of the first floor.

(CCC) hired 2.5 million men over a nine-year period to plant trees, dig drainage ditches and fish ponds, build firebreaks and reservoirs, and create or restore national park areas. The Public Works Administration (PWA) harnessed 4.75 billion man-hours and more than $6 billion over a six-year period to construct about 10 percent of all new transportation facilities built in the country at that time, as well as 35 percent of new hospitals and health facilities, 65 percent of city halls, courthouses, and sewage disposal plants, and 70 percent of all educational buildings. The PWA was the financier; the Works Progress Administration (WPA) was the planner and director of the multitude of projects. The WPA also hired artists to preserve national folklore and to entertain the public in free concerts and plays.

Like other civic-minded institutions, Bloomingdale's, now under its new leadership, did what it could to help out. When contributions were needed for the Emergency Unemployment Relief Committee, the new president of the store, Michael Schaap, rallied more than 2,500 employees to contribute. Bloomingdale's also placed advertisements in newspapers, encouraging the public at large to contribute as well. More than 25,000 letters from readers expressed surprise and gratitude at the largesse of the public-minded store, and Bloomingdale's gained a reputation for being active in the rehabilitation of the local economy.

The store also developed a fashion scholarship program, put on Christmas parties for poor children from a day nursery, and raised funds for the Henry Street Settlement with an exhibit of souvenirs from Admiral Byrd's second Antarctic expedition. In 1937, Bloomingdale's built a little house in its basement, to help the Federal Housing Administration publicize the low-cost building plans it had developed to help low-income families afford homes of their own. The four-room model house was furnished by Bloomingdale's, which offered to provide furniture without charge for people who agreed to invest in low-cost housing.

Bloomingdale's continued to hold its annual essay contests for employees, and it is noteworthy that in 1932 the essay subject was "The Department Store As an Economic and Social Institution in the Life of the Community." Bloomingdale's had always identified itself strongly with the Upper East Side community, and that sensitivity helped the store to know its customers' needs—and frustrations—and help them deal with both. The store lived up to its responsibility as a central and long-standing neighborhood establishment.

In August 1931, Lehman Brothers issued an analysis of the Federated Department Stores, Inc., and described what it saw as the character of Bloomingdale's: "Such a store is generally accepted as a local public institution of permanent character; its continued existence, given proper management, is practically assured; the nature of its business and its operating methods make it to a large degree depression-resistant; it participates in prosperity without dependence on sales outside its own trading area, and its current and fixed assets are readily convertible into cash."

It was evident that such "proper man-agement" was very much at work. Despite tight money, Schaap elected to install new fixtures, greatly improving the appearance of the store's interior. He also instructed that merchandise be grouped by price range. Thus, for the customer who was, of necessity, on a tight budget, higher-priced items were placed far enough from thrift goods to remove the irritation of temptation. Customers appreciated the sensitivity and consideration that this grouping implied. The policy also helped strengthen the growing suspicion that Bloomingdale's had values for every customer.

Even throughout the time of the stock-market crash and deepening Depression, Bloomingdale's determinedly kept its outlook optimistic and continued to expand. Right after Christmas 1929, the store announced plans to construct an eleven-story addition, complete with a restaurant and solarium penthouse. The ceremony laying the cornerstones of the addition, to be erected on Lexington Avenue at Fifty-ninth Street, was held the following April, with several hundred city officials and businessmen in attendance. Sealed within one cornerstone was a box of articles which symbolized the present day: a radio set and cocktail shaker, both with instructions for their use; a telephoto picture of Colonel and Mrs. Charles A. Lindbergh; a baseball autographed by Babe Ruth; stock ticker tape with the previous day's quotations; a subway strap; current sheet music; a wedding ring; and a bound volume of forecasts of the future written by prominent theologians, scientists, businessmen, and artists.

The contents of the second cornerstone were rather remarkable. Beside the usual copies of the *Congressional Record*, current issues of a number of newspapers, and photographs and a history of the present store, there were three bank books with deposits of $25 each, on which interest would be compounded annually, so that when that cornerstone would be opened in 200 years, according to the plan, each deposit would be worth $614,000, to be divided among three city hospitals.

Bloomingdale's also constructed a tunnel under Lexington Avenue at Fifty-ninth Street for the safety and convenience of pedestrians and subway travelers.

The store celebrated a couple of anniversaries in the thirties. In 1931, it pulled a creaking horse car from its carbarns at Second Avenue and Ninety-sixth Street to make an old-fashioned run across Fifty-ninth Street in commemoration of Bloomingdale's fifty-ninth anniversary. Several young women in hoopskirts and bonnets rode in the carriage to remind the public of fashions from that bygone era.

The same car was dragged out again the following year for the store's sixtieth anniversary. The driver steered the carriage toward City Hall. This time Samuel Bloomingdale was the passenger; he presented a Japanese table garden to Mayor Walker.

One hugely successful recurring project at Bloomingdale's was the dog show, begun in 1931. Bloomingdale's devised every possible variation on this theme. Ribbons were granted for the smallest dog, the fluffiest dog, and the oddest-looking dog. A four-year-old chihuahua named Gary Cooper won second prize in his class. His irreverent name was accounted for when it was discovered that his mistress was the young daughter of Ziegfield Follies comedienne Fanny Brice. Other children entered their dogs in such categories as Cutest Dog Raised and Owned by Child, Dog with the Most Spots, and Funniest Dog. One dog show was for nonpedigreed dogs only, and it was called the "just dogs" show. Chico Marx stopped in one day to serve as a judge. He said after the show that "it was a nice and funny show" but that he preferred the talking picture, adding that a vote should be taken to decide which end of the leash a dog belonged on.

In 1934 a crisis struck. The American Kennel Club, reversing its stand of the previous year, refused to license the Bloomingdale dog show since it was held inside a department store. The club's refusal came a bit late; entries had already been registered, and ribbons and cups and programs prepared. So Bloomingdale's, like a fine trouper, decided to "go on with the show." The mini-furor created a camaraderie among dog owners and viewers alike, and the winners happily accepted their unsanctioned trophies.

Bloomingdale's also became known for its imaginatively conceived and staged exhibits. These ranged from an animated crew of Tarzan, Brer Rabbit, Cinderella, Robinson Crusoe, and the Three Bears visiting the toy department before Christmas, to an exhibit of Hungarian embroidery, lace, and tapestry. Owners of antique furniture could visit displays that demonstrated how the furniture could be integrated well into a modern room—a precursor of the semiannual model room exhibits that later became, and still remain, famous.

The heads of four Latin American consulates in New York once attended a luncheon at Bloomingdale's to mark the opening of the store's new Central and South American shop, which featured native handicrafts. Perhaps the most exotic exhibit of 1933 demonstrated the amethyst wonders of fluorescent paint. It showed the inside of a dining room in which various objects, including the hostess's lace gown, had been sprayed with invisible fluorescent paint. Upon the lighting of an ultraviolet ray machine, the entire setting took on the glisten and dreamlike colors of an underwater scene.

Bloomingdale's sponsored bridge tournaments and, in conjunction with the Parks Department, sponsored model boat races at the Conservatory Lake in Central Park. Small steam, sail, electric, and spring-powered craft competed. Boys and girls carted their boats to the lake in paper bags and toy wagons, and several thousand people showed up to see which would prove victorious.

Bloomingdale's crowning glory, however, was just that: a reproduction of Great Britain's crown jewels, set in a reproduction of the Tower of London's mossy Jewel Room, guarded by two "Beef-Eaters" in traditional red uniforms and plumed hats, bearing halberds.

During the Depression it was particularly important to pay close attention to the way goods were advertised, to make sure that the messages of high value for low cost got across. And with the advent of synthetic fabrics, it became important to identify whether a gown was made of silk, rayon, or cotton crepe. Bloomingdale's became one of the first stores to stress consumers' rights when it decided to require its manufacturers to place informative labels on their merchandise so customers would know exactly what it was they were getting for their valuable dollars.

As the thirties came to an end, Bloomingdale's was able to congratulate itself for being the only store in the country which showed a profit right through the Depression years. In 1932, for example, a year which saw the closing of many businesses throughout the country, Bloomingdale's sold more merchandise than in any other single year of its existence, including the boom years of the late twenties. Sales went up each year, proving the value of sensitivity to customers' wants and needs, aggressive advertising and promotion, and realistically optimistic expansion and renovation programs that looked toward a healthy economic future.

The thirties deserved a big celebration to herald its end—and the New York World's Fair in 1939 was the grandest, most costly and ambitious celebration anyone could want. "It was the paradox of all paradoxes," wrote Sidney M. Shalett in *Harper's* magazine in 1940. "It was good, it was bad; it was the acme of all crazy vulgarity, it was the pinnacle of all inspiration." Millions walked along the fairground's sixty-five miles of paved streets and footpaths, staring at the various exhibitors' views of the future—and hoping it would not hold in store another decade like the one they'd just gone through.

But in the next few years, World War II shocked the country and absorbed its material and human resources to the utmost. Overseas, American soldiers witnessed the trauma of war and the horror of Nazi atrocities, while at home the economy

Northeast corner of 59th Street and Lexington Avenue. The area was served by both subway and elevated trains. Although cars and clothing look dated, the building itself looks much the same as it does today.

boomed. Men joined the armed forces; women ran the factories, sold war bonds, or joined the Red Cross. American citizens planted Victory Gardens again, saved toothpaste tubes for scrap-metal drives, and tried again to get used to rationing. Little books of food stamps suddenly dictated the limits of each day's menu, and people counted food point values as assiduously as calories.

Rationing hit manufacturers, too, creating shortages of certain items. Trying to accentuate the positive, Bloomingdale's put on a special exhibit of plastic goods, to encourage people to accept them as substitutes; the metal that was normally used to construct these products was now needed for vital war industries.

Nineteen forty-five brought the end of the war. It also signaled the end of an era, for isolationist America and for American business as well. For Bloomingdale's, it heralded a time of intense, deliberate change, and of growth far surpassing anything that had come before. Perhaps, for some people, it would continue to be the neighborhood store. But by the end of the Second World War, both the neighborhood and the store were evolving into something new, something far more cosmopolitan. The family store was about to shift gears.

Part 2

The Making
of the Phenomenon:
1945–1970

Summer 1945: The Allied powers triumphed in Europe. Japan surrendered. After years of anguish, the Second World War was over. Nothing would be the way it had been.

President Truman proclaimed a two-day victory holiday. Like most of the nation's stores, Bloomingdale's closed its doors in celebration of the hard-won peace. A huge flag covered the upper part of the building, flanked on both sides by flags of the Allied nations. The windows were covered with paper flags; across them ran streamers with quotations from "The Star-Spangled Banner."

As American troops began pouring home from the far corners of the world, the country they'd left seemed, superficially, much the same on their return. The pennant races, the morning paper, and the friendly faces of friends and neighbors provided reassuring normalcy. *The Lost Weekend* won the Oscar as Best Picture of the Year, and Bess Myerson was named Miss America. Edward R. Murrow, H. V. Kaltenborn, and Elmer Rice, whose radio commentaries had given the nation continuous news of the war, now turned their attention to problems of peace and domesticity.

Outside the Third Avenue side of Bloomingdale's, peddlers set up their rickety tables each day, as they had in years past, offering a potpourri of merchandise to the trusting consumer. Inside, Bloomingdale's bargain basement still featured its tables of shoes tied together in a leathery mass.

But beneath the surface, subtle changes had taken place that altered forever the fabric of American life. Some of the changes were obvious. Senator Arthur Vandenberg, one of the famous isolationists in the Senate, announced that such a policy was no longer viable in the postwar world. Without realizing it, the American people, for their own reasons, dictated the inevitability of that reality.

World War II brought an end to the insular naïveté that had been enforced by the Depression. Lack of money had kept all but the very wealthy tied to their own country, and Americans did not travel extensively during the thirties and early forties, even within the United States. An unintentional chauvinism had made people wary of different places with their odd-sounding names and odder customs. The way we did things around here was just fine, thank you.

Then the troops returned, bringing with them an awareness, even if superficial, of foreign cultures, and an acceptance of "differentness" that they conveyed to their friends and families who had remained at home. Service in Europe and Asia may not have imbued the American with the ability to distinguish one style of furniture from another, but it exposed him, or her, to various commodities—furniture, clothing, and other consumer goods—that were unlike what was available back home, and now these items were seen as highly desirable.

As the postwar economy moved into gear, the frugality that had started with the stock market crash of 1929 was thrown aside. There was money to be earned. And for more families, there was now another member to help do the earning. Out of wartime necessity, millions of American women had taken the places of the departed men on the "home front." Now that the war was over, they were released from the assembly lines of munitions plants, and they no longer needed to volunteer at USO clubs, Salvation Army and Red Cross units, schools, or hospitals. But women had learned that they could be extremely useful outside the home, as well as within it; and gainful employment meant that much more income for the family. Acquisitive instincts, long suppressed, began to reassert themselves—and there was beginning to be money to spend on luxuries as well as necessities.

Many American businesses attempted to pick up where the war had interrupted them. Some incorporated new ideas, but changes are generally made slowly, cautiously. Although the new mood was exuberant, business tenets usually hark back to the voice of long experience. But Bloomingdale's, and its parent company, Federated Department Stores, Inc., were about to innovate.

In 1944, Fred Lazarus, Jr., head of F. & R. Lazarus & Company of Columbus, Ohio, took a trip to Texas to visit his son Ralph, who was then a lieutenant at the air force base at Ellington Field. En route to the base, Fred stopped in Houston to investigate the local department stores.

The largest store was Foley Brothers, then forty-four years old. To Lazarus' amazement, it was doing only a fourth of the business of Shillito's, one of the department stores his family owned in Cincinnati. The following year, Lazarus became president of Federated. He urged that Federated expand into Houston, and finally persuaded the consortium to build a new store there. Aware that Federated's agents were actively acquiring land, Foley's de-

cided to step out of the race; late in 1945 it sold out to Federated, which elected, however, to continue construction on the new building. At its completion in 1947, the $13 million store, the first entirely new department store built in the United States in almost twenty years, was a showcase for Fred Lazarus' merchandising theories. It contained movable walls and stock rooms located around the perimeter of the building adjacent to selling departments, and was operated far more scientifically than other stores of its day.

Under Federated's leadership, meanwhile, staid Foley's underwent a revolution in management which increased its sales from $6.5 million to $16 million in one year. This success confirmed Lazarus' belief that department store merchandising should embody a new philosophy and more dynamic, aggressive techniques.

is assumption to the presidency of Federated marked a major turning point in the consortium's history. Until then, it had functioned as a holding company for existing stores, which continued to be managed independently. Now Federated began to actively participate in the construction and modernization of its stores, and to influence their management—or who their managers would be. And Fred Lazarus began the practice of hiring experts to research and put into effect ways in which the various stores could better share their most successful techniques. Myron S. Silbert, who with Paul Mazur co-authored the definitive *Principles of Organization Applied to Modern Retailing*, was made head of the research division.

The new dictums—expand, modernize,

innovate—were brought to Bloomingdale's by a new management team. In 1944, James S. Schoff became president of the store; former president Michael Schaap was named chairman of the board. Schoff welcomed the challenge of constructive change, but recognized that any improvements in the store and its profits would only come about if Bloomingdale's management itself could be further improved.

In the late forties, and primarily in 1947, he began to assemble an extraordinary team of executives, some promoted from within and many drawn from the managerial staffs of other leading department stores. James P. Mitchell (who later became U.S. Secretary of Labor) was elected a vice-president of Bloomingdale's, in charge of personnel and labor relations. Mitchell had been director of personnel and industrial relations for R. H. Macy & Co.

Sidney Reisman was made vice-president and general merchandise manager of the store. Harold Krensky became senior vice-president in charge of merchandising and publicity, a position he held until 1959. (Krensky, a brilliant merchandising executive, left Bloomingdale's in 1960 to take charge of William Filene's Sons Co. in Boston, returned to become chairman of the board and managing director of Bloomingdale's from 1967 to 1969, then went on to become an official of Federated Department Stores, Inc., itself. In 1973 he was elected president of Federated.)

Lawrence Lachman joined Bloomingdale's in 1947 as treasurer; he went on to become president in 1963, chief executive officer in 1966, and chairman in 1969.

But the man who would have the most immediate effect on Bloomingdale's was J. Edward Davidson, who was elected chairman of the board in June 1947. Davidson had been executive vice-president of R. H. Macy & Co., president of William Hengerer & Co. in Buffalo, and until 1946, president of McCreery's. He joined Bloomingdale's in 1947 at Schoff's urging. Davidson and Schoff's association led to new merchandising objectives for the store which were so all-encompassing, and so radical, that they ultimately led to a complete change in its very essence.

After more than seventy years of selling mass-produced, generally inexpensive merchandise, Bloomingdale's remained a hard-sell store with a flair for attention-catching promotions. In the late 1930s, Louis E. Kirstein, then chairman of Federated's executive committee, asked Bloomingdale's sales promotion director, Ira Hirschmann, to make a study of the store and its future prospects. The resulting report, "Bloomingdalia (N.Y.)," urged that the store change its image, upgrade its taste and its merchandise, direct its focus to a more educated, more affluent customer (the report suggested that the store strive to attract people who habitually read the *New York Times* rather than the *Daily News*), and provide high-quality merchandise for a Park Avenue clientele, instead of lower-priced items for the residents of Third Avenue (which, at that time, was lined with tenements and low-rent brownstones).

Such a radical turnabout required an enormous risk, and it held the potential for an equally enormous financial loss. Bloomingdale's, without any changing or improvements, was an extremely successful business. Sales and earnings at the beginning of 1946 were at a new high. Sales for the fifty-two week period ending February 2 were $44,167,573.

Nonetheless, despite the store's success, Schoff and Davidson decided to change the concept of Bloomingdale's. Their goal was to create a store that would carry higher-quality goods, directed toward more sophisticated customers with a "higher" taste level. All of this was, of course, intended to bring in a greater profit.

Their undertaking was immense. It meant that they would have to totally revamp the store, to make the building and its decor as elegant as the new merchandise they intended to carry. More sophisticated, affluent customers would have to be wooed into a store they were unaccustomed to shopping in, or hardly even thought of walking into. Lawrence Lachman remembers going to a dinner party shortly after he joined the store in 1947. "The lady next to me said, 'And what do you do?' I told her I had just joined Bloomingdale's, and she responded, 'Oh, yes, my maid shops there'!"

The store would have to develop good working relationships with a new set of suppliers. Manufacturers and designers would have to be persuaded to supply Bloomingdale's with quality lines. And meanwhile, in conjunction with what Davidson and Schoff knew would be a long, costly evolution, the existing store would have to maintain its business, keep selling something to somebody, to ensure a continuation of profits.

Businesses do grow, expand, diversify, but very rarely does a successful business turn back upon its own proven procedures to reject the very basis of much of its success, on the extreme risk that another, wholly new direction would prove more profitable. Backed by Federated, Schoff and Davidson made the commitment: Bloomingdale's would undergo a metamorphosis.

The decision was not without foundation. Until the end of the war, most of Bloomingdale's customers lived in the tenements that extended to the north and south of the store, from the east side of Lexington Avenue almost to the East River. These working-class people sought low-priced merchandise, and the vast array and selection of consumer goods lured buyers from the rest of the city as well. The Third Avenue El brought customers to the store, but it also made for a noisy, somewhat dingy neighborhood.

"But after the war," Lachman explained, "we realized the area would change. We saw it as a potential business and residential area."

The new management considered expanding its merchandising line to include many different price levels, and then decided that it was impossible to be all things to all people. Like Samuel and Lyman Bloomingdale before them, they assessed their location and predicted that the neighborhood was headed for a radical change. The United Nations Organization (as it was then known) was about to construct its elegant headquarters on First Avenue and Forty-fifth Street, not too far away. A Second Avenue subway was planned, to replace the Third Avenue El. There was already the nucleus of a high-income population. The store was a convenient distance from wealthy Fifth Avenue (whose fine shops were steadily expanding to the north, toward the south end of Central Park—nearly Bloomingdale country), and Bloomingdale's management foresaw an upward shift in the residential and commercial population that surrounded the store. If they were right, Bloomingdale's would have to change just as radically, in order to attract and make sales to this new potential clientele.

It was easier said than done. Schoff and Davidson conceived a master plan which would effect the change in stages. One of their first goals was to begin to make the buying public aware of Bloomingdale's as an uncommon store, a store worthy of attention, a store newly interested in fashionable and unique merchandise. And the device they chose to catch the public's attention was a gigantic, extraordinary, and extraordinarily expensive party.

James S. Schoff lights the candles as Samuel J. Bloomingdale looks on.

Nineteen forty-seven marked the seventy-fifth anniversary of Bloomingdale's opening. Top management had begun to plan for the event in January 1946, seeking a theme and a point of view for the celebration. Most stores hold traditional anniversary sales; Bloomingdale's wanted this occasion to be much more. They decided to hold a month-long program based on the theme of "Bloomingdale's Continued Story," focusing on the store's role in New York's community life. With this commemoration of their store's long and colorful past, management intended to make a transition leading to a very different, but even more successful, future. So they needed much more than an ordinary anniversary sale. They needed— and they created—a media event. It was an accomplishment at which they would grow increasingly adept over the years.

"Monday evening, February 10th, Lexington Avenue and 59th Street teemed with a thousand men and women in formal evening gowns and tux," the columnists enthused. "Bloomingdale's had all the brilliance of an opening night on Broadway." . . . "A red carpet was spread throughout the arcade." . . . "On the main floor, beaming above were 75 birthday candles in a tremendous candelabra sprinkled with roses." . . .

The 1,000 guests included prominent figures in the political, social, and industrial life of the city. Following a preliminary cocktail party on the rose-bedecked street floor, they were offered a lavish dinner (catered by Sherry's) on the seventh floor, which had been temporarily transformed into a formal turn-of-the-century restaurant.

Seated at the speaker's table were, among others, Police Commissioner Arthur Wallander; Vincent R. Impellitieri, president of the City Council; Hugo E. Rogers, president of the Borough of Manhattan; and Mr. Francis Henry Tayler, director of the Metropolitan Museum of Art.

After dinner, James S. Schoff rose to commence the ceremonies with an opening-night speech. In it he stressed the responsibility of a large retail establishment to the community in which it is located, and in so doing he set the tone for the entire anniversary celebration.

Instead of receiving gifts on its birthday, Bloomingdale's gave them out. First, a recreation building was donated to the Police Athletic League's camp in the Adirondacks; it would come to be called "Bloomingdale Hall."

Next, ten gemlike dioramas of New York City in the 1870s and '80s were presented to the Museum of the City of New York. They were to be added to an already existing collection on display in the museum, to be lent out to libraries and schools for educational purposes.

Finally, in a careful study of receipts and credit histories carried out months before the anniversary celebration officially began, Bloomingdale's had discovered the names of 2,117 people whose families had been charging purchases at the store for fifty or more years. To honor this faithful patronage, the store had gold charge plates made for each of these families. Mrs. Charles Dana Gibson, widow of the famous artist, was on hand to accept from Mr. Schoff a token gold charge plate on behalf of all those customers.

Following the presentations, Sidney Reisman, first vice-president and general merchandise manager of the store, greeted the 600 manufacturers at the dinner. After thanking them for their long association with the store's past, he subtly revealed to them, and to those who would read his remarks in the business pages, that the store had some different ambitions for its future. "Our task, as a retailer, is to investigate all marketplaces, both here and abroad. We must bring to our customers and our community the very best products at the lowest prices accompanied by the kind of service we believe our customers have a right to expect."

To demonstrate its longstanding commitment to its community (the quintessential "neighborhood store"), and to provide a hint of the glory to come, Bloomingdale's had transformed the store's interior into a museum of past and present, spiced with a bit of future consumerism. It was, after all, Bloomingdale's Diamond Jubilee, so the jewelry department featured a special display of 5,000 diamonds. But it was also a night—and a month—of nostalgia: mannequins were dressed in museum costumes of the 1870s; the men's robes section displayed old dressing gowns; in the infants' department were christening clothes and a shining baby's stroller from the last century; the picture department showed original Currier and Ives prints; the "Largewares" department had a display of kitchens, old and new, including a group of patent models of old washing machines. And because the store was always eager to bring its customers the first taste of new items, the radio department showed, beside the display of old and new phonographs and the Lear Wire Recorder, one of the

February 1950. Disembodied hands, feet, and featureless heads grow out of a pile of driftwood. The information card, standard in 1950s displays, calls driftwood "the natural stimulant . . . seen in the pages of *Glamour*." Edward von Castelberg was the display director.

first models of a television set.

Up until 1947 Bloomingdale's had never been noted for high fashion. It would be another two decades before quality clothing became associated with the store, but to further prepare the buying public—and the designers and manufacturers—for the store's change of image, Bloomingdale's assembled a major apparel collection called Woman of Fashion 1947.

The spring of 1947 had marked the first time in five years that the supply of fashion materials in any field began to approximate the normal. With the end of the war came a

slow return of the delicate European cloths, English tweeds, Irish linens, and fine French laces. Cumbersome wartime restrictions governing the making of all clothing were removed just in time to influence the tail end of the designing of the spring collections, so for the first time since 1942 American designers were absolutely free to make what they wanted, and the result was a blossoming of new fashion creativity.

The Bloomingdale Collection totaled twenty-six costumes—suits, coats, ensembles, daytime dresses, cocktail and evening gowns, summer cotton dresses, play clothes, a swimsuit, lingerie, a lounging robe, and a hostess pajama—all by celebrated American designers, among them Claire McCardell, Adele Simpson, Davidow and Pauline Trigere. Major accessory designers such as John-Frederics, Eric Bragaard, and Sally Victor were also represented.

The collection was not for sale. It was displayed in the Lexington Avenue windows for ten days, then presented to the Costume Institute of the Metropolitan Museum of Art, "with the purpose of furthering research, education, and artistic effort in the field of creative fashion design." This was the first collection of modern costumes ever housed by the Mci.

The highlight of the anniversary celebration was the miraculous transformation of Bloomingdale's sixth-floor furniture department. The store had sponsored an "architectural competition" for the design of private dwellings suitable for the New York suburban area, which was experiencing an unprecedented housing boom. The context was intended to acquaint the public with the possibilities of fine architect-designed small homes.

Six miniature model houses were on display near the sixth-floor elevators, representing the first-prize winners in each classification. Well-known furniture designers such as Norman MacGregor, George Nelson, and Edward J. Wormley were enlisted to create life-size model rooms from the winning plans, using either contemporary or traditional furniture to best complement the architectural designs.

The traditional rooms were characterized by wood-paneled fireplaces, pale beige walls and ceilings, rich old mahogany furniture, and creamy white porcelain lamps. The contemporary rooms were marked by Norman MacGregor's big, armless, spacious chairs upholstered in bright, clear colors, free-form rugs, and built-in cupboards.

All visitors to the furniture floor during the anniversary month received a printed brochure, "Prize Winning Designs in the Architectural Competition."

The month-long celebration was designed to attract attention, and in that it succeeded wildly. Major newspapers and magazines, both for the general public and for the trade, ran numerous feature stories on the seventy-fifth anniversary. It was discussed on radio shows in New York, Boston, and Philadelphia, and featured in *House Beautiful, Mademoiselle,* and *Today's Woman.*

Bloomingdale's had announced its intent to "trade up," to become a marketplace for high-quality merchandise. The public heard, and suspended judgment: It was a fascinating idea for a store to change its image in midstride. But could it be done?

Yes—but with great difficulty. The store's then-current "image" turned out to be a liability with suppliers as well as customers. As a former merchant of low-priced items, Bloomingdale's couldn't very well go to better ready-to-wear manufacturers on Seventh Avenue and ask to begin buying their lines of clothing. The manufacturers would have laughed at such an outlandish notion, and strenuously objected to the damage their own reputations might have suffered if their merchandise were sold in the same establishment as inexpensive, low-quality goods.

American furniture manufacturers reacted in similar ways. But there were other sources of furniture, sources that didn't care who the buyer was, as long as the price was right: the European marketplace.

With the worldwide postwar economy still somewhat chaotic, and men newly home from the war and eager to work, there were many more willing and able hands in Europe than there were buyers for their services. So Bloomingdale's turned to Europe as the source of high-quality, unique, exciting merchandise.

Under Davidson's guidance, Bloomingdale's began to transform its character, concentrating its attention first on home furnishings, bringing in high-quality merchandise from wherever it was available. Davidson, who had traveled widely and was extremely knowledgeable about furniture, art, and antiques, encouraged his buyers to travel to small towns and out-of-the-way places as well as to the traditional sites, to find samples of furniture which, with only slight alterations, could be used in American homes. His theory, based upon his own prewar observations, was that the big showpieces in the palaces of Paris, Rome, Versailles, and Madrid would lose significantly in the translation down to practical size. But in museums and public buildings, as well as private homes, in the smaller towns of Europe were numerous pieces which could be reproduced readily for export to the United States. Further, Davidson sought to have pieces designed by Bloomingdale's own staff which would then be made in Europe by individuals or small groups of craftsmen who possessed great skill but desperately needed orders to help rebuild lives shredded by the war. Bloomingdale's personnel were instructed to aid these people as necessary. In one instance of mercantile patronage, one of the store's buyers discovered a talented potter whose pieces she thought Bloomingdale's customers would love to have. But there was no mass production here; each piece was made by hand and fired in the potter's small, old kiln. At his normal rate of production, he simply could not produce pottery in sufficient quantities to fulfill the store's needs. The buyer and the craftsman discussed the problem, and he mentioned that he could make many more pieces each day if there were some way to fire them. So Bloomingdale's bought him a new, much larger kiln, and he went to work creating his line of pottery for shoppers in faraway New York.

Schoff and Davidson both had home furnishings backgrounds, but Davidson's was coupled with a sophistication that he began to impose on the store and its then-small staff. Davidson became the spiritual father to the

A home furnishings display, circa 1949

store in general, and to the home furnishings department in particular, culling the best of the existing staff and hiring a group of new young people, including Marvin Traub (who would later become president and then chairman of the board), Carl Levine (who went on to head the increasingly prestigious home furnishings department) and Barbara D'Arcy (whose design sense made Bloomingdale's model rooms a mecca for the fashionable and the curious). Collectively and individually, these people would come to change the gestalt of the store so profoundly that their innovations eventually broadened and changed American taste and style.

D'Arcy grew up around the corner from Bloomingdale's, and vividly remembers her mother pushing her through the store in a stroller. "My mother, even then, was interested in the furniture department," she says. "It's come a million miles since then, but the home furnishings department was always looking forward."

When D'Arcy joined the store on May 5, 1952, Henriette Granville was the fashion coordinator for home furnishings. Known as a woman with "great taste,"

Granville had designed two of the model rooms with white marble floors and walls, and modern Widdicomb furniture. The store was already beginning to display fine taste, dramatically instituted.

D'Arcy began as a junior interior decorator, assigned to a desk in the fourth-floor fabric department, where her job was to answer customer inquiries about fabrics. Three months later, she was promoted to the fifth floor. At that time, some of the prestigious decorators in New York were initiating the use of mattress ticking for furniture upholstery and draperies. It's not unusual today, but at the time the idea was, as D'Arcy recalls, "very new, very fashionable." Bloomingdale's carried some open-stock sectional pieces covered with the narrow-striped fabric, and they sold slowly, cautiously. Then a South American family came into the store and walked around thoughtfully, looking at the furniture. D'Arcy asked if she could help them. They had, they said, an enormous beach house for which they wanted draperies, slipcovers, everything. D'Arcy suggested that they use mattress ticking for a unified, summery look, and wound up with the largest order the department had ever gotten. Bloomingdale's began to take notice of the smiling young woman with the flaming red hair, and the use of mattress ticking as a decorative element became a fad which lasted for several years, becoming one of the first Bloomingdale's ideas to be picked up by other stores.

From then until 1957, D'Arcy was Granville's assistant. Bloomingdale's was not the only store to hire fashion coordinators, but it was one of the few, and this gave it far greater authority and responsibility, even at that time, than many stores have today. Granville's taste led Bloomingdale's buyers to bring in well-made modern furniture. Clean lines were the most popular (though the furniture was invariably wood; glass and metal were not yet a part of the picture). Granville, fluent in several languages, educated abroad, seemed ideally suited to Davidson's desire to internationalize the store. Then, in 1957, Granville resigned. The "look" of the furniture department was ripe for a change.

One of the primary instigators of the change was the young Marvin Traub. Traub had joined Bloomingdale's in 1950 as assistant to the vice-president in charge of the separate basement store. A *magna cum laude* graduate of Harvard, with a master's degree from that university's School of Business Administration, he had grown up in a retailing family. His father had developed Christian Dior's original line of brassieres and girdles, and his mother was Bonwit Teller's longstanding chief fashion consultant. Traub went through the sales and executive training programs at Macy's, Alexander's and A&S, then rose very rapidly through Bloomingdale's ranks, becoming a merchandise manager in charge of home furnishings in 1956. He was the heir apparent, the crown prince in Schoff-Davidson's empire-to-be. He was the one marked to continue the work they began, and Davidson, in particular, began grooming him, as he groomed them all, to perpetuate his dream.

Traub, under Davidson's guidance at first, went on to groom his own team. Shortly after Granville announced her decision to leave Bloomingdale's, Traub phoned

Barbara D'Arcy designed this room for George Balanchine, Artistic Director of the New York City Ballet.

A studio-den for author Truman Capote.

For Leonard Bernstein, musical director of the New York Philharmonic.

Barbara D'Arcy created this Mediterranean studio using her favorite colors and textiles.

D'Arcy incorporated *treillage*, the Edwardian architectural style, into an octagonal pavilion lit entirely from behind through white plexiglass. The eclectic accessories range from pre-Columbian artifacts to white Noguchi lanterns.

Fall 1978: This is the environment area, featuring French Provincial fabrics and imported furniture.

Spring 1979: Richard Knapple designed this area in front of the model rooms. Accessories and lamps, both contemporary and country traditionals, are all imported from Italy.

Spring 1979: "Palermo" was inspired by an actual 18th-century villa, designed for the exiled King of Naples. The ceiling is a giant umbrella, the floor is stenciled. This is the dining pavilion. The rattan furniture was designed by Knapple and produced in the Far East.

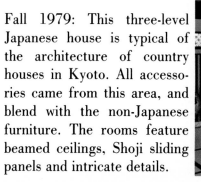

Fall 1979: This three-level Japanese house is typical of the architecture of country houses in Kyoto. All accessories came from this area, and blend with the non-Japanese furniture. The rooms feature beamed ceilings, Shoji sliding panels and intricate details.

Pratt's mannequins are always so calm in the face of surrealistic calamity. Notice how casually these models lounge about, totally ignoring the chandelier that has fallen into their midst.

During the Bloomingdale's celebration of "Milan Week," the store highlighted the work of four Italian designers. Howard Meadows carried the message in a single window, using the broken column as a device to present the four designers' names, as mannequins display their clothing.

For the "launch" of Ralph Lauren's fragrance *Tuxedo,* Meadows created what he calls "an entrance." The tiny penguins climbing the brass staircase convey both elegance and the pun on the name of the perfume, which can be seen on the small pedestal table. And, presumably, on the tuxedoed model.

D'Arcy and asked if she would like to make a trip to Grand Rapids with him, to visit the American furniture manufacturers. D'Arcy said yes. She and the rest of the home furnishings department had, in the meantime, been speculating about who would be appointed to take Granville's place.

On the plane, Traub turned to D'Arcy and asked, "Are you wondering why you're making this trip?" D'Arcy said, "As a matter of fact, yes, but I figure it's market time, and you have no fashion coordinator and you need someone in the interim to carry through and know what's happening."

Traub told her she was both right and wrong; she, he had decided, was going to be the new fashion coordinator.

Shocked, D'Arcy refused at first, but Traub insisted, convincing her finally to take the job on a one-year trial basis. She held the job for sixteen years, during which time she became one of the major trend-setting forces in the American home furnishings industry.

D'Arcy's promotion teamed her with Carl Levine, who later became senior vice-president of the home furnishings department. Levine had been hired in 1956 to work in the budget dress department in the basement. After successfully completing Bloomingdale's executive training program, he progressed to assistant buyer of bedding, chafing at the assignment but determined to move into the increasingly more interesting home furnishings department.

"Furniture at Bloomingdale's, at that time, even though we hadn't gained *any* reputation or image, had more image than

Casa Bella, the first import fair, was held in the fall of 1960. It began a series of import promotions that were held annually for the next ten years. The fair was limited to home furnishings and accessories for the home. This was the area through which Bloomingdale's changed its image.

Bloomingdale's developed new merchandise in Europe and imported it as well as antiques. Elaine McAllister sought antiques and discovered craftsmen to produce home accessories for the store. Imported glass, china, pottery, and decorative accessories were interspersed with antique opaline pieces from Florence.

Barbara D'Arcy had reproductions of furniture made for the store. The mural on the wall was hand-painted.

The antique figures at the entrance of the fifth-floor home furnishings department were intended as decoration, but were quickly purchased.

after graduating college. About a week after he'd been hired by Bloomingdale's, flush with the headlines of his new-found success in the big city, he encountered Jim Schoff as the two were walking toward the store one morning. Schoff smiled at the young Levine's air of instant sophistication, then said gently: "You think you're going to learn a lot at Bloomingdale's, and I think you're going to contribute a lot, but don't demean Pompton Lakes, New Jersey. You're going to find out, after you've been here for six or eight months, that you know an awful lot about retailing as a result of growing up in your father's small-town business." And, Levine now adds, "He was right."

Levine, moving into the home furnishings area, could sense the movement beginning in that department, and as yet absent from the rest of the store. In 1957, Traub, Levine, and D'Arcy, by then beginning to function as a smoothly integrated

ready-to-wear or men's wear. We had model rooms at the time . . . and people were beginning to recognize certain fashion, especially modern. We were carrying Baker modern and imports. Things were happening on the furniture floor, in china and glass, and there seemed to be more happening there than there was in the rest of the store." Levine, too, had grown up in a retailing family; his father operated a small department store in New Jersey, where Carl worked for a year and a half

French millinery boutique on the second floor

The Blue Room in Bloomingdale's was inspired by the Hall of Mirrors in the guesthouse of the Nymphenburg Palace outside Munich. Reproduced in Florence, it was shipped here in sections.

The 1961 fair was L'Esprit de France. It covered several areas of the store.

Entrance to the import area

Barbara D'Arcy had furniture made to her specifications in France. In the model rooms, she often used imported antiques to add touches of elegance.

team, decided to hold a Scandinavian show—a collection of model rooms and furniture pulling together the most beautiful of the modern furniture. The three had decided that the great consumer interest in the modern period was drawing to a close. They knew it would continue to sell, but in lesser degree. The pendulum was swinging back toward traditional. So Bloomingdale's created a bravura show to culminate the modern theme—then turned away from it, even as other stores and designers were embracing it. Bloomingdale's increasingly sensitive antennae had determined that it was time to move on to something else. All they had to do was find the right direction—or set it.

Davidson had by then instilled Traub with his penchant for traveling, encouraging him to see what was happening in Europe, to investigate the possibilities of new suppliers, new types of merchandise, to explore different kinds of items that might be, or might become, important to Bloomingdale's. The two men proceeded to "educate" the rest of their staff. Levine was scheduled to make his first scouting and buying trip to Europe in 1958, with Traub. Shortly before they left, Davidson called Levine upstairs to his office. "He started to show me pictures of various Louis type furniture—Louis XV, Louis XVI—saying, 'You ought to have that, you ought to have this.' Luckily, I knew a little bit about it because I'd studied a little architecture and history of design in school, so it wasn't all foreign to me. But he could really intimidate young, inexperienced executives by telling them what they should do. He'd throw out some names of furniture or antiques, and we'd have to go back to our

dictionary to find out what he was talking about. We not only had to find out what to do, but we had to find out what he was telling us to do. He assumed that we understood and knew. He was a highly educated man, very well versed in home furnishings and fashion."

Traub, by that time, was the chief disciple. In the late 1950s, he had made several trips to Europe, particularly to Italy, Spain, and France, looking for directions that Bloomingdale's might take in the area of imported furniture. One day, he called D'Arcy and Levine into his office and pointed to some pieces of furniture he'd discovered during his foraging and had shipped over. "What do you think of these two chairs?" he asked nonchalantly. "We thought they were fantastic," D'Arcy recalls. "Terrific! We asked where he'd found them. There was also a little table he'd brought over from France. That was really the beginning."

It was, indeed. Traub had brought them back to see what his key staff members thought of them, and whether they could be made to sell in New York. D'Arcy was faced with the challenge of using these pieces in her model rooms, and Levine, by then the furniture buyer, had to consider the problems of finding ready sources of supply. Those three pieces of furniture marked the beginning of annual buying trips by the buyers in the furniture department, and radically increased Bloomingdale's focus on imported furniture.

But the store didn't merely buy what was offered. During the late 1950s, Bloomingdale's began the practice that became one of its most significant hallmarks: *the merchant as*

Poster announcing the 1962 import fair

glass, housewares, and decorative accessories.

By the end of the decade, Bloomingdale's was ready to demonstrate its new-found prowess. In late 1959, a team of about twenty buyers (a vast entourage for that day) swarmed all over Italy with a special purpose: to obtain or create merchandise for an "Event." Management had decided to fill the store with *Italia:* not only Italian wares, but Italian musicians and artisans would also be imported for the occasion.

The store had still not gained the stature it sought, so the fashion buyers could not convince a Valentino to place his line of elegant clothing in Bloomingdale's. But the store could, and would, create its own elegance, to make the public, and the Valentinos, take notice.

D'Arcy, for example, poring through books on fine furniture, had come across a lovely writing table from a palazzo in Venice. She showed the picture to Levine, saying "I think this would make an interesting design for the furniture floor. Do you think you could sell it?"

creator. Barbara D'Arcy, acting as fashion coordinator of home furnishings, spent hours poring over art books, selecting beautiful pieces of eighteenth-century furniture that she felt would—almost—be appropriate additions for the American home. Then she created designs for the pieces, modifying them slightly to make them more appropriate to American interiors. Levine would discuss and approve the designs, then bring them to Europe and negotiate with manufacturers there to have the pieces made to Bloomingdale's specifications. While D'Arcy concentrated on furniture, Elaine McAllister, who also reported to Levine, was spending four months out of every year in Europe, developing what the store calls "resources"—craftsmen and manufacturers—of china,

Storefront heralding the 1963 import fair, Tradition.

An Empire drawing room inspired by a room in the Casita del Labrador, a palace outside Madrid

A vacation cottage in Portugal

Copies of Givenchy and Balenciaga gowns

"Johnny's So Long at the Fair" was Bloomingdale's salute to 1964.

Hand-painted murals stood at the entrance to the third-floor imported fashions area.

Levine said yes, and the two then decided what size it should be (to conform to the height of most American desk and table tops, they often made reproductions of tables or desks the standard twenty-nine inches high). Levine then suggested that the piece would be more practical if it had a few drawers in it, so D'Arcy took the picture to her drawing board and managed to incorporate the practical needs into the design, without losing the flavor or charm of the original.

Then, in Italy, Levine and his buyers went to skilled craftsmen who custom-made each piece of furniture. Because they were reproducing antiques, Bloomingdale's came up with the then-revolutionary idea

Entryway to a second-floor shop area was copied from the old Foire St. Ovide near Paris. It is now called the Place Vendôme.

that the furniture finishes should look the same as that of the original pieces. So they asked the Italian craftsmen to reproduce the patina of the eighteenth-century origi-

Interior of Foire St. Ovide housed special accessory and perfume shops.

The shop for imported accessories and perfumes

"Fruit Stall" on main floor carried European soaps.

Pompeiian murals set the background for a room combining 18th-century English Regency with French Directoire.

Musicians mark the entrance to room settings and displays on the fifth floor during the 1965 import fair, Symphony in B.

French Provincial pieces are mixed with Spanish.

nals. The resulting pieces bore a "distressed" finish that was totally new for the American market, where even the better furniture manufacturers, such as Baker and Henredon, which were already copying some European styles and lines, used glossy new finishes. When Bloomingdale's "antique finish" appeared in the store, it was widely copied, opening up a new era of creativity for the American furniture market.

In 1960, Bloomingdale's opened the doors to its Casa Bella. Compared to the parties the store throws today to launch its import fairs, this one was insignificant: a little cocktail party for the press, called for six o'clock in the evening before the Italian promotion was opened to the public. Levine remembers that "Maybe thirty-five people appeared. We had rolled-up prosciutto and a few jugs of Chianti, but we got publicity, which was the purpose of it. And customers started to come in, and they were buying all those unique things that we brought from Europe. When word of mouth spread, we had to reorder immediately. I was sent back to Italy six weeks later by the gentleman upstairs, Mr. Davidson, to expand that reorder."

D'Arcy credits Davidson with being "one of my great guides" during the years she first began designing Bloomingdale's model rooms. "The great temptation, once we'd learned to do something well, was to do it again. But he constantly moved us to reach out in other directions." And so, having developed an enormous knowledge of Italy, and a network of craftsmen and manufacturers who had been patiently taught to produce merchandise to Bloomingdale's exacting specifications, the store

turned around the next year and moved on to unknown terrain: France.

L'Esprit de France, Bloomingdale's 1961 import show, gained enormous notice from the American public. The store had learned from its earlier venture, and this time the preview party was carried out in the manner to which the store was to become accustomed. On September 26, shortly after the doors closed behind the last customer, Bloomingdale's played host to more than 850 invited guests. Some were members of the press, some were celebrities, and most were members of society with the wherewithal to purchase their admission on behalf of the Etraide Française. (Most of Bloomingdale's "galas," as the store refers to them, are fund-raising benefits for various organizations, and the public relations department is constantly deluged with requests by assorted charities, societies, schools, and miscellaneous causes wishing to be the recipient of such an event.)

andering through the store sipping champagne (and ultimately fed a lavish dinner featuring steak au poivre), the guests found what Bloomingdale's customers would discover the next day: *objets françaises* were everywhere. While the hallmark of the show was the fifth floor's model rooms, home furnishings no longer had a corner on the imported items. More than forty buyers and fashion coordinators had spent more than a year preparing for the exposition, traveling more than 250,000 miles within France, gathering and commissioning items which were eventually shown in fifty-five departments throughout the store. It was the

largest single undertaking Bloomingdale's had attempted as of that time.

French perfumes, packaged especially for this show, were available for sampling in the main floor's Perfumery Shop. On the third floor, Bloomingdale's had constructed a faithful recreation of the famed Rue Faubourg St. Honoré, lined with small shops displaying elegant and exquisite fashions and accessories. The store had even managed to acquire some examples of French couture: sportswear by Jacques Heim, Gres, and Lanvin, coats by Madeleine de Rauch, Guy La Roche, Michel Goma, and Heim, Boussac print raincoats, and, most impressively, evening dresses by Dior, Givenchy, Balmain, Balenciaga, and Nina Ricci. There was specialty food, more perfumes, and, on the second floor, a collection of French knitwear and children's *prêt-á-porter* from Esterel.

Preparation for L'Esprit de France marked Barbara D'Arcy's first trip to Europe on behalf of Bloomingdale's. Instead of combing books for furniture designs to adapt, this time D'Arcy went to France with Levine, to scout the whole country.

Their mission was guided by a significant aspect of Davidson's philosophy: Don't confine your traveling to the museums and tourist spots, and don't bury yourself completely in your work. Instead, learn the culture of a country as well as its merchandise. At the end of the day, have a good meal in a good restaurant. Davidson was a wealth of information on out-of-way restaurants and country inns. D'Arcy recalls meeting with him before each trip to discuss her goals and plans, and invariably, at some point in the conversation, he would recommend places for her to visit.

The 1966 fair was called Color. In this room, Barbara D'Arcy depicted "The Color of Japan," adapted from a country farmhouse in Kyoto.

"You're going to Lyons? Well, then, you must drive forty minutes into the country to this great little restaurant. . . ." The object, he taught his young team, was to get to know the ways of the people, to develop one's own taste. Before and during each trip, the travelers were expected to do an enormous amount of research in libraries, museums, and so forth. Then, while they were in each country, they were to make firsthand explorations to see how the people there live. "When you get to that wonderful restaurant," he'd muse reminiscently, "enjoy the food! But notice, also, the furnishings, the big farm tables and country chairs, the architecture of the country."

"You couldn't buy the cookware of provincial France and not understand what you were buying, how these things were used," D'Arcy still says, paraphrasing Davidson. "Many of the decorating concepts that seemed so chic and sophisticated were ideas we got from a provincial restaurant."

But Bloomingdale's, becoming adept at

"The Color of Gracious Dining," an 18th-century dining room

"The Color of Southeast Asia," combining contemporary furniture with old Indian miniature paintings.

The 1967 model rooms were named for famous plays. This was "The Country Wife," a replica of a room in the Basque Museum in Bayonne, France.

creating its own style, transplanted country items for big-city tastes. Functional kitchen implements became decorative accessories, adorning walls or countertops instead of being hidden away in drawers. Their utilitarian purposes were not ignored either; the store redefined itself, taking on the role of educator and entertainer as well as merchant. If the American woman was accustomed to beating her eggs with a fork, Bloomingdale's would provide demonstrations to introduce the wire whisk. If the New York customer thought baskets were only for carrying laundry or picnic fare, Bloomingdale's would introduce baskets of every size, shape, and design, and display them filled with everything from croissants and colorful fresh vegetables to clusters of shining Christmas ornaments.

And always, there was the unexpected. For L'Esprit de France, Bloomingdale's had reproduced an eighteenth-century French provincial kitchen on the fifth floor. The essence of the Gallic spirit, it was complete down to the last detail: terracotta floor, tiles imported from France, a Normandy fireplace, a smoke-blackened *crémaillère,* and an alcove bed with feather mattress. But amid the wood and brick stood a gleaming modern electric range. During the first weeks of the promotion, the stove was presided over twice daily by M. Georges Pesquet, head chef of the French liner *Flandre.* His cooking demonstrations drew huge crowds.

More than any other single event in the history of the store, the French merchandising promotion raised Bloomingdale's image. The remarkable model rooms filled with custom-made furnishings, the extraor-

dinary taste reflected in both the traditional and the unique furniture and accessories, succeeded in changing the public's perception of the store. Schoff and Davidson's master plan, conceived fifteen years before, was at last bearing fruit. But Bloomingdale's new image was still shaky; there were those who wondered how long the excitement would last, and when, if ever, the rest of the store would catch up with the front-running home furnishings department. Well aware of these doubts, Bloomingdale's began to expand its horizon, raising the quality and taste level of other areas of the store, still relying heavily on European merchandise to add uniqueness, and gradually gaining access to some of the better-quality merchandise from American manufacturers. Bloomingdale's was not the only store to import merchandise, or even to hold import fairs: Neiman-Marcus in Dallas had been holding its "Fortnights" every October since 1957. But Bloomingdale's applied its own level of taste, its own brand of creativity, both to

"All the World's a Stage" was Bloomingdale's 1967 promotion. The second floor's apparel area carried out the theme.

the buying of existing merchandise and to the creating of special items for the store. Buyers and fashion coordinators regularly explored new countries, identifying more and more suppliers and ordering custom lines of virtually every type of merchandise—even, finally, clothing. The massive promotions became annual events throughout most of the sixties (and were reinstituted in 1978), each different from the one before, each done with the flair and panache that were becoming the hallmark of the store.

One of the more unusual of the import shows was held in 1963. Titled "Tradition," it featured items from many different nations, reflecting a wide range of themes. Once again, Barbara D'Arcy won acclaim for her model rooms, which this year were as eclectic as the exhibition itself. One of the rooms was a delicate French pink and white boudoir, inspired by a queen's bedroom in a Spanish palace. Soft pink fabric was draped from the ceiling, enhancing the feeling of a fragile, feminine retreat, and setting off the custom-painted Louis XVI–flavored furniture. In stark contrast was a dimly lit bullfighter's tavern that seemed to have been transported directly from Spain. A plaster-walled Portuguese hut featured a rope bed and a hay loft. All furniture and accessories, with the exception of the hay, were available for sale.

Once again, special boutiques were set up all over the store, even in the downstairs store and the budget shop. In the main floor men's store, Bloomingdale's had re-created Peterborough Row, which featured British men's wear and Irish tweeds.

In 1964, Bloomingdale's created a fair about fairs. The New York World's Fair of 1964–1965 had opened the preceding spring, and shut down for the winter months before opening once more. During the interim, Bloomingdale's filled the entertainment void with its trade show entitled "Johnny's So Long at the Fair." The staff had worked more than a year researching museum archives and peasant villages to learn about big and little fairs throughout history.

Dominating the whole was the balloon. Bloomingdale's designers created balloon lamps, chandeliers, tea sets, planters, ashtrays, coasters, tiles, glasses, wrapping papers, bread boxes, chairs, wall sculptures, bedspreads, and dozens of other items. A five-minute segment of a film about balloons called *The Stowaway in the Sky* was projected on a wall along with slides of famous old European fairs and a moving abstract painting that kaleidoscopically shifted its patterns. The store was filled with balloons, hanging singly or bunched in clusters, many bearing the slogan "Johnny's So Long at the Fair." Clementine Paddleford of the *Herald Tribune* summed up her review of the promotion simply: "The balloon is everywhere."

But so was a lot of unexpected merchandise, some of fine quality, and some items of whimsy. A large produce market was set up on the main floor. Its bins held packages of luscious-looking tomatoes, radishes, bananas, and strawberries—all made of soap! Three green onions sold for 50 cents, a corn on the cob was 75 cents an ear, and $1.25 bought a bunch of three

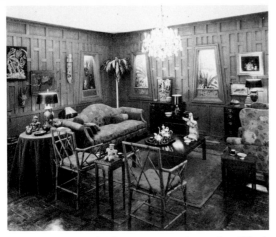

"The King and I" was a version of a Thai house. Note the grilled tapered windows. Lighting and murals behind them suggest a sunny garden in Thailand. D'Arcy often used such a technique with her windows, to enhance the mood and setting of the rooms.

The 1968 theme was "New York, New York." Barbara D'Arcy's model rooms were each created with a famous person in mind. This traditional drawing room was created for Mayor and Mrs. John V. Lindsay.

For architect Edward Durrell Stone

gloriously yellow bananas. Bloomingdale's was cultivating a mercantile sense of humor: how better to sell edible-looking soap than at a fruit and vegetable stand?

More serious fare was displayed throughout the store. Suits and coats designed by Italy's Valentino were presented on the lower level, along with the requisite handbags, shoes, boots, scarves, and textured stockings, all color-coordinated with the clothes. This was a signal that the former bargain basement had finally been successfully transformed into the more reputable "downstairs store."

Entrance to the Street of Shops during the 1969 fair, Art Beat

British men's wear was featured on the main floor, in addition to the fruity soap, while the second floor was a series of accessory shops modeled after the Foire St. Ovide, formerly held at what is now the Place Vendôme in Paris. On three, the central motif was a big carousel complete with papier-mâché horses. It was encircled by ladies' fashion shops, including the Green Room where Givenchy evening clothes made by Adele Simpson were featured. The Sutton Place room showed Spanish-inspired evening dresses by Luis Estevez and Junior Sophisticates, while the new Young East Sider's shop was given over to styles by young London designers including Kenneth Sweet, Angela, Gerald McCann, Susan Small, and Jane and Jane.

On five were Barbara D'Arcy's seven model rooms. They included a Victorian room inspired by London's Crystal Palace Exposition of 1851, another room inspired by the 1925 Paris Exposition, and one representing a St. Bartholomew Fair of twelfth-century England.

A crew of sixty staffers had prowled the world in search of interesting items to sell. The resulting potpourri titillated all of New York City's quality newspapers, and reporters and columnists flocked to cover the event and its tangential aspects. Articles about balloons themselves appeared, as did stories about famous fairs of bygone eras. But the Bloomingdale's fair was newsworthy enough in its own right.

The store had sent out a team of apparel buyers with instructions to search every offbeat village in Europe, to assemble a collection of custom sweaters. They came back with an assortment not only from such predictable places as France, Holland, and Scandinavia, but even from such villages as Land's End, the farthest point in southwest England, on the Cornish coast.

The foods drew critical reviews. Bloomingdale's assembled an exclusive collection of fifty-six cheeses not usually imported at that time, forgoing popular imports for a palate of uncommon varieties that were unavailable anywhere else in the United States. Many of these cheeses became regular items at Bloomingdale's, and some gained wide acceptance throughout the country. An enormous mustard display was

Replica of the French art gallery Denise René Rive Gauche

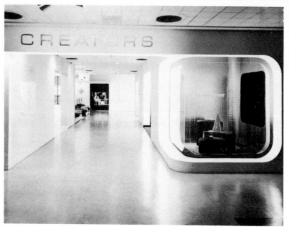

The theme for the 1970 show was "The Creators." This is the entrance to the shops.

Barbara D'Arcy dedicated this stainless-steel environment to Victor Vasarely.

Barbara D'Arcy's inspiration for this 17th-century bedroom was Pieter de Hooch's painting *Boy Bringing Pomegranates*.

D'Arcy called this sophisticated feminine setting the Mary Wells Lawrence room, and contrasted satin, fur, and brass.

built around a collection of reproductions of old mustard pots dating back to 1777, copied from the famed Grey Poupon mustard store in Dijon, France. There were Bunderfleisch beef strips dried in Alpine air 6,000 feet above sea level, and truffles from Perigord, and biscuits from Brussels, and a banquet of other edibles.

The fair was an assault on the senses, epitomizing the motto displayed throughout the store: "The unusual is a fact of life at Bloomingdale's." Ten months in the planning, it produced the desired results: publicity, approval, amazement, excitement. And by the mid-sixties, Bloomingdale's was well on its way to achieving the goal its management had set for it two decades before. Spurred first by the changes in the home furnishings department, and enhanced by the excitement of the import fairs, the store was inexorably improving its image. The quality imported merchandise, the enormous excitement of the storewide promotions, and the crowds of people—including both middle-class and affluent shoppers—who flocked to the furniture floor and stayed to wander through other departments, did not escape the notice of manufacturers of quality articles. Bloomingdale's had demonstrated, in a highly visible way, its commitment to "trading up"—to carrying better and more expensive lines of merchandise. It had also proven that it had learned how to attract the "better" customer.

And so, after more than a decade of parrying, the American furniture manufacturers were suddenly more than willing to allow the store to sell their top-quality lines. The store graciously accepted the manu-

facturers' envoys; the additional merchandise would provide the means to generate increased profits. Only now there was a difference: this time, it was Bloomingdale's that was discriminating. The store set rigid standards of quality and demanded adherence to shipment schedules, high levels of design, and, in some cases, willingness to work with the store's own fashion designers in developing unique merchandise. Some manufacturers found these expectations too demanding to comply with; others realized that the ugly duckling had come into its own, and that the situation was by that time so reversed that it would enhance a manufacturer's image to have his line carried by Bloomingdale's.

The store sorted out its new friends. It would continue to use Europe—and the Orient—to develop unique and customized goods, especially "hard" furniture, accessories, and apparel, but domestic resources were crucial, especially for certain areas. To provide customers with the options for custom upholstery, for example, American suppliers were vital—ordering customized upholstered goods from overseas simply took too long. On the apparel end, toward which the store began to focus more of its interest by the mid-sixties, domestic manufacturers were again highly useful whenever Bloomingdale's needed to rush through an order for a brand new "look."

But the two factors that were mainly responsible for changing the store's image were the import fairs and the remarkably innovative and tasteful home furnishings department. These carried Bloomingdale's through its crucial transition and established its image as a purveyor of excellence, in quality and in imagination.

When Bloomingdale's used its seventy-fifth anniversary in 1947 to herald its intent to upgrade its merchandise, it was faced with the very real need to continue making a profit, somehow, in the midst of its self-induced changes. It was decided that the home furnishings department would be the front-runner, the avant-garde division that would pave the way. But the rest of the store did not, could not, follow all at once. Someone had to stay back and tend to the business of selling, of serving the long-loyal customers of inexpensive goods, of ensuring a sound monetary base which would support the expensive experiment. And so, in effect, from 1947 until the early 1960s, Bloomingdale's survived by developing a split personality.

Schoff and Davidson decided, for the foreseeable future, to maintain the basement store as an almost independent business, with its own buying and stocking systems and its own merchandising manager and staff. It continued to deal in high-volume, low-price merchandise, almost oblivious to the changes taking place above it. In 1945, the basement had set a record for sales volume, and the postwar consumer explosion resulted in even greater sales records.

But management was now carefully re-evaluating all areas of the store in light of the image it wished to move toward, and this resulted in some surprising changes in merchandising. Like other department stores, Bloomingdale's had long carried a line of home appliances—stoves, refrigerators, vacuum cleaners, etc. With the post-war housing boom, demand for both homes and furnishings steadily outstripped the supply. Manufacturers, straining to switch from war production to consumer goods, were lagging far behind as the public clamored for new appliances. Virtually all major department stores initiated a policy of requiring buyers to sign up in advance to purchase home appliances. Bloomingdale's response was radically different. The store eliminated its home appliance department! From a managerial point of view, the move actually makes considerable sense. These products, at this time, were a distinct liability; to continue to stock them prolonged, in the public's mind, Bloomingdale's status as the East Side version of such low-price department store operations as May's and S. Klein, and conveyed images of merchandise strewn on table tops, with eager women piling over one another to grab items marked down on sale. Refrigerators and stoves were simply not consistent with the new image the store's leaders were determined to achieve. Thus the whole department was closed.

A combination of factors led to another significant development at Bloomingdale's. Paris during the 1940s was the fashion capital of the world, and Elsa Schiaparelli was one of its most talented designers. She operated her business from an elegant building on the Place Vendôme. There she combined her design studio, workrooms, and showroom salon, where the elegant women of the world came to see her latest creations. Shortly before World War II erupted on the Continent, Schiaparelli opened a small shop inside the downstairs salon. It was, in effect, a shop-within-a-shop, a rather strange concept, and its effects on the marketing industry have been revolutionary. Tiny boutiques, often designed around a central theme, popped up in other fashion houses in Paris, and then spread to stores themselves. A few American department stores adopted the notion, creating minidepartments for special areas or, more likely, for special occasions (like the ubiquitous Christmas decorations shop that appears every December). New York City's Henri Bendel, a store carrying fine clothing and accessories, created a series of elegant little shops on its main floor and has never seen fit to revise the concept. But it was Bloomingdale's, more than any other store, that took the idea as its own and ran with it. For Bloomingdale's, the boutiques, the minishops, the store-within-a-store concept became a way of life that continues to influence its merchandising philosophy.

It began in 1948. By then, the war had created a shortage of decorative accessories, which had the net effect of turning the United States into a giant market for Mexican handicrafts. So Bloomingdale's opened the Latin American Market on the seventh floor. Instead of simply setting up a display in an area of the floor, store designers created a special shop, featuring hand-carved hardwood figurines from Brazil, fancy tin objects from Mexico, and rugs from Chile, Mexico, Peru, Arizona, and New Mexico. A Colombian weaver demonstrated his craft for two hours each afternoon during the opening week.

The basement store, still carrying lower-price goods but trying to find a way to move out of the "bargain basement" image, noted the success of the boutique concept and adopted it as its own. In the spring of 1953, it opened the Capri Shop, billed as "the first attempt at a budget downstairs

September 1953. A stylized racoon joins three legless mannequins to display square umbrellas. "The news is in the shape," the card proclaims, "and the shape is square, an idea we picked up in Paris!"

shop devoted entirely to foreign-inspired fashions and accessories." Some of the items were imported; many were based on Capri fashions. The shop combined clothing and accessories such as straw hats and handbags, espadrilles, and "inexpensive but exotic" jewelry. But everything had the spice and flavor of sunny Italy. Most of the merchandise was sold out in the first week.

The success of this first budget import shop led to the much more ambitious London Mart the following autumn. Almost $250,000 worth of merchandise was brought in, and this time 90 percent of it was imported. A leather exhibit from London's Museum of Leathercraft was used as the central motif, and the shop was filled with leather goods, brass items, and home accessories.

Some of the apparel, such as raincoats

and men's golf jackets, was imported, but a good deal of the ready-to-wear clothing was manufactured in America from British fabric. By producing the items locally, the basement store was able to sell them at lower prices than would have been possible with direct imports. Although it was still virtually operating as a separate business, and still concentrating on low-priced goods, the basement was beginning to generate an aura of individuality; it was also following the "main store's" focus on importing merchandise. To help further shed the old bargain-basement image, it now began calling itself The Downstairs Store, and its import events were planned as carefully as those upstairs.

Work on the 1954 event began in the summer of 1953, immediately after the huge success of the Capri Shop, and it provides a case study of how Bloomingdale's operates, even today. Management of The Downstairs Store had immediately decided to try to copy their success by picking another unusual location as the theme for the next summer's promotion. They selected a Mediterranean locale, which would feature merchandise and ideas from the islands of Majorca and Sicily: the new shop would be called Piazza del Mare, place of the sea.

Milton Goldberg, a vice-president of the store and general merchandise manager for the downstairs operation, visited Majorca and Spain in July 1953, buying items representative of native styles and colors. He then went to Sicily to place orders for shoes, hats, and accessories, knowing those take a long time to manufacture.

But it turned out that Majorca and Spain could not provide the variety and merchandise the store needed for its pro-motion. No matter—Bloomingdale's would find a way. So Goldberg returned to New York, laden with clothing and trinkets. He assembled them in his office and began calling in buyers from all the related departments: sportswear, shoes, accessories, children's wear, fabrics. After several meetings, the group selected the colors they wanted to feature; several domestic fabrics were then selected, to complement the fabrics purchased abroad. Gloria Wasserman, stylist for The Downstairs Store, was assigned the task of coordinating merchandise, developing styles, and developing some original merchandise ideas which would be produced for the store.

In January, Goldberg returned to Italy and Spain with two key buyers to place orders for accessories, sportswear, and home furnishings. The three men were armed with fabric swatches and color samples they asked the manufacturers to work with. As many as 100 Italian firms, some large, some little more than cottage industries, were involved in producing items for the store, to careful specifications. Straw for wine bottles was even dyed to match the selected color scheme.

The buyers picked up ideas for other merchandise, which were then discussed with Wasserman. The job of coordination was prodigious. For logistic purposes, for example, certain sportswear was manufactured in the United States—following Majorcan styles. Different types of straw trimming were imported and attached to the clothing in the American factories. Hand-crafted items were all imported, as a major focus of the promotion was to emphasize the craftsmanship of the Spanish and Italian artisans. Several famous Italian design-

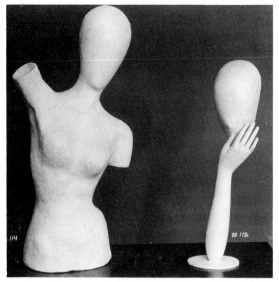

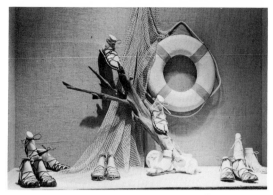

July 1951. Beach sandals are shown in a beach scene, complete with netting, drift-woods, sea shells, a life preserver, and dis-embodied feet.

1947. For its 75th anniversary, Blooming-dale's began to upgrade its fashion image. Siegfried Liebmann, a noted mannequin sculptor, was commissioned to create sev-eral models to display accessories. One of his designs was ultimately placed in New York's Museum of Modern Art.

October 1953. Display director Edward von Castleberg favored thematic window treat-ments. The props here are all fire-fighting equipment. A paper ribbon attached to the ladder is labeled: "Accessories! Save my costume!"

In 1955, Bloomingdale's imported a line of French millinery. Liebmann designed this head for the show. It came in various fin-ishes, all with standard hat sizes.

April 1965. Easter bunnies and Easter "eggheads" combine for the inevitable spring hat display.

June 1950. Hats are sale priced at $5.90.

February 1952. Hollow rectangles focus at
tention on the "outside corsets ".

January 1952. A white fur
stole, and copies of *Vogue*
made these inexpensive
gloves seem fashionable.

March 1952. Bandbox
purses and a corsage at the
collar.

March 1953. Von Castle-
berg's designs were often
more cute than sophisti-
cated.

ers were commissioned to create original items for home furnishings, housewares, fabrics, and ceramics; these were then specially produced for the promotion.

While merchandise in the Piazza del Mare ultimately sold for from 25 cents to $17.98, 99 percent of the items were priced beneath $10; this cost factor was a feature of the event. Import fairs in the main store, then and now, carry higher price tags, but the mechanics of "buying the world" are much the same.

The Downstairs Store continued to open new import shops annually throughout the 1950s. They were still bargain-priced, but the concept of bargain changed in 1955, with the Pavillon d'Or. Bloomingdale's stylists had immersed themselves in costume museums and libraries to re-create the French Directoire period. Two guilded tea pavillions (which one spectator said looked like "enormous golden birdcages") were the centerpieces for displays of clothes, accessories and gifts inspired by the period. But this time, the pricing consideration was considerably changed. Imitation jewelry could still be had for $4, but there were also one-of-a-kind hand-painted ceramic plates selling for $100 and French brocade coats priced at $69. Directoire-period paintings ranged from $18 to $25, and real—and quite elegant—birdcages were available at $100. True, these were good prices for the items offered, but who would expect to see a $100 price tag in what was, after all, a store's basement?

nce again, one was reminded of that seventy-fifth anniversary promise. It would be another decade before The Downstairs

Store was completely phased out and high-quality merchandise (and high prices) evenly dispersed throughout the building; and in the meantime, lower-priced shoes and corsets continued to be sold in the lower level. But The Downstairs Store continued its penchant for imports and its habit of having high fashion designs especially made for it by American ready-to-wear manufacturers, so they could be sold at "value" prices. It could never again be categorized as a mere bargain basement. The Downstairs Store, like its above-street-level counterpart, had begun the ticklish process of "trading up."

The process was completed in February 1967, when The Downstairs Store ceased to exist as a separate entity. All below-street-level areas, revamped and renamed to reflect their new status, were also shifted on the organizational chain of command, and each became a part of the appropriate division of the upstairs store. Howard Goldfeder, Melvin Jacobs, and Franklin Simon, who at that time were all merchandise vice-presidents reporting to Marvin Traub, by then executive vice-president and general merchandising manager, absorbed the lower-level merchandising areas into their domains, and thereafter Bloomingdale's was a single entity. But that's corporate paperwork. With Bloomingdale's penchant for self-contained boutiques, what the public now saw was a large building housing numerous departments, each created to display and sell a particular type of merchandise. But no more bargain basement.

On August 1, 1955, Mayor Robert Wagner led a cavalcade of New York City

November 1950. Though Bloomingdale's was still two decades away from setting fashion trends and declaring itself in favor of a style too new to have gained general acceptance, this window is a precursor of the new management's willingness to suggest a particular fashion look.

August 1953. The window card says: "Handbag News in Three Dimensions," and the display is a study in three's. Each handbag style is shown in three different sizes. A triple frame holds three cutout figures, and each figure holds a pair of the then new 3-D glasses.

November 1953. The black-dressed mannequin wears a fox stole and a face mask. Fox stoles are draped around the wire head-and-shoulder forms mounted on the circling vines. The window card declares: "No one outfoxes us!"

officials and dignitaries on a three-hour tour from Chatham Square in Lower Manhattan to 125th Street in Harlem, celebrating the demise of the Third Avenue El. Demolition began at noon, and the "wake" was the occasion for outdoor festivities arranged by business organizations and members of the forty-five nationality groups who had settled in its noisy shadow.

By the mid-1950s, the East Side neighborhood around Bloomingdale's was one of the fastest-growing in the city. New businesses moved in at a rapid rate, and the convenient, modernized apartments were attracting a young, trendy constituency. Bloomingdale's postwar survey had been correct.

The store began making some strong efforts to gain the attention of the neighborhood's new residents and career people. In 1955, the remodeled third floor was opened as a showcase for fashion. Entitled "Glorious Third," it began with an all-American show, wrapped around a big promotion. Fifteen thousand handbills were distributed to female employees working in the office buildings within a five-block radius of the store. The flyers invited customers to attend a fashion show and, while they were in the store, to consider opening a "career girl credit account." Along with the fashions was an exhibition of pieces done by members of the New York Sculptor's Guild. Half-hour fashion shows, conveniently scheduled at lunchtime, were held every weekday, with a twenty-minute commentary and a ten-minute interview with a leading fashion editor. More than 500 customers came each day to see fashions by Vera Maxwell, Hannah Troy, Jo Copeland of Patullo, Adele Simpson, Tina Leser, Mollie Parnis, Brigance, and Anna Miller.

"If New York City's working girls are now more conversant with fashions from top American dress designers," said *Women's Wear Daily*, "they can thank Bloomingdale's."

Early in 1956, ads were run in four newspapers to announce the opening of a new bridal shop. Readers were invited to make reservations for a formal bridal show to be held after regular store hours on Tuesday, January 18. Almost 2,500 ticket requests were received for a space which could hold about half that number, and a repeat performance had to be staged to accommodate the rest of the interested customers.

In 1957 the entire Third Avenue side of the building was remodeled. With the El down, Third Avenue was becoming a major thoroughfare, and the store built a new facade of marble, glass, and granite and installed a series of new elevators. (This created the street-floor face that exists now on the Third Avenue side of the building

Within the modern exterior, the men's store had been remodeled and expanded into a 27,000-square-foot shop. Roughly half of it was given over to clothing, and the other half was occupied by a smoke shop, a gift shop, and a camera department. Here, too, the boutique concept dominated.

Russell Webster of Bloomingdale's advertising and publicity department used the occasion of the renovations to continue the store's policy of introducing itself to the newcomers of New York's East Side. He became an unofficial greeter, visiting nearby hotels and new apartment and office buildings, inviting new residents of the neighborhood to shop at Bloomingdale's. Webster was particularly creative in greeting the neighborhood's new set of international neighbors. The United Nations building complex was completed, and Webster sent the diplomats and staff members illustrated booklets, in five different languages, describing Bloomingdale's merchandise and services.

The store continued pushing American fashion designers, soon merging this interest with its focus on boutiques. In 1959 it opened an elegant little shop called Sutton Place (named for the exclusive East Side neighborhood) on the third floor, and had showings of dresses by Shannon Rogers for Jerry Silverman, Robert Morton, Kasper of American Editions, Richard Cole, Frank Adams for Deb Time, and Betty Carol for Mam'selle, among others.

But Bloomingdale's, with its taste for foreign imports, still hungered to gain access to the top couturiers of Europe. While some of their doors would continue to be barred to the American changeling for the next few years, France had a burgeoning fashion industry that was open to all buyers: the *prêt-à-porter.* As this European ready-to-wear supply increased steadily, Bloomingdale's became a bigger factor in the Paris buying market. By 1959, Madge Carroll, the buyer for the store's fashionable Green Room, and Patricia Snyder, the fashion coordinator, had become regulars at all the Paris showings.

That spring, they were the first to buy a line of chignon-like hats from Dior. And later that year, Dior signed its first contract for patterns, a trend it had long opposed. By the following fall, Madge Carroll's acquisitions had expanded to include apparel and accessories by such major designers as Pierre Cardin, Jacques Heim, CMC, Guy La Roche, Lanvin-Castillo, Madeleine de Rauch, Nina Ricci, and Claude Rivière. The items were priced from $65 to $285. A fashion show was held in Paris for the benefit of the press, to demonstrate this expansion of the store's purchasing power. The Bloomingdale's models were done up with sooty eye makeup and a light lipstick shade called Cannella. The cosmetic line, created by Stendahl of Paris, was offered at Bloomingdale's in September 1960.

Bloomingdale's transformation of its own image had the net effect of changing the way the rest of the retail industry viewed the Upper East Side of Manhattan. In late 1964, rumors began circulating that at least two major department store chains would join it in the East Fifty-ninth Street area. The *New York Times* went so far as to predict that "the area around Bloomingdale's department store at 59th street and Lexington Avenue will soon rival, if not surpass, 34th Street as Manhattan's busiest shopping center."

While that lofty projection never quite materialized, the success of Bloomingdale's did draw one major rival into the neighborhood. Alexander's, a six-unit group headed by George Farkas (under whom Marvin Traub had apprenticed in 1949), opened a store on Fifty-ninth Street immediately south of Bloomingdale's, which became the flagship of its chain.

Shortly before the opening of the Alexander's store in the summer of 1965, Farkas mused that if he were Bloomingdale's, "I'd have bought the land and built a big apartment building. I wouldn't want a competitor so close."

The new Alexander's developed into the kind of store that Bloomingdale's had been long before it began its great transformation. It served as a general store for the immediate neighborhood, featuring discount merchandise.

In 1947 Davidson and Schoff diverged from Bloomingdale's long single-store history to open a branch in New Rochelle, an affluent suburb just north of New York City. It wasn't a new store; it had been Ware's, a regional department store that had operated in Westchester County since 1881, and Bloomingdale's purchased both the building and its stock. Sidney Reisman, a first vice-president of Bloomingdale's, was given charge of the fledgling branch operation, and Milton Mandelson, who had been manager of Ware's, was kept on as manager of the store.

It didn't take long to determine that the purchase of existing stores could mean the acquisition of existing problems as well. Store location is crucial, and careful planning and design of a building, with allowance made for future needs, can avoid the pain of being stuck with an obsolete physical plant. New Rochelle was the first branch, but it was also the last time Bloomingdale's bought an existing business.

Bloomingdale's in Fresh Meadows, 1949

n May 24, 1949, the first "custom-built" branch store opened in Fresh Meadows, Queens. The new building was two stories high, with a basement of then highly modern design. Emblazoned on the white marble above the main entrance was the distinctive Bloomingdale's "B" in the ornate script style that had long been identified as the store's own. A covered porch was provided outside the main entrance for mothers to park their baby carriages, not an inconsequential consideration in the days of the postwar baby boom. The building was located at the corner of Horace Harding Boulevard and 188th Street, beside a new apartment development.

The day before it opened, the store gave a preview: a picnic lunch held in a large tent pitched outside the south entrance. When it officially opened to the public the following morning, a crowd totaling more than 25,000 people poured in, taxing both the 1,000-car parking lot and the detail of New York City police on hand to help with crowd control. After careful consideration, Davidson and Schoff and their team had decided that the new branch would sell all merchandise available at the main store, with the exception of home furnishings (and the heavy appliance line that was being discontinued anyway). A large number of charge accounts were opened the first day, presaging the success the store quickly became.

As the branch operation expanded, problems developed that required long-term thinking about logistics, training, and merchandising policy. Personnel became a particular problem—how to ensure that the staffs of the branch stores would successfully implement Bloomingdale's attitudes and policies. What could be readily communicated to the compact staff of the Fifty-ninth Street store became a bit trickier when the operation was geographically dispersed.

"You can't expect employees to commute from the city every day," Davidson observed, "and so you've got to depend on local residents. These are generally inexperienced and you have an almost complete training job to do." Many of the better people staffing the branches were part-time employees who had no interest in working full time. This problem was partly solved by shifting some experienced people from Fifty-ninth Street to a new branch that might be in the suburban area in which they lived.

Schoff was particularly adept at handling personnel and training issues. He had once been a personnel director, an unusual accomplishment for a merchandising head, and he was extremely interested in establishing a training program, particularly for executive personnel. A very strong leader, he became known for his ability to spot executive potential, back his people, and fill staff positions by promoting from within.

The Bloomingdale's executive training program became legendary. By the mid-sixties, it had produced an extraordinary number of executives who went on to become leaders in the retailing field. Some stayed with Bloomingdale's; some moved to Federated or another of its divisions; and some went to "rival" stores. Here's what they were doing in Bloomingdale's then, and what they're doing today:

Arnold Aronson was divisional merchandise manager of home furnishings; he is now chairman of Saks Fifth Avenue.

Jim Coe was manager of Bloomingdale's Bergen County store; he is now president of Meier & Frank.

Howard Goldfeder was a vice-president of ready-to-wear; he is now president of Federated Department Stores.

Lester Gribetz was a divisional merchandise manager (DMM) of housewares; he is now Bloomingdale's executive vice-president and general merchandise manager for home furnishings.

Richard Hauser was vice-president of ready-to-wear; he is now chairman of John Wanamaker.

Mel Jacobs was a senior vice-president and general merchandise manager of ready-to-wear and accessories; he is now vice-chairman of Federated.

Carl Levine was DMM of home furnishings; he is now a senior vice-president of Bloomingdale's.

George (Phil) Kelly was a DMM of juniors; he is now president of Marshall Field & Co.

Ronald Ruskin was DMM of coats; he is now president of Gimbels.

James Schoff, Jr., was vice-president of home furnishings; he is now president of Bloomingdale's.

Franklin Simon was senior vice-president and general merchandise manager of men's and home furnishings; he is now chairman of Bullock's.

Bob Suslow was DMM of ready-to-wear; he is now chairman of Saks Corp.

Marvin Traub was executive vice-president and general merchandise manager of Bloomingdale's; he is now Bloomingdale's chairman of the board.

Schoff brought James P. Mitchell on board to handle personnel and labor relations because Mitchell had a reputation of sensitivity to labor needs. Mitchell left in 1952, and treasurer Lawrence Lachman became head of operations, incorporating the personnel department. Lachman had worked for Davidson when the latter had been head of McCreery's, and the two had a mutual respect. Vincent Brennan, who'd also been hired in the late forties (away from Macy's, where he'd run the training squad program), took over the development and running of training and personnel, and implemented Davidson's plan to retrain Bloomingdale's existing executives to upgrade their taste and knowledge of fine merchandise.

Brennan, now senior executive vice-president, occupies what was once Davidson's office. He remembers Schoff and Davidson as being a perfect match in the operations and merchandising ends of running the store: "There was a synergistic approach and energy between the two men and the two areas, although Schoff and Davidson were very different people." Schoff is a good-natured "regular guy" whose amiable personality never lets his intelligence become threatening. Davidson was always the sophisticate, the debonair man of the world. But each had another, less obvious side. Brennan recalls that "Schoff's people policies were very fair and very sensitive, but he demanded very high intellect, taste levels, and sophistication on the part of his executives." Davidson, on the other hand, for all that he was a connoisseur of everything from art to fine foods, was also "tough-minded about the need for profit, and highly knowledgeable about European markets and merchandise." Under this dual leadership, Bloomingdale's became one of Federated's most profitable units.

The teams they assembled tended to work together as smoothly and as closely as they themselves did. There is, today, a nucleus of people who have been with Bloomingdale's for a very long time. Many of today's vice-presidents came up from this core of young, energetic, talented people. As Brennan says, "We all grew up together." Executives and staff tend to stay with Bloomingdale's during their professional lifetimes, and this has resulted in a *continuity of thought process*—a concept engendered by Davidson and carried on through top management since then.

After the opening of the Fresh Meadows branch, Schoff and Davidson and group took five years to retrench, to intensify the planning and retraining of personnel necessary for the beginning of their determined upgrading of the main store, and to consider what direction to take with their brand-new branch operation. They didn't want the branches to become inexpensive promotional stores, destined to compete with Sear's, Montgomery Ward's, and other high-quantity, mass merchants of the suburbs. The main store was working hard to move away from that image. Obviously, any new branches shouldn't even be

Bloomingdale's now has a chain of sixteen stores. This is the one in White Plains, N.Y.

The Chestnut Hill branch in suburban Boston opened in 1978, right across the road from a Bloomingdale's home furnishings outlet.

opened until Bloomingdale's was fully ready and able to implement its new image in the new stores as well as on Fifty-ninth Street.

In 1954 they opened a branch in Stamford, Connecticut. Moving slowly and carefully, they waited another five years before opening the next store, in Hackensack, New Jersey. By 1959, Bloomingdale's, now energetically developing lines of quality imported merchandise, had created a complete circle of branches around the flagship store.

In time, more branches were added. In the early 1970s, Bloomingdale's even set up a completely separate group of stores carrying only home furnishings, under the leadership of James Schoff, Jr., who had by then become a skilled executive of the corporation. The original plan was to im-

plement a series of home furnishings outlets throughout the Northeast, selling fine furniture and accessories. This idea was later dropped, and while the outlets in Manhasset and Eastchester were retained, a men's wear section was later added to the large outlet in Jenkintown, Pennsylvania. The Chestnut Hill branch outside of Boston was retained as a home furnishings store, but a second store carrying clothing and accessories was opened in 1978, just across the road.

Before Bloomingdale's moved into its heavy colonization stage, personnel were able to remain in one position for a long time, developing a high degree of specialization. (This policy is now radically different.) They'd also had years of working together in teams. D'Arcy recalls that "there was a very strong singleness of mind and direction." And when the store started actively expanding its branches, key people from the New York store went out to lead them.

It wasn't just that there were fewer employees than there are today; it was also that there were very few key people. Communications were very open. The network of senior managers, merchandise managers, and the myriad of people necessary to deal with the increased work load weren't there yet, so staff and management were much closer, and training and education of the obviously talented individuals occurred almost on an ongoing basis. D'Arcy says, "We were all hopped up to find something new, all the time, to constantly look in all directions to give the customer something new"—in the branch stores, as well as on Fifty-ninth Street.

The stated purpose of the branches was to export the style and reputation of Bloomingdale's to the suburbs. The goal had varying success (it had incredible results with the two stores built in the nation's capital in the 1970s), but the attempt itself was significant. Branches of other retail stores tend to be shaped by the existing tastes of their locations, rather than by the philosophical judgment or taste of the parent store.

"In going to the suburbs," Carl Levine observed, "our philosophy, at least in my area, has been that we will not contribute anything to a new suburb unless we go in like Fifty-ninth Street. We have to have the same impact, the same image, the same quality. We would not compromise that if we were going across the river to New Jersey or across the bridge to Long Island."

Betty Ford was the guest of honor at the opening of the branch store in Tyson's Corner, Va., in September 1976. On her left is Bloomingdale's President Marvin Traub; to her right is Chairman Lawrence Lachman.

Sometimes this notion met with considerable surprise. "When we were going into Philadelphia" (to build the Jenkintown store, which is still dominated by and was then exclusively devoted to home furnishings), Levine remembers, "I was told by my counterpart, a friend at a competitor store in the area, 'Gee, Carl, I hope you're not going to go in with all that modern stuff you have in New York because it just doesn't sell to these pilgrims here in Pennsylvania. You want a lot of Early American and English type.' And I listened to him and thanked him for his information. But, again, we used the philosophy that we're going in so we can bring something new to this community. And a third of our floor was modern and the rest was typically very 'up-traditional,' bright fabrics and so forth. Philadelphia turned out within two years to be our most successful store for modern furniture."

When the branch opened at the White Flint Mall in Bethesda, Md., in March 1977, the guest of honor was Elizabeth Taylor. At left is Bloomingdale's Margot Rogoff. At right is Taylor's husband, Senator John Warner.

In part, this approach succeeded because Bloomingdale's was the only place customers could buy fine lines of modern furniture. "Now the answer is obvious," Levine says. "Nobody else credited modern with being viable in Philadelphia. But this and similar experiences have further convinced me, and I think most of the merchants in this store, that the Fifty-ninth Street image in the suburbs is very important."

Right from the start, the branches were really extensions of the main store. All of the buying and designing continued as it had for Fifty-ninth Street, except larger quantities were produced. This gave Bloomingdale's something of an edge when its buyers contracted for original merchandise. The larger quantities needed to supply the new branches helped cut down the cost per item through volume purchasing.

This factor still accounts for the surprisingly reasonable prices of certain merchandise (notably customized pieces of furniture and some "made for Bloomingdale's" ready-to-wear). Prices of home furnishings in the branch stores, however, are sometimes the one exception to this. Carl Levine explained that "when something is *very* experimental in my division, we will buy for four to six stores out of the group. Then, if it goes well, the next season we'll add it to the stores that were left out. This is because it's very expensive to bring in a new furniture line. Samples themselves are very costly."

Once the first group of new branches was in operation, a system of meetings, usually on a quarterly basis, was begun in which representatives from the branches were brought into New York to learn about the upcoming shows and the new lines in the various departments. Branches are encouraged to use their creativity to generate individualized "events" appropriate for their respective communities, and merchandise displays (including model rooms) are designed and implemented by the separate stores. But always, always, the major creative and merchandising impetus comes from the Manhattan store. Color schemes and master design and selling plans originate there, and while each branch may modify the canons, the leeway is carefully controlled. Bloomingdale's is selling the Fifty-ninth Street image. The suburban customer goes to her local Bloomingdale's only as a convenience—it's easier than trekking into the city. But the branches can only continue to exist if they are perceived as an accurate reflection—not quite as deliberately, breathlessly hectic, not

Chestnut Hill

Marvin Traub flew to Denmark to persuade sculptor Björn Wiinblad to create the ceramic fountain center for this Stamford restaurant.

Provence restaurant in White Plains. Notice the counter in the rear of the main restaurant. "Quarante Carottes" is the branch-store version of Forty Carrots.

The shop for juniors in the Chestnut Hill store. The clothing hangs from pipe racks.

The gourmet shop in Stamford

quite as avant-garde or provocative or naughty as today's main store is—but still a glittering semblance of the one and only Bloomie's.

Around 1950 Bloomingdale's began to change its whole approach to advertising and promotion. The store's media buys for almost half a century had been concentrated in the mass-circulation morning tabloids—the *Daily News* and *Daily Mirror* and the splashier afternoon newspapers like the Hearst-owned *Journal American,* which had had the largest evening sales in New York since the early 1920s. The readers of these papers were largely those people who inhabited the residential area around the store, dwellers in the tenements under the elevated tracks.

As a promotionally oriented mass retailer, this was the audience the store had sought—people seeking moderate- and low-priced goods, enticed by specials, sales, and bargains, working to stay within their tight budgets and outfit what was normally a good-sized family. When the determination was made to move out of this market, the advertising and promotion had to shift into other areas, too. Under Harold Krensky, this was one of the major thrusts that helped improve the image of the store. More and more of the ad budget was allocated to the quality newspapers, and the ads themselves were redesigned to reduce the clutter and emphasize sleekness.

By the early 1950s, the store's moves were attracting the attention of the industry. The profit picture was running counter to the general trend of the New York retail business, which was markedly down. Krensky cut the advertising budget by 25 percent in 1952, to preserve capital. But of greater significance was the shift away from promotions for low-priced items, in favor of advertising which was "tonier" and talked about such things as the exclusive "Manhattan Green" fabric developed for home furnishings by Miron Mills. The same year, the store achieved one of its major breakthroughs in the American market when Hathaway shirts agreed to provide a line "designed exclusively for Bloomingdale's."* Only Wallach's and Lord & Taylor had previously had the privilege of this arrangement with Hathaway.

Krensky was also reshaping the advertising budget. In the mid-1950s he put fully half of the ready-to-wear advertising allowance into prestige fashion copy which was not designed to bring any immediate results. Instead, it was geared to build high-fashion business in the years to come. This was considered a key part of the education of the new Bloomingdale's customer, as well as a kind of institutional promotion, intended not to sell specific merchandise, but rather to keep the public apprised of Bloomingdale's improved domestic and imported goods.

---

* Bloomingdale's often carries items that are labeled "exclusive." The sheer amount of unique merchandise is part of what makes the modern (post-1967) store so exciting, and knowing this, Bloomingdale's promotes its "exclusives" highly. But the word means different things at different times.

In some cases, a manufacturer produces an item, or a line of merchandise, "exclusively" for a given store. In these instances the manufacturer decides, on its own, to limit its distribution to a single store within the "trading area" so that the retailer can advertise the item as an exclusive. This is probably what happened here. Hathaway may well have made the same decision to limit its distribution to specific other stores in other parts of the country, probably stores that have a merchandising image—expensive, trendy, etc.—like Bloomingdale's. Each store thus becomes the only one in its area to carry that particular item.

A "one-of-a-kind" is a different situation, though. Here, Bloomingdale's buyers have literally brought in items that are totally unique—things such as hand-painted porcelains or handcrafted furniture or accessories. In these cases, the customer is literally buying an original.

Bloomingdale's pioneered in sending its buyers to Europe, the Orient, all over the world, to search out unique, attractive, as-yet undiscovered merchandise. Simply by dint of these efforts, many of the store's items are unavailable in other retail shops.

On many other occasions, Bloomingdale's has itself designed various pieces of merchandise, which are then manufactured for it according to the store's own design.

Some merchandise becomes "exclusive" because Bloomingdale's buys out the entire manufacturer's stock—so it isn't possible for any other store to carry that particular merchandise. And some items are "exclusive" for a limited amount of time, as decided by the manufacturer. This happens often with cosmetics and with linens. Perhaps Estee Lauder will bring out a new lipstick, or a new line of cosmetic colors; or Springmaid will come out with a new design in sheets and pillowcases. They may want the prestige of having the new items "launched" by Bloomingdale's. So they'll decide to give the store the exclusive right to introduce this merchandise for a specific amount of time—say, two to four weeks or so—after which other stores will sell it also. This merchandising technique has advantages for all concerned. The manufacturer gets the prestige of associating its merchandise with Bloomingdale's, at least for a while. The store gets a jump on the market; it's the first one out with a great new thing. This fact, in itself, helps keep Bloomingdale's the trend-setter it wants to be. And the customer who wants to be first with the latest knows where to go to find it. After all, by the time it gets to the rest of the department stores, last month's novelty has become, for some people, as interesting as last month's news.

Another radical departure was the absence of price emphasis, which had been a trademark of Bloomingdale's ads for the previous three decades. Hardly any millinery or shoe advertising stressed price, and steadily less of the accessory ads trumpeted pricing as a factor in buying at the store. Instead, they carried slogans like "the hat we regard as the most important of the season."

Supporting the new advertising program was a major change in the decoration of the store and the way items were displayed for sale. Schoff and Davidson were keenly aware that all of the new and unusual merchandise their buyers were acquiring had to receive maximum display and the highest possible public awareness, if it was to sell. They instigated innovations in the presentation of merchandise inside the store and in the exterior windows. The creative displays changed the entire aura of the store, pulling the focus away from the "bargain" image and spotlighting the uniqueness and quality of the merchandise. The store's ambiance grew both more lively and more tasteful.

In addition to display, the whole area of promotion and publicity was being emphasized. Krensky realized that news stories, even more than advertisements, would help give the store a more "active" image. To gain the attention of the press, the store began to stage at least one "special event" each month, learning in the process what types of activities titillated the press and the buying public.

In September 1955 Bloomingdale's experimented with a sculpture exhibit on the third floor. Doris Caesar, Maldarelli, Key-Oberg, and other members of the Sculptors Guild of New York showed their works, all of which were for sale. The *New York Times,* while admitting the "singular" nature of the event, disapproved of the mix of art and mercantilism: ". . . bravely, figures and abstracts . . . try to project their absolute value amidst the merchandise even as the Midtown Galleries paintings in the windows, swamped by fall fashions."

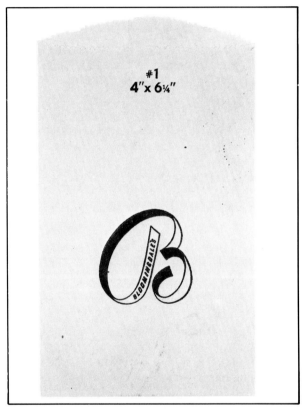

#1
4"x 6¼"

But two months later Bloomingdale's staged a major food demonstration in the Au Gourmet department. Each Tuesday and Friday morning for six weeks the store hosted a "how to" series on the preparation of such dishes as veal scallops Viennese, omelet aux fines herbes, veal kidneys flambé, and cheese beignets (fritters, to the uninitiated). The series also dealt with some other culinary tactics such as the boning of poultry.

In charge of this particular set of demonstrations was what the *New York Times* called "neither a home economist nor a professional chef, but a round-faced young man." That "round-faced young man" was Craig Claiborne, just two years out of his Swiss cooking courses. In time, he would become the *Times*'s own food critic, probably the best-known in America, and the author of numerous exceptional books on food and its preparation. This early and almost serendipitous endeavor was the genesis of a longstanding mutual affection between Claiborne and Bloomingdale's, and laid the foundations for a romance which eventually led Claiborne to his position as high priest of the New York kitchen.

With rare exceptions, these happenings were staged only in the main store, but a program of special events for the branches was developed simultaneously. Run by the public relations department of each store, it included the predictable fashion shows and demonstrations of health and beauty aids, but spiced the program with art exhibits, discussions by prominent authors, and charity affairs, which led one suburban customer to comment that a large part of her education had come from "Bloomingdale's U." All of this was in addition to the regular model room and fashion promotions tied in directly with merchandise. Eventually, the huge import fair themes were also extended to the branches.

Another aspect of the Bloomingdale's changeover was the emphasis given to the display windows. With the removal of the El, chic art-movie theaters were built in clusters along Third Avenue and the windows on that side of the store became as commercially important as those on Lexington. Under Edward von Castelberg, the retail display director, the window displays assumed a storytelling mode in the 1950s and early 1960s. One of the best-known was the "Dig We Must—for Growing New York" windows of 1959, which showed city planning ideas in combination with a fall fashion line. Von Castelberg convinced Con Edison to lend the store the heavy drills and wooden frames needed for these displays and prevailed upon the George Fuller Construction Company for other tools and construction materials to display alongside the mannequins. The whole display was staged in front of highly stylized drawings of the city under construction.

It all helped. After fifteen years of intense effort, Bloomingdale's was closing in on the outer limits of high chic. But despite the dramatic change in home furnishings, the emphasis on imported and unique merchandise, the new direction in advertising, display, and promotion, and the initial attempts at upgrading the apparel lines, one of the most important elements in improving the popular view of Bloomingdale's was a fluke. For all the careful planning and intentional changes, the element that finally succeeded in getting the public to associate Bloomingdale's with high quality and high fashion was, ironically, a fad-within-a-fad: the shopping bag.

In the late nineteenth and early twentieth centuries, fashionable women looked upon the shopping bag with the disdain normally reserved for something the other side of the maid's day off. The wealthy sent their servants to pick up purchases or had them delivered. Even Bloomingdale's had its shiny black horse-drawn delivery vans and liveried drivers. The status-conscious "carriage trade" established an element of snobbery that kept the social elite extremely conscious of which delivery truck stopped at whose house, for where people shopped was considered ever so revealing of their taste and bank balance.

Today stores like to keep deliveries, particularly of small items, to a minimum ("The package you carry arrives today"). The shopping bag, which came into existence in its modern form in 1933, thus serves several genuine needs: it enables the servantless customer to carry home lightweight purchases, and it makes a personal (and very public) statement about her level of taste and consumerism.

At the same time, the bag is a portable advertisement for the store, an extension of its persona. Up through the 1950s, the shopping bag was considered, by shopper and store, primarily as an object of necessity. Stores had them manufactured and dutifully dispersed them, and people used them to cart home purchases and, afterward, for sundry other domestic purposes.

There used to be a small laundromat on Third Avenue, right near Bloomingdale's, and beside it a Chinese laundry. Clients of these establishments frequently brought in their laundry in Bloomingdale's shopping bags, and as they piled up in the window, the little shops looked like odd appendages of the department store. The proprietor of the laundromat kept track of the seasons by the colors of the bags: "I knew it was spring when the blue ones showed up."

But the 1960s ushered in a revolution in graphic design. Quite suddenly, art was no longer exclusively intended for museums and wealthy collectors. For the first time, it was created for and directed toward the general public, and it took new and varied forms: posters, advertising, packaging, book covers, menus, record jackets—and shopping bags. And this time, Bloomingdale's literally got there first with the finest.

It happened in 1961, when the store was planning its monumental L'Esprit de France import show. Artist Jonah Kinigstein was commissioned to do a design for a shopping bag. The idea he came up with was so daring as to be almost impudent. First, he rejected the muted colors and inconsequential design stores traditionally used. He suggested reproducing two classic drawings from a set of old French tarot fortune telling cards, one for each side of the bag. And he suggested they be reproduced in the vivid red, blue, and gold of the original cards. Finally, in the most audacious move, he decided to omit the name of the store from the bag.

Bloomingdale's agreed to gamble on the idea. Remove the obvious commercialism, and let the bag be a thing of beauty, a work of art. And, indeed, that's precisely what it would have to be if they were to successfully pull it off. Anything less than spectacular would provoke ho-hums, and Bloomingdale's wanted gasps.

It worked. The tarot bags created a sensation at the press preview, and although the store hastily placed a reorder, the first supply of bags was virtually exhausted before the promotion was a week old. Even that was not enough. Everyone wanted the fantastic, unlabeled, but unmistakable Bloomingdale's shopping bag. It became a fad. Eventually a drugstore chain copied the design and produced (and sold) an imitation of the tarot card shopping bags, but the quality of the original was unmistakable. Having a genuine Bloomingdale's bag became an instant status symbol.

Thus was born the nameless "designer shopping bag," or as one newspaper put it at the time, "ambulatory art." Never one to ignore a good thing, Bloomingdale's hired Kinigstein to design the following year's bag to coincide with its "Romance Everlasting" import fair. This time Kinigstein, matching his own act, incorporated characters from Italy's seventeenth-century *commedia dell'arte,* again using vivid colors that were atypical of other shopping bags.

Other retailers were, of course, quick to pick up the cue, but although the general level of design improved greatly, most corporations were too conservative, certainly for the first few years, to make radical changes, and virtually no one shared Bloomingdale's self-confidence in releasing a bag that didn't carry its name or logo— the symbol or typographical design by which the public identifies a company or brand. (One noteworthy exception was Bonwit Teller, whose Philadelphia store reproduced a famous Renaissance painting on its waterproofed bag. And of course Halston has since issued his own red bag of courage—an immediately identifiable solid red shopping bag. Both of these are, like the Bloomingdale's bag, what the industry calls "pure"—unblemished by an identifying name.)

"Over the past two years, the rise of the paper shopping bag has been fantastic," columnist Eugenia Sheppard of the New York *Herald Tribune* observed in 1963. "It had a long way to go, since its prestige started from scratch. . . . That the shopping bag is no longer a completely frumpy item linked with the cook's day out—can be credited mostly to Bloomingdale's."

Being both a status symbol and an object of convenience, the bags saw a lot of use. Sheppard described a scene in Bendel's exclusive "Fancy" room one day: "Into the hush-hush that always precedes a fashion show came an ominous crackle. Two well-dressed, tweedy women were settling into their chairs with Bloomingdale's paper shopping bags on their arms. One of them had a $300 Hermes handbag on the other. This incident wasn't reserved for Bendel, either. At Saks Fifth Avenue's show of expensive Dior clothes the other day, the rattle was loud enough to be funny."

Within two years of its paper revolution, Bloomingdale's was distributing in excess of 2.5 million shopping bags annually and was still struggling to keep up with the demand. A national survey indicated that shopping bags were not only a prime advertising medium but also conveyed a store's image. Two hundred midwestern women unfamiliar with six eastern department stores were shown their shopping bags and asked to react to them and to describe the impressions they imparted. Bloomingdale's bag attracted the younger, fashion-oriented, middle-income women. The shopping bags, all by themselves, were conveying the store's new image and drawing in a new type of customer.

Undoubtedly, tying each season's new, nameless bag to a highly publicized, increasingly successful retailing promotion was a considerable help. The bags didn't really have to say where they came from. The affluent society, and its zealous watchers and imitators, knew at once. Bloomingdale's 1963 import fair was "Traditions," and the third designer shopping bag, inspired by Epinal prints, depicted the Royal French Guard of the nineteenth century. The following year, the bags flaunted gaily colored, giant balloons, and simply *everyone* who was *anyone* knew that the balloon was the symbol of "Johnny's So Long at the Fair." Nineteen sixty-five saw the regal "Symphony in B," and in 1966 the theme was "Color."

By then the once-ignored shopping bag had been fully recognized for what it was—a form of portable graphic art which, carried incessantly by customers and by those who wished to appear as customers of a particular establishment, resulted in millions of dollars' worth of free advertising. Newest of the crown jewels of retailing promotion, the industry appreciatively rechristened the shopping bag "the Paper Icon."

By the mid-sixties, Bloomingdale's was establishing a firm reputation for its seeming ability to create trends. Lawrence Lachman, who had assumed the presidency of the store in 1963, pointed out later that this was not entirely the truth of the matter. In reality, he believes, Bloomingdale's staff is able to sense a change in the marketplace and respond to it with such daring and clarity that it gives definition and identity to the trend.

Perhaps. And that is certainly a large and important part of it. But by this time, its old image totally cast off, the store was ready to confront the bastions of high fashion, the one frontier left to conquer. It *did* develop an ability to create trends. In the process it also shattered several of retailing's longstanding tenets, while establishing some new ones of its own making.

Part 3
The Present

In many ways Bloomingdale's is like a mini New York: large, sparkling, intimidating, and a place where anyone and everyone can be found. It is the city slicker of department stores.

Mademoiselle, *August 1974*

Tongue in Chic

Today, Bloomingdale's fashion department is the trend-setter for the retailing industry. It holds a position of such eminence that it inspires almost religious devotion from its customers, who make repeated pilgrimages to their temple of style. When circumstance or distance prevent the true habituée from her regular visits to the store she calls Bloomie's, withdrawal symptoms have been known to set in. *Village Voice* reporter Blair Sabol, who moved to Los Angeles, managed to live there only a year because it was too far away from the store. "I had to come back to New York every three months, to get my fix of Bloomingdale's," she told CBS News correspondent Morley Safer during a 1976 "60 MINUTES" television feature about the store. "I had to move back to New York—this is terrible to say—because I had to live near Bloomingdale's. And I even found an apartment two blocks away—now, that's pretty awful—so that I could be close to Bloomingdale's."

While Sabol's reaction might be a bit extreme, there is a sizable cult of people who maintain a dedicated loyalty to Bloomingdale's. And yet, little more than a decade ago, such a thing would have been unthinkable. By that time the store did, indeed, have its "model room groupies"—people who tracked the seasons by Bloomingdale's model room openings. But fashion? Well, it hadn't quite happened yet.

In the fall of 1966, Harold Krensky, who had left Bloomingdale's to head Filene's in Boston, returned as chairman of the board and managing director. A director of the Fashion Institute of Technology, Krensky had a strong background in ready-to-wear clothing, and an even stronger impulse to build the store's fashion sense. He recognized that Bloomingdale's had succeeded in changing its image from a promotional store for inexpensive merchandise to a respectable leader of exciting, innovative, high-quality merchandise—in the area of home furnishings. Now, Krensky insisted, the time had come to make the transition in apparel, as well.

With the full accord of then-President Lawrence Lachman and then-Executive Vice-President Marvin Traub, Krensky initiated a change in the direction of the store's fashion thinking. The key element in facilitating this change was the hiring of Katherine Murphy Grout as the store's vice-president and fashion director. Katie Murphy had trained at Macy's, then gone on to gain considerable experience at Lord & Taylor, Bergdorf Goodman, and Bonwit Teller. By the time she came to Bloomingdale's, she was already a legend in the fashion industry.

Brought on board in May 1967, Murphy proceeded to create a new fashion direction for Bloomingdale's. She developed an excellent working relationship with vice-presidents Mel Jacobs and Dick Hauser, who headed the departments of ready-to-

In 1967, better dresses were housed in the third floor's Green Room, the boutique that ultimately became today's Place Elegante.

wear, accessories, and cosmetics, and they began to actively implement her ideas, even when she suggested doing some rather unconventional things.

Murphy believed in designers—here, there, and everywhere; nationality didn't matter, domestic or foreign. What counted was talent, and she ferreted it out, courted it, nurtured and nourished it until it blossomed into creativity.

She tried, audaciously, to persuade Yves St. Laurent to open a boutique in Bloomingdale's; it would have been his first in this country. But St. Laurent, who was being actively courted by established fine stores throughout the United States, wasn't quite ready to cross the Atlantic, yet. She did succeed in persuading Givenchy to present his latest couture collection at the store, however, and along with it came the designer's own beauty experts, to demonstrate his new line of makeup. Afterward, five of his haute couture models went on a storewide shopping trip. In 1969, *Women's Wear Daily* reported that "Bloomingdale's will go anywhere in the world—to Paris, Copenhagen, and even Timbuktu—to find designers who are truly talented and who really understand and know what young people want in fashion."

Murphy took chances on new, sometimes outré styles, carrying the midi even when other stores were loath to risk it. And these items sold in Bloomingdale's, in part because of her conviction, which she passed on to Bloomingdale's next generation of fashion buyers, that fashion is a total look. She emphasized the importance of explaining to a customer how an item of clothing might fit into a wardrobe (as opposed to selling a single item and letting the customer flounder about trying to combine it with other clothing and accessories). The midiskirts were left hanging on the clothes racks of most stores; in Bloomingdale's, they sold, even to fashion-conscious Jacqueline Kennedy Onassis, who began to be a frequent customer. *Women's Wear Daily,* whose reporters shadow her constantly, reported: "Jackie O did the Bloomingdale's bit Tuesday [October 10, 1969] . . . a black suede Midi wrap coat and a long black jersey wrap dress from the Halston boutique."

The Halston boutique. And the Mic Mac boutique, featuring Gunter Sachs's new fall collection. Designer boutiques. Traub's penchant. Katie Murphy loved boutiques, too, and set about creating a series of them, something not at all usual for Bloomingdale's fashion floors at that time. By 1969, Krensky had left Bloomingdale's for Federated; Lachman had stepped up to the chairman's role, devoting himself even more to the operations end of Bloomingdale's. And Traub, now president, retained

The Halston boutique on the third floor

the title and functions of general merchandise manager, and began to actively support Katie Murphy's attempt to lure top designers into the store. Designer's snakeskin jackets slithered onto the sleek shoulders of chic women who had not shopped at Bloomingdale's before.

In January 1970, another new boutique opened on the third floor. It was called Paradox, and began with a collection of unusual knits from France, Italy, and Scandinavia. As aficionados of Bloomingdale's know, Paradox went on to become the home to the newest, most avant-garde fashions, forever featuring items that jolt the imagination. Its clothing is what Bloomingdale's projects will be at the height of fashion *tomorrow*. Its customers are, like Katie Murphy, willing to take a chance on being wrong; better that than sit back cautiously and wind up at the hind end of fashion.

Marvin Traub said at the time, "I see my new job as making sure business keeps growing through continued emphasis on fashion for young thinking people." The former manager of home furnishings had now adopted fashion as a new priority for the store.

Boutiques continued to open: Workmen's Compensation, a second-floor shop for denim clothing; and the more elegant John Kloss boutique. Finally, in the summer of 1971, Bloomingdale's held a cocktail party for top designers: Giorgio di Sant' Angelo, Anne Klein, Bill Blass, Geoffrey Beene, Kasper, John Kloss, Oscar de la Renta, and Jerry Silverman, among others. The gathering signaled the beginning of a renovation and expansion of the third floor, which would thereafter focus on better apparel, more experimental fashions, and more designer names. The renovated third floor would also include the long-awaited Rive Gauche boutique, which opened in September. A couple of months later, Yves St. Laurent ventured to New York to take a look at his newest outpost.

The move toward boutiques allowed Bloomingdale's to spotlight merchandise in a new, exciting way. Not that boutiques themselves were that new; Place Elegante was established in 1950 by Bloomingdale's fashion accessory coordinator Janina Willner, as an accessories shop that magi-

The third floor used to have a traditional main aisle, with a display "island" that ran down its center. Today this area is filled with designer shops.

A 1979 view of Paradox, here featuring Thierry Mugler's designs

Workmen's Compensation was one of the first shops to use reality to sell fashion.

cally appeared each Christmas, and other stores experimented once in a while with the boutique concept. By the early seventies, however, Bloomingdale's had embraced and developed the concept on a much larger scale than anyone had ever attempted. The store's second and third floors became collections of these small worlds, islands in a galaxy of new designers and ever-changing "looks." The boutique became a way to express a belief in a designer, or to get behind a trend as long as it was hot. When the trend began to wane, the boutique would dissolve and the next trend could come into its own.

One designer for whom Bloomingdale's had long wanted to open a boutique was Valentino, creator of classically tailored clothing. Negotiations with Valentino continued for months, finally culminating successfully in the autumn of 1974. The daring Katie Murphy broke convention and marked the new boutique with a fashion show at the unheard-of hour of 10:30 in the morning, though she was warned that fashionable women would never show up so early.

But they did. Jacqueline Onassis, Arlene Dahl, Polly Bergen, and other social Bloominaries turned out in droves to ap-

The first Yves St. Laurent shop, with sculptured logo

plaud Valentino's collection and christen it with cash.

Bloomingdale's fashion campaign moved fast and steadily upward. Marvin Traub and Leonard Rosenberg, then vice-president of ready-to-wear, visited Paris one year and saw all the French women wearing a bright and different "lips" sweater. They tracked down the designer, a young man named Kenzo, and introduced him to the American public. Bloomingdale's became the first American store to sell Kenzo and the popular Sonia Rykiel.

Katie Murphy and her small staff continually sought out the younger, newer designers, as well as the established leaders. She ranged from the refined Dorothee Bis

and Rosita and Tai Missoni, to the more outrageous French designers. But she also developed American talent. Ralph Lauren had first approached Bloomingdale's in 1967 with his heretical new wide men's ties. With the store's encouragement, he went on to develop the Polo line of men's wear. Vice-President Dick Hauser also became interested in him, encouraged him, and helped him make a transition into designing women's clothing. In 1971, Lauren created a line of man-tailored but feminine shirts for women. Bloomingdale's immediately rewarded the notion by building an entire boutique around the shirts. They became one of the store's most popular items, and the newly spotlighted Lauren quickly became one of today's most prominent designers of women's clothing. Lauren's relationship with Bloomingdale's was so strong that when he won the 1979 Coty Award for fashion design, the presentation speech was made by Marvin Traub.

Katie Murphy died suddenly in 1975. Devastated, 1,200 members of the international fashion industry gathered in the ballroom of New York's Waldorf-Astoria for a Bloomingdale's-sponsored tribute to her. The evening garnered donations of a quarter of a million dollars, which Traub presented to the Fashion Institute of Technology for the construction of the Katherine Murphy Amphitheater. Murphy had been an exceptionally warm, vibrant person, but that's not quite enough to explain why people like Sonia Rykiel, Ungaro, the Missonis and all the rest flew in from around the world to pay their respects. Ralph Lauren's comments about Murphy help explain, in part, the relationship she had with designers. Lauren said that having Murphy's

Ralph Lauren's original Polo shop, in 1970

guidance "was like having a coach who watches over you when you are a kid. You remember everything he said. She always made me feel special."

Not all of Bloomingdale's fashion discoveries are serious designers or profound stylistic changes. Many are whimsical; but certainly all are reflections of the moment. Father's Day gifts one year included boxer shorts imprinted with stock market listings, and ties embellished with little (male chauvinist) pigs. Bloomingdale's presented slick cartoon strip belts featuring Brenda Starr and Dondi—and Juicy Fruit and Doublemint gums. When the *Superman* film opened, there was a super-mania boutique. The buyers travel incessantly in search of a new idea, a gimmick, a "statement." Once they get the idea, if merchandise isn't available, Bloomingdale's arranges to have the items manufactured.

As Bloomingdale's gained momentum, it became increasingly important to its customers. The Bloomingdale's secular religion began. The store manufactured bikini underpants emblazoned with the famous nickname: bloomie's™. The sobriquet soon appeared boldly splashed across the front of T-shirts, nightgowns, and virtually anything imaginable. What other store creates such a chord of identity with its customers that they carry its name so close, like an amulet or a charm?

Today the Bloomingdale's fashion mystique is a fact of urban life. Lois Gould wrote in the *Saturday Evening Post* that she was a "hard-core Bloomingdale's freak; the kind who, twenty minutes late for her own wedding, would only be halfway down the aisle of the Young East

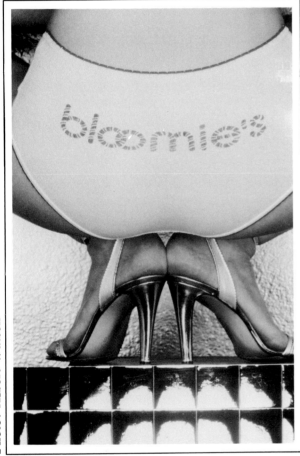

Sider department, rummaging frantically for something new, something blue. . . . I seem constitutionally unfit to shop any place but Bloomingdale's."

ow does the store wield this magic and voodoo such addiction? Spinning out much of Bloomingdale's fashion sorcery is a coterie of professional crystal-ball gazers called

fashion coordinators. Their insights, the store's speed in implementing their suggestions, and the backup given by tremendous advertising and promotional support create such a climate of vitality and constant change that customers come to feel that Bloomingdale's *knows* what next month's "in" look will be, and which item of today's wardrobe will be passé. And, for the woman who wants to be first with the newest, to be certain that her dress will bespeak an in-the-know, with-it image, Bloomingdale's becomes the logical, if not inevitable, place to shop.

The wizard in charge of the crystal-ball gazers is Kalman (Kal) Ruttenstein, vice-president of fashion direction. His smiling round face can belie the control and energy that power him, but Ruttenstein understands, and can verbalize, the need for his department to maintain relationships of mutual liking and respect with the fashion buyers. For the role of the department of fashion direction, created for Ruttenstein when Traub hired him in September 1977, is complex, and possibly unique to Bloomingdale's. There are fashion offices in several of the better department stores, and others are beginning to recognize their value, but in many stores the role of fashion coordinators is usually fuzzy and weak.

Bloomingdale's coordinators operate in all areas of fashion: ready-to-wear, men's, children's, accessories, intimate apparel. (There is also a fashion office for the home furnishings–gifts–home accessories area.) Each has been a buyer, all have strong merchandising backgrounds, and they are storehouses of fashion and retailing information, thoroughly knowledgeable about their markets (customers, manufacturers and suppliers, established designers, up-and-coming designers, and individuals who have not yet made a name for themselves but have talent and should be watched), and they're uniquely qualified to predict coming trends, or to create them.

The fashion coordinators advise the buyers, who do the actual purchasing. Of course, a buyer doesn't have to listen, but the coordinators come fully armed with ample evidence to support the wisdom of their suggestions. And, since most coordinators were once buyers themselves, they're sympathetic to the buyer's needs. As Ruttenstein explains, "They're unlikely to advise a buyer to buy a shirt with no buttonholes, because they know how it feels to mark it down if it doesn't sell."

The fashion office does constant research, finding out colors of fabric in advance of the season, shopping the competition to find out what other stores are going to do, doing market surveys on consumer wants, learning about resources (manufacturers and suppliers) for each of their departments. They channel this information to the buyers.

Ruttenstein and his staff have little nostalgia for the present, and none at all for the past, unless it can be recycled as a retro fad. They decide when a fashion item becomes a basic, and when a basic dies, and they are not hampered by sentiment for the current rage. (In merchandising, it can be disastrous to hang on too long.) The coordinators know what sold well, what is now on the decline, and what is about to taper off. Their territory is the future; they foretell it and they shape it.

One recent winter, cowl sweaters were among the industry's biggest sellers. Many buyers wanted to restock them heavily for the following year. The fashion coordinators said no: The cowl had had its day. But their advice is just that—suggestion, not mandate; and for buyers who weren't convinced, the fashion department could only provide a gentle caution: "Go easy, then. Don't stock too many."

To the surprise of many manufacturers and some buyers, the cowl sweater was, indeed, unable to sustain itself for a second year. Some did sell, to women who valued the flattery of the soft collar over the virtue of being *au courant,* but most shoppers turned to a new sweater style, with which Bloomingdale's just happened to be very well stocked. The fashion office had sensed, and correctly interpreted, the nuances that subtly indicated the customers' desire for change.

The coordinators also sense when better items are ready for general acceptance, and they assist the buyers in getting merchandise reinterpreted at more moderate prices. What's selling now in Place Elegante might be appropriate in Plaza 2 Sportswear next season.

The fashion office operates under the credo that Bloomingdale's does not constrain itself to the same timetable as the rest of the world. Sometimes it will deliberately hold back, letting other stores rush precipitously into a new fashion direction that the world is not ready to accept; and, after the new style has made its uneasy way through the ranks of fad and moved into firmer acceptance, Bloomingdale's will bring it in, as an item that has now become fashionable.

Most of the time, of course, Bloomingdale's timetable requires that the store be first. And being first requires advance knowledge, accurate predicting, and the ability to do it yourself. During an annual fabric show in Europe, one of the store's fashion coordinators made it a point to find out which fabrics were bought by the designers she respected most. Polka dots, updated and multicolored, appeared to be a possible trend. The coordinator bought bolts of the dotted cloth, designed styles for it to be made into, and rushed both to a manufacturer that the store had worked with in the past. That January, Bloomingdale's ran a series of "conviction ads," powered by fashion illustrator Antonio's dramatic chiaroscuro renderings, informing New York that "We believe in dots!" Polka dots were all over the store: on shoes, jewelry, combs, handbags, junior wear, smocks, dresses—and nowhere else in the country. Until the spring, that is, when the regular ready-to-wear merchandise, which had been ordered from Europe in the conventional manner, arrived at the other stores.

Then there's the story of the baggy jeans. Ruttenstein has a network of forty to fifty people in Europe whose jobs, in addition to the normal visiting of shows, dealing with designers and manufacturers, or presenting of information to the store's buyers, is to Be Aware of What's Happening. Bloomingdale's sometimes uses Europe as a sounding board; if something begins to move there, it might well be the beginning of a trend that could spread across the Atlantic.

Last summer, there were baggy jeans at the Paris show, for the first time. *Fantastique!* Rushing the news to its readers in the States, *Women's Wear Daily* ran a banner headline over its story. "Baggy jeans!" they said wonderingly, predicting that the loose-fitting style would hit America hard by the following spring.

Bloomingdale's "conviction ads," illustrated by Antonio, here proclaim: "We believe in dots!"

some like it dot

e hottest dots in town— premiering tomorrow in our lexington windows, in accessories and throughout our second and third floors. new york and all fashion store

bloomingdale's

One week later, on August 3, Bloomingdale's ran a huge ad in the *New York Times* for "Sasson's rendition of the hottest, newest jean shape out of Paris and St. Tropez. . . . Remember when you thought only tight was right?" Now, when a Bloomingdale's ad appears in the newspapers or on television, it means that the advertised item is on the racks and ready to be bought. How could the store have baggy jeans *in stock* one week after *WWD* heralded their appearance on the Paris runways? Even more confusing, how did the ad appear little more than a week after the show, when it takes at least a month to prepare and place such an advertisement?

Obviously Bloomingdale's had a bit of advance knowledge. Ruttenstein heads an informal network of fashion spies throughout the world, who operate a bit like undercover police informants, keeping an eye on what the smart young women are wearing, watching for inspirations that could become trends. They had reported that women were wearing white cotton anklets with sophisticated outfits, presaging that fad. And through them, Ruttenstein had learned about the baggy jeans that were showing up on the streets of St. Tropez, and he predicted that the designers would pick up on the fad, polish it a bit, and present the new style at the Paris show. So, to beat the crowd, Bloomingdale's approached Sasson, urged them to create their own version of the loose-jeans look way before the fad hit the States, developed an ad, and timed it for release a couple of weeks after the show would create a flurry of interest in the new look. It was, to say the least, going out on a thin limb. After years of skin-tight jeans, with a sales

history that indicated the style was here to stay for the foreseeable future at least, Ruttenstein's educated instinct told him that the baggy jeans would catch on as an auxiliary jeans look both with the French designers and with the American public. If he'd been wrong, Bloomingdale's would have been left with a lot of denim hanging around the third floor.

He wasn't wrong.

Kal Ruttenstein, former president of Bonwit Teller and vice-president of Saks Fifth Avenue, says he's always wanted to work in Bloomingdale's. Why? "Because Bloomingdale's traffic pattern allows buyers to take risks, even make mistakes. The sheer volume of customers will eat up the mistakes. No other store has a traffic pattern like Bloomingdale's." Therefore, presumably, no other store can afford to take such risks second-guessing the quicksilver fashion industry in a constant attempt to have tomorrow's style available today.

The predictions are made not only by means of a thorough knowledge of the fashion industry, but by an intuitive sense of fashion itself, and by keeping abreast of life styles of Bloomingdale's customers. One freezing January day, Ruttenstein's staff urged him out of the warmth of the store. They piled into cars and headed south to Soho, that area of Manhattan just south of Houston Street and west of the more affluent Greenwich Village. Soho is today what the Village was many years and many dollars ago, the home of the avant-garde, of artists living in lofts carved out of unfashionable office buildings and factories, of craftspeople selling their unique wares in tiny shops or in the lofts they live in.

The uptown group explored the out-of-the-way storefronts where undiscovered young designers were cooking up the future. They showed Ruttenstein the kinky little shops that had all of the new, "in," or soon-to-be-"in" merchandise they predicted Bloomingdale's customers would soon be buying. The fashion coordinators are a lively group of active people, selected in part for their ability to stay in touch with what's happening. They don't rely on newspaper columns to learn that the Mudd Club is in and "the Studio" out; they know because the city's trends are part of their own lives, and the lives they lead are often similar to the lives their customers lead, or would like to lead.

One of Bloomingdale's greatest strengths is its extraordinarily developed ability to have merchandise developed for itself. Fashion coordinators and sometimes buyers are adept at having their creative ideas turned into unique merchandise. When the store held its India import fair, fashions were created in a myriad of ways. Fashion coordinators bought quantities of silks, gauzes, and cottons in India and carried them to designers in Europe and in the United States and said: Here, make us five hundred blouses of this fabric. The store was simultaneously placing an order and providing the fabric; how could anyone refuse?

Sometimes they went to Indian designers with fabric from Europe or the States. They also scoured the Indian markets for antique clothing, or for specific items of everyday wear that they felt their customers would like. Or they went to Indian manufacturers and said, We love what

you're making, but we'd like you to make some for us that are slightly different, in this specific way.

It doesn't just happen in India, of course. With so much of every store's merchandise the same as that sold by every other store, Bloomingdale's has developed a penchant for involving itself in design or manufacture, to ensure that at least some of the items it carries will be unique. This quest for the different explains the store's constant search for new designers. When one is found, Bloomingdale's will often commission some of his or her work, but request adaptations to make the merchandise more attractive to the store's customers. The store rarely encounters a designer who refuses to accept such suggestions. Respect for Bloomingdale's fashion sense has a definite effect on the creative exchange.

Ruttenstein is quick to point out that not all of Bloomingdale's merchandise is avant-garde, because not all its customers care to wear Claude Montana's exaggerated fantasies. ("But it's important that we carry them," Traub insists, "that we know of them and showcase them. Because that's part of our image.") Still, and to the surprise of the unknowing, Bloomingdale's maintains a broad base of good basic, quality merchandise. "We project the advanced merchandise in our ads," Ruttenstein says. "That gets the customers in. They like to see the newer things. But not every woman wants to wear them. So for her, we have the classics, the clothing she's comfortable wearing. But she feels good knowing it comes from the store that features the latest. And by displaying the new looks, we're educating her. Next year, or the year after that, maybe today's far-out design will be modified a bit, and she'll be more used to seeing it on the mannequins, and she'll be more likely to try it on and find that she likes the way it looks on her."

The interaction between the fashion office and the buyers, who are in fact the merchants of their specific departments or boutiques, is delicate, and carefully nurtured. If a coordinator recommends a designer or a trend that falls flat, it's the buyer who has to live with the unsalable merchandise and the diminished profit line. But Ruttenstein's office maintains enormous impact on the buyers.

The tenuous relationship works, in Bloomingdale's, because buyers and fashion coordinators have learned to hold each other in mutual respect. It works because the fashion coordinators continuously share their knowledge with the buyers, acting as a resource, providing immediate data that the individual buyers would not have time to gather for themselves. It works because the individuals in the two groups like and respect each other, see each other as members of the same team. Their common job is to predict what the public will want to buy and wear, and to get that merchandise into the store.

And, as with many things in Bloomingdale's, it works because Marvin Traub believes in it. He backs the fashion office, and that gives it an extremely important status. Ruttenstein, with his highly organized, sizable staff, is after all the successor to Katie Murphy. Traub is only too aware that Bloomingdale's fashion leadership can only be maintained by retaining an in-house corps of experts who regularly attend every European *prêt-à-porter* (as does Traub himself), who can distinguish the significant from the faddish, and who can enable the store to turn that knowledge into sales and profits.

Of course, once the clothing and accessories are in the store, they have to be moved from the racks into the customer's Bloomingdale's shopping bag. To do this, Bloomingdale's has become a master of advertising and promoting, letting the consumer know what's available, making her want it, and drawing her into the store to buy it. Because fashions at Bloomingdale's are constantly changing, the advertising department can't keep up with the nuances of the new. So fashion coordinators and buyers select the merchandise to be displayed in the windows, delivering it to display director Howard Meadows with explanations about what it looked like on the Paris runways, or how it might best be accessorized for a total look. They mastermind the conviction ads, and get involved with conceiving new shops—whether it's a shop for a "look" (e.g., designer blue jeans) or for a particular designer (Ralph Lauren or Perry Ellis or a fantastic young woman from Idaho whom no one else has heard of—yet). They'll sometimes stay up all night, perhaps with the advertising staff, and have a brainstorming session that results in a concept for a new promotion or a new, temporary boutique. Your Strong Suit was conceived that way; it was a boutique that featured every type of suit: skirt, pants, jump, walking, and basic black.

The boutiques are the delight of some customers and the dismay of others. Even today, Bloomingdale's will be visited by the shopper who wails, "But where are the

Long, long ago, it used to be called "Plaza 2 Juniors." Since the early 1970s, though, this second-floor shop has become one of the most changeable areas in the store. These are just a few incarnations of a shop that is the epitome of Bloomingdale's constant search for the ever-changing trend.

skirts?" Well, there are some over here, and some over there, and then there are some more. . . .

But the frequent shoppers soon learn the trick: learn which boutiques carry lines by certain manufacturers or designers who make clothes that look good on you. And when you go to the store, head for those sections, just as you'd go to specific stores along Madison Avenue and avoid others that don't carry your type of clothing. OK, solved that one. Now what about the problem of the constantly shifting locations? You've discovered a boutique that seems to have things made just for you. Every time you visit it, you find something simply fabulous! The only trouble is finding that peripatetic boutique. The store keeps moving it from one place to another.

Not really, shopper, it only seems that way. Actually, most of the shops are really rather immobile. What do change are the seasonal shops, open only for limited periods of time, and the transitory shops carrying trendy items—like The Feather Shop, or Super-Mania—which appear suddenly, remain for the duration of their trend, then disappear. These instantly appearing, suddenly disappearing boutiques, which can and do pop up anywhere in the store, help create the uneasy feeling that Bloomingdale's boutiques are like mobile homes, enabling the store to shift whole floors at Traub's capricious whim.

Traub, of course, denies this. But truth to tell, even the "standard" shops have been known to ease on down the floor upon occasion. Paradox did it, for example. Possibly the best-known boutique in Bloomingdale's, Paradox features the newest, freshest merchandise: pre-trend. It

was originally located within the Young East Sider department, under the assumption that the Y.E.S. shopper would be attracted to its with-it wares. Yet, while this was certainly true, the location had the undesirable effect of removing Paradox from the travel routes of many customers who did not patronize or explore the Y.E.S. department. So one night after the store closed, Bloomingdale's simply picked up Paradox and transplanted it into the central aisle, where it now thrives.

Jill Robinson wrote in *Vogue* that "when one wonders where the efficient workmen have gone, Bloomie's has them all. Transformations are effected overnight, reflecting the mobility that is the operative characteristic the Bloomie's personality wishes for. Unlike life, nothing does stay the same. Bloomie's does not have to wake up and see itself all over again tomorrow. It can enjoy the change the rest of us only attempt."

These flickering changes within the store are transitory. They will change with the season, with the mood, with the trend. The substantive change seems permanent. Bloomingdale's has succeeded, as retailers rarely do, in totally changing its image, even to the skeptical eyes of the fashion watchers. The store that once took three years to lure Yves St. Laurent into its boutiqueries has now become authoritative, decisive, a force in its own right. It takes risks other stores would never dream of, for it is an aggressor in the world of fashion, an actor instead of a reactor. By now, Bloomingdale's has a position of such eminence that it becomes difficult to say whether the store recognizes a trend and promotes it, or creates the trend and watches others copy it. In fact, it does both, at different times. And that almost religious devotion the store inspires in its "regular customers"? It comes from the organic process of acquisition of merchandise, much of it unique; the creation of original items; one of the most aggressive, creative advertising and promotion departments in the business; and the willingness to move damn fast to bring the very latest merchandise to its customers before anyone else has realized that yesterday's big craze is about to die.

Service, Bloomingstyle

Devoted Bloomingdale's customers may thrill to the store's carnival of merchandise and incessant hum and buzz of traffic, but others feel too overwhelmed to do anything but sigh over catalogs at home. The people at Bloomingdale's understand how awesome and forbidding a task shopping can be, so there are three shopping services to demystify the process and provide a personal bridge between the customer and the store.

The Beatrice Dale shopping service is the oldest of the three. First invented as B. Dale, short for Bloomingdale, the service handles all merchandise except for furniture and rugs (which require the specialized knowledge of home furnishings sales personnel). An enormous variety of customers uses the service—foreign and out-of-town customers, people without charge cards who want to buy items throughout the store but make only one payment, and others who want items shipped to them, even when the postage may cost more than the merchandise itself.

Joan Cuomo, director of the service, and her five-member staff do everything from Christmas shopping on behalf of a shut-in to helping a new customer get acquainted with the layout and offerings of the store.

"We don't have any limitations on the word 'service,' " says Cuomo. After a dozen years with the shopping service, she is used to the busy doctors who dash into the store at 4:00 P.M. on December 24 each year to start their Christmas shopping. (And yes, personal deliveries can be done that night, if necessary.) Comedienne Anne Meara visits Bloomingdale's every Christmas, too, bearing her own wrapping paper, cards, and lengthy list. Cuomo peruses the list, tells Meara where to find everything, advises her on new or unusual items, then awaits Meara's arms-loaded return hours later. Marie Osmond stopped in with her mother one day, and she also wanted to do her own looking and choosing. So Cuomo guided them on a quick tour of the departments they were interested in, gave them a Beatrice Dale coupon book, and the pair went off to shop the store. As Marie selected items, they were instantly shipped to Cuomo's office (that's part of the normal service) so that by the time the Osmonds returned, all their purchases from throughout the store were there waiting for them, and they could pay for all the merchandise with a single payment.

U‌nited Nations employees and spouses of diplomats take advantage of the service's multilingual information and shopping service, and tourists from virtually everywhere stop by to inquire about unique gifts to send back home.

One Bloomingdale's customer has developed her own solution to the problem of gift giving. The moment this customer receives her Christmas catalog in the mail, she runs the bath water, settles into a bubble bath, reads the catalog, and then calls Cuomo with her order. This routine has been going on for years, yet Cuomo and the customer have never met.

Perhaps the most unusual request for aid came from a longtime Bloomingdale customer whose husband had just been transferred to Moscow.

"I don't want to go to Moscow," the lady lamented, "but if I have to go, I want to take some Bloomingdale's with me."

Cuomo at first thought the woman merely wanted a souvenir of the store. But no, she wanted an entire roomful of furniture—and within two weeks' time. The two went to the home furnishings department, where, as luck had it, some model rooms were about to be dismantled. The customer chose a room of chrome and glass. Within one week, the entire room was packed up, piece by piece, and shipped off to Moscow.

Beatrice Dale is listed in the phone book and openly promoted throughout the store. In great contrast, "At Your Service" is rarely publicized. It is the open secret of a network of affluent women—their treasure and salvation, to hear some describe it. Most of its customers reach the service through word of mouth and personal referral. More often than not, they are women in search of skilled fashion guidance and assistance in wending through the labyrinthine "terrors" of the store. For sophisticated as these customers might be, they are frequently overwhelmed by the complexity of the store and the variety of the merchandise. They are women who are used to having things done for them. Many of these customers are extremely wealthy or extremely famous, or both. This is the haven for the visiting celebrity, for wives of UN diplomats or multinational industrialists, for the woman who travels a lot, and does a lot, and is used to having a personal staff to smooth the way and take care of the details.

But despite expectations, many of the users of "At Your Service," while financially comfortable, live in a less rarefied strata. Judy Krull, director of the service, identifies her average customer as "about thirty-five, with an income of about fifty thousand dollars. About twenty-five percent of my customers are wives and mothers who have jobs." Since the woman has probably been referred by a friend, Krull or her staff can guess fairly easily which hairdresser she goes to, what jewelry she prefers, what restaurants she frequents.

A visit to the service begins with a private discussion about the customer's needs, tastes, and fashion perspective. The aim is not to make the customer fit Bloomingdale's available merchandise, but to enable the staff to understand, or to help the customer develop her own personal style, while also considering what items she already has that must be included in the overall buying plan. Even wealthy women no longer seek new wardrobes at the expense of discarding the old, but rather seek to add to treasured clothes they already have. A *Ladies' Home Journal* article once noted that fashion collector's items "no longer come with an invisible label that reads 'Self destruct at end of season.' . . . Fashions have new-found staying power."

Then comes a lesson on how to actually "shop the store." Krull or an assistant often has to literally walk with her arm around the waist of a customer to reassure her that everything will be all right. The walk through the store is primarily restricted to the third floor, couture wear. Both women discuss which items they like, and pull some for the customer to try on. Trying on is done back in the "At Your Service" rooms, and staff members run for larger or smaller sizes and additional items to go with or accessorize outfits.

"Our customers get hooked on the service," says Krull.

Men use "At Your Service" also, to buy substantial gifts for their wives or female friends. And sometimes the staff serves entire families. One well-to-do woman from Virginia sent her daughter north to Bloomingdale's for a college wardrobe. The store arranged for the girl's limousine transportation to and from the airport, meals, and consulting, and sent her home after a twelve-hour trip with a wardrobe that satisfied both the girl and her mother.

"At Your Service" does not advertise because they might, Krull fears, be swamped with customers. She prefers to keep the department small so that she and her staff get to know the customers well. She also feels that customers should be made aware of the on-floor service they can get from sales personnel, since "At Your Service" concentrates almost exclusively on higher-priced clothes.

Lady Bird Johnson, Diana Ross, Farrah Fawcett, and Jacqueline Onassis are among the service's customers. Mrs. Onassis brought her entourage with her at first; now she feels so comfortable in the store (and with the store's own security officers) that she leaves them—and her famous sunglasses—behind.

"This is Bloomingdale's. You expect to see movie stars here, and president's wives," says Krull. "If they're going to be anywhere, they're going to be here."

Right next to Ralph Lauren's Polo collection is a quiet door that says "At His Service." This is Bloomingdale's own gift to male customers and their women, a place that can save time, declassify what seems to a bewildered shopper to be top-secret information, and generally serve the customer in any ways he can dream up.

Not surprisingly, this unusual department is another of Marvin Traub's inspirations. He realized that men need a personal shopping service at least as much as women do, and maybe even a touch more. Often relegating their personal shopping to the category of onerous, perhaps intimidating chores, many men want to walk into a store, find what they need, and walk out again as quickly and as efficiently as possible. "At His Service" understands.

The newest of Bloomingdale's shopper services, "At His Service" began quietly in October 1978, headed by Susan Schaenen, who had gained experience working in the female-oriented "At Your Service." Schaenen and her assistant, Ken Hershman, have found that men's shopping needs and preferences are somewhat different. "At His Service" is virtually all-encompassing; though its focus is men's clothing, it is more like the Beatrice Dale service in its willingness to assist customers with purchases throughout the store. Schaenen explains that the service will help men with "all their needs: clothes for him, bought by him or by her, and clothes for her, bought by him as gifts. It also means anything else in the store that a man needs, be it china and glassware or a Cuisinart or silk flowers to match his living room's prize painting."

Most of the service's clients are men over thirty-five, business-oriented, whose income is probably over $50,000. The typical customer is busy, and prizes service above any other criterion in shopping. He likes coming in for a two o'clock appointment and walking out promptly at three, with all purchases taken care of. In an emergency, he likes being able to depend on the service to deliver a suit by the next morning at eleven sharp, when he needs it for a business trip. He likes the shopping service to get to know him, so when a Missoni sweater for $450 that he liked but could not quite afford gets marked down to $225, Susan Schaenen will remember to call him and ask if he still wants it.

When a man or his secretary calls for an appointment, Schaenen tries to get an idea of what he is looking for so that, if possi-ble, she can pull some merchandise beforehand, to save him time upon his arrival. She knew a lot about men's wear in the first place, but when she started this service, she took private lessons in men's fashions from each buyer in the men's wear and shoes and accessories departments, exploring each one's line piece by piece, going over design details, fabrics, terminology. She keeps a card on every man who uses the service, recording his size, what he bought, and what he likes, but she also depends on her memory and intuition. Customers include European businessmen who frequent New York, the store's own executives, and many women who nearly always choose their husbands' clothes. (One woman does it indirectly. She tells Schaenen, "When my husband comes in to see you, I want him to get . . .")

Sometimes the service goes a bit above and beyond normal expectations. One very overweight customer decided, in despair, that the only good way to motivate himself to lose weight was to forbid himself to buy clothes until he pared himself down to size. He mournfully discussed his problem with Schaenen, and thereafter, to his delight, she phoned him once a week with a friendly reminder that when he's ready, she'll be there to help him choose his nouveau-skinniness reward.

Schaenen is accommodating but not fawning. She believes it's best for the department to be honest with its customers. If something does not look good on a client, she tells him. If a combination of shirt and jacket is garish, she tries to keep him from buying it. And customers appreciate the feedback. In the first month of business, the service sold $40,000 worth of merchandise. At their first Christmas, sales totaled $65,000.

Bloomingdale's latest shopping service is in the food department, of all places. There Pam Krausman helps customers select gift baskets for Christmas or other occasions—they can have baskets filled with their choice of edibles—or helps with large orders for private or corporate accounts. The service injects an atmosphere of calm into the frazzle that shopping can sometimes be. Customers can sip tea from a china cup while Krausman explains the store's latest unusual culinary item.

All of Bloomingdale's shopping services are quite successful. Perhaps it is because of the merchandise. Perhaps it is because of the privacy. Perhaps it is because of the security of having expert advice. Or perhaps it's simply that, as Judy Krull puts it, "Customers get hooked on the service."

Vanity Flair

When Myron (Mike) Blumenfeld took over Bloomingdale's cosmetics departments, he was given one piece of advice by David Falk, then vice-president of fashion accessories: "Don't louse it up." Falk told him that the department ran just fine, was quite profitable, and needed someone to keep the $2 million volume stable and the customers happy.

Fortunately for Bloomingdale's, Blumenfeld was a man who couldn't just sit tight and keep track of pigment shipments. Perhaps his name has something to do with it. Myron, in Greek, means "perfume," and Blumenfeld, in German, means "field of flowers." A man with poetry in his name, he was destined to make the cosmetics area a thing of beauty, and to increase its sales volume more than fifteen times over.

He moved into cosmetics from a four-year post in home furnishings and men's wear at Bloomingdale's Fresh Meadow store. For him, cosmetics were simply another way to beautify America. If there was hype in the product, he accepted and even enjoyed it as part of the inevitable effervescence of the game. Glamour, for Blumenfeld, is fun.

Free of worry about the deeper, darker meaning of rouge, Blumenfeld has learned about the cosmetic business, and so have his customers. He has guided his departments in the direction of improved service, trying to educate as an integral part of selling.

Bloomingdale's cosmetics department has long been awesomely comprehensive, carrying one of the most extensive selections of product lines in the country. A woman traveling the aisles encounters everything from the scientific aura of Clinique, to the exotics of Shiseido. There are products from small new firms as well as from giant established ones. Blumenfeld has tried to provide the customer with easier entry into this mind-boggling array by emphasizing personal service far

1968. Designed by Jack Lindsay ↑   ↓ 1970. Designed by Joe Bellesi

The Beauty Spot was the first cosmetics demonstration area, near the center of the main floor. Displays changed monthly throughout the 1970s. This area introduced the new lines of most key cosmetic manufacturers and gave women an opportunity to get advice from experts. Note the identical location in these two pictures, despite the variation in display design. Note also the display cases that used to exist around the walls of the main floor.

beyond the normal call of salesmanship.

He started, in 1967, by encouraging vendors (the manufacturers) to hire permanent resident makeup consultants. While itinerant consultants always drew crowds at the store during the week or so they visited it, Blumenfeld wanted customers to feel that they could, at any time, find a consultant at the store with whom they could develop a personal relationship. He wanted them to spend more time in the department, sitting down, settling in for personalized instruction, and learning about new merchandise to buy.

"So many women have never used a moisturizer or a freshener," he explained to *Women's Wear Daily* in 1967. "They haven't the foggiest notion about eye make-up, and they are hungry for instruction on facial improvement. So we will seat them, and the experienced sales personnel and consultants will give them the personal attention that is absolutely necessary these days."

Suddenly the department was filled with consultants in peach-colored smocks, and with stools for customers to sit on. The consultants handed out personalized business cards, and would even write to customers they came to know personally to suggest setting up another appointment or to inform them about new items that might interest them.

And new items were always coming in, many of them launched at Bloomingdale's—always a high-status accomplishment. The idea for a launch might come from any one of a number of sources. Vendors, naturally, might suggest introducing a new product at Bloomingdale's, but quite fre-

quently the idea comes from Blumenfeld, from one of his buyers, or even from Marvin Traub himself. For example, Traub, with his infallible memory, once remembered that Estee Lauder and the Missonis were good friends and had once paired in a promotion at Bonwit Teller. When that department store met its demise, Traub thought the pair might look for a new place to team up, and asked Blumenfeld to ask Estee Lauder if she would be interested in developing new colors to coordinate with the Missonis' collection. All were delighted with the idea, and the promotion eventually included three other Italian designers as well: Fendi, Armani, and Basile.

Blumenfeld comes up with ideas by relentlessly scouring trade magazines and by staying within earshot of whispering European trend-setters. He has made Bloomingdale's one of the most exciting launch pads by pioneering promotional techniques such as cosmetic "outposts" on ready-to-wear floors, and a small theatrical staging area, The Beauty Spot, whose presentation changes every two weeks to highlight some new theme, idea, and product.

Blumenfeld's buyers also join in the brainstorming process. There are six buyers, six assistant buyers, and a clerical staff under Blumenfeld's direction. The cosmetics division is divided into thirteen subdepartments, each consisting of from one to as many as thirty different vendors. The buyers must control their specific inventories (within their budgets). They also make sure that they have the best personnel on the selling floor; even though some salespersons are hired by the vendor, all are required to meet high Bloomingdale's

In 1922, years before there were such things as shopping bags, Bloomingdale's printed a special Fiftieth Anniversary message to its customers on the face of its small brown paper bags. It was far from great art, but it was the store's first recognition that the bags in which its merchandise was carried could be used to make a statement about the store itself.

The shopping bags we use today, expansive paper sacks with strong twisted handles, weren't manufactured until the mid-1950s, and Bloomingdale's adopted one in 1954. The design was pleasantly innocuous: a rose on one side, a gloved hand with an umbrella on the other, and the store's old-fashioned script signature to make sure everyone knew where the bag and its merchandise came from. With slight variations, this design was used throughout the fifties. It changed color each year, and at Christmas the rose and umbrella were replaced with a sprig of evergreen and a candy cane. Otherwise the design seemed fine; why tinker with it?

In 1961, the store found reason enough to tinker. Bloomingdale's held the first of its storewide import fairs, and commissioned a special shopping bag for the occasion. The French tarot-card design, which flagrantly omitted the store's name, became the first in a long series of "designer" bags that raised the medium to a level of pragmatic art. Today's bag may be the creation of an artist, a photographer, a graphic designer, or even a fashion designer, and a customer may casually carry over her arm an original creation by a designer whose clothing she'd pay dearly to wear.

Most bags are seasonal. Some come back for repeat performances. And some bags used by specific departments within the store have been used for so many years that they are immediately identifiable. The dates below refer to the first year each bag appeared.

The Ultimate Shopping Bag is not a shopping bag at all. It's Bloomingdale's recent Shopping Bag Jigsaw Puzzle, a montage of the store's favorite bags, and the proof that for Bloomingdale's the shopping bag is no longer a means but an end unto itself.

1922 Fiftieth Anniversary

Spring 1954

Christmas 1954

Fall 1961

Fall 1963

1970–1979

Fall 1970

Spring 1971

1975–1980

Fall 1975

1976

1976

Spring 1977

Au Chocolat 1970–1980

The Ultimate Shopping Bag

Spring 1978

Spring 1978

Spring 1978

Fall 1978

Spring 1979

Spring 1979

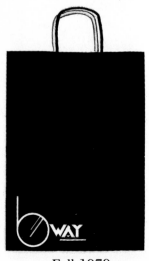

Fall 1979

Fall 1979

Winter 1980

standards. In Blumenfeld's words they must be "well-trained, informed, and enthused."

Blumenfeld thinks the "most sexy" aspect of a buyer's job is promotional activity and advertising. Buyers work in close collaboration with vendors, sharing ideas and co-designing displays. As an idea cooks, all buyers are let in on it to make sure there is no conflict of interest and to give feedback. The display, advertising, and store design departments join in, and pretty much everybody—from vendor to buyer to designer—has to be satisfied before the idea can finally reach the customer.

In a cover story on the cosmetics industry, *Time* magazine once estimated that only eight cents of the cosmetics dollar go for a product's actual ingredients. The rest goes for administration, promotion, and eye-catching packaging. Bloomingdale's own promotional gimmicks have ranged from Diane von Furstenberg herself, swathed in sable, spraying her Tatiana perfume on the wrists of lunchtime shoppers, to far more indirect methods. In May 1975, for example, street grime met the sublime when seventy-five Brooklyn cab drivers attended a caviar breakfast at Bloomingdale's to witness thirty-two new Charlie eyeshadows by Revlon, presumably because, as a Revlon spokesman explained, a cabbie is "an eye man" (among other things) and would tell his female customer to shop at Bloomingdale's. In 1967, Blumenfeld announced that "we are giving the excitement of the entire world to our beauty customers" by setting up outposts on the floor where international experts will advise customers on makeup application.

A second Beauty Spot was opened a couple of years after the first. It was on the main aisle, just before the entrance to the men's store.

Also in 1967, *Women's Wear Daily* excitedly announced that Blumenfeld had "bagged a first" with Elizabeth Arden beauty classes at the store. It was the first time the classes had been held anywhere other than Arden's snazzy Fifth Avenue salon.

In 1977, Bloomingdale's set up The Beauty Center, where "Paris-trained aestheticians" provide deep-cleaning facials and massage, leg waxing, foot pampering, and makeup, while hairdressers top the effort with the latest coiffures. Customers at The Beauty Center are even given the opportunity to do some beautifying from the inside out. They can order light lunches such as croissants and cheese, fresh fruit, *crudités,* or "lunch in a glass," a brave blend of ricotta cheese, apple juice, lecithin, and brewer's yeast.

Blumenfeld sees facial rooms as increasingly important in the overall beauty scene, pointing to the success of outposts—in both the main store and branches—of Adrien Arpel, Orlane, Lancome, and Payot.

Men are not neglected at Bloomingdale's; in fact, Jed Davidson himself recognized the potential for men's cosmetics. He also perceived that men felt timid about exploring the area and needed a very different kind of attention.

So in 1963, Davidson decided to open a "bar." Harry's Bar, an oak-paneled handsomeness haven, was set back toward the men's wear department as an exclusive counter where men could spray colognes and test after-shaves and try on Braggi's bronzer in a reassuringly male ambience full of manly wood and rope textures that would make even Ernest Hemingway feel comfortable. It was a stunningly successful innovation. Each year, more men not only approached the area, but learned to ask for products by name. The cosmetic bartenders gave painstaking individual attention, informing customers about useful products—and almost frivolous ones, such as Arden for Men's cologne packaged in a bottle shaped like a domino.

In 1978, Bloomingdale's won the right

Pierre Cardin (left) signing autographs during the introduction of his fragrance, *Cardin for Men*, at Harry's Bar, in October 1971

to launch Yves St. Laurent's new fragrance in the United States. The controversy over its name—Opium—had kept many other stores away, but Blumenfeld had a strong hunch that the perfume would sell fantastically well. So the store shouldered a hefty promotional budget and brought out the perfume to a huge celebrity-studded fanfare. Opium's name did indeed create a furor, but it became an instant sensation—perhaps because it was associated with St. Laurent, perhaps because it smelled good, or perhaps, at least in part, because of the very outrageousness of its name. Bloomingdale's, which was for a time the only store in the United States allowed to sell the perfume, sold more than half a million dollars' worth in only three months.

Blumenfeld's cosmetics department became so successful that by 1979 it had outgrown itself. He and his staff listened to customers' wants, and decided to tamper with their own success. The heightened intimacy of increased service, personal attention, and resident cosmetics experts required a major change in the layout of the sprawling cosmetic orchard. It was time to reshape the look of the main floor.

In the fall of 1979, Bloomingdale's radically converted its huge vista of endless cosmetic counters, raising and lowering ceilings to create an optical illusion of small, intimate shopping areas that enabled customers to experiment with different cosmetics more comfortably. Many women had objected to having themselves made up in full view of staring customers, although the concept of having vendors' cosmeticians teach them new makeup techniques was very popular. Facial salons were set up behind some shops to respond

Entering ⬚ from the men's store

La Parfumerie

Baubles

Rain Checks

to the ever-increasing demand for pampered, deep-cleaned, "naturally beautiful" skin.

The cosmetics and Lexington Arcade section of the store was completely overhauled, with the cosmetics department enlarged by 35 percent, bringing total selling space to 10,000 square feet. The ceiling was lowered to give a greater sense of intimacy, and a twelve-foot-wide central aisle of black and white marble squares led from the Lexington Avenue escalator to the edge of the men's shops on the Third Avenue side. (Bloomingdale's sent its own people to personally select the marble. The white marble is Carrera, the black is Belgian.) Major vendors, such as Estee Lauder and Revlon, were situated in their own "private shops" which lined the sides of the floor. Even center counters were redesigned to be more accessible.

Harry's Bar, which had become a landmark, was retired after long and faithful service. Blumenfeld said it "was out of keeping with the sleek, modern, new look for the main floor." The Board Room took its place, looking like a very modern office lined with giant panoramic photographs of New York.

The new main floor was designed by Ann Larkin and Sylvia Pontecorvo, working under Barbara D'Arcy's direction. Its inspiration came from the sixth floor's Main Course, with its Street of Shops featuring housewares. For a long time, Marvin Traub had wanted to do something spectacular with the floor. It had not been redone in twenty-five years, and the redirection in the cosmetics department's focus provided the impetus for the design change.

Rechristened the redone floor

Bloomingdale's celebrated the opening of with its own perfume: bloomie's .

is a drama of black marble and brass: deep, rich, velvety blackness offset by the constant glint of gold, with brass and glass counters warmly lit from within. The transformation was total, and totally stunning. Paul Goldberger, writing in the *New York Times,* called it "perhaps the most daring piece of large-scale store design in a decade. . . . This design is right for Bloomingdale's, and it feels very much as an elegant, fashion-conscious New York department store should look—sleek, dark and glossily elegant."

Along with the floor's new look came important new services—more private consulting spaces, a group discussion room in the Clinique complex, a myriad of built-in audiovisual equipment to give customers televised demonstrations and to allow greater flexibility and drama in display.

Most of the floor is devoted to cosmetics, featured in an area called *Vanities.* There are also several new shops, selling a variety of fashion accessories. The redone balcony even boasts a "fashion eyewear" boutique (formerly located in the late Bonwit Teller) which will fill your prescriptions and tint your lenses—on request, of course—to match your eyes or your outfit.

Myron Blumenfeld feels that Bloomingdale's is at the top of the cosmetics field because it has the largest selection of products, the best-trained, best-informed salespeople, and the most inviting ambience. Now that he has doubled and redoubled the department's volume many times over, he claims that it is "hard to remember just what I did or didn't do" to achieve such success.

Caviar on Wry

Saturday's Generation loves to eat. Not just eat, as in tuna on rye, but eat *well,* as in caviar and Brie and crisp, delicate wafers. Whetting and catering to their customers' appetites has become a major area of Bloomingdale's business.

Many of the foods are to be taken home and served there, on silver or crystal or earthenware or china, for Bloomingdale's People give a lot of parties. And, in a process of mutual education, they and their bloomie's have developed a decidedly exotic palate.

Many stores sell cheese. Some of the good ones sell many different kinds of cheeses. Is it remarkable that Bloomingdale's has 350 different kinds of cheeses on its control books? Well, let's not exaggerate; that is, after all, an annual figure. There are only from 110 to 150 different types of cheese actually on the shelves at any one time. Recently, the store started carrying fresh French cheeses on a seasonal basis. Surely everyone realizes that, for example, the goat cheese in

the spring tastes different than the goat cheese in the fall. Why? Difference in the grasses, of course.

Then there are the vinegars: from red wine, from champagne, even a twenty-five-year-old sherry wine vinegar. Bloomingdale's carries one of New York's foremost selections of vinegar and oil, including an extensive selection of olive oils.

Who can tell the difference between spring cheese and fall cheese? Between one type of olive oil and another? Ah, Bloomingdale's can. Though the whole store is concerned with good taste, in the Delicacies department, good taste is an art. And for divisional manager Ray Berger and creative director Pam Krausman, it's also something of a science. Manufacturers, importers, and distributors are forever seeking an audience with them or with one of the buyers.

So Bloomingdale's has developed several rules of tongue. Each new product is sampled and compared with its nearest competitor. Foods are tasted in proper context—for example, sauces are sampled only on the appropriate meats. To do things right, the staff has been known to carry their work home with them. After all,

one can't determine the quality of a sauce by sampling a bit on the tip of a spoon.

They have even learned *where* to taste things. Sharp cheddar cheese, for example, should be savored at the back of the mouth. Buttery cheeses are most appreciated at the sides, and salty cheeses (or salty flavors) should be tasted on the tip of the tongue.

Taste is only one standard the store insists on before agreeing to carry an item. Quality and packaging matter, too. All these criteria are even more rigid for items to which Bloomingdale's affixes its private label. Bloomingdale's own line of fruit syrups and domestic honeys, for example, are all of excellent quality. Krausman, who is truly knowledgeable about food, says

Bloomingdale's Chinese Food Packs, complete with packaged ingredients and recipes, come in basic, intermediate, and advanced.

very seriously, "I won't put our name on anything that is not the best there is." This doesn't keep the whimsy off the shelves, though. The store carries myriad lines of honey, including something labeled "Killer Bee Honey." Presumably the perfect gift to give to someone you really don't care for.

Though a great percentage of the items sold in the Delicacies department are imported, Bloomingdale's doesn't favor imports for their own sake—it's just that some items aren't made here. Sometimes, though, the buyers will find a phenomenal European product which is too expensive to bring back. In that case, Bloomingdale's will go to another manufacturer, perhaps one in the States, and have the product made for Bloomingdale's.

The department is a paradox of prices. There are some unexpected values for the discerning customer. The store carries clams packed in brine; compared with the brands carried in supermarkets, which are heavy on the brine, this item, which has a higher proportion of clams, winds up being a very good buy.

But many of the people who shop for delicacies at Bloomingdale's aren't looking for bargains. Film director Robert Altman and actors Danny Kaye and Robert de Niro have bought the store's customized gift baskets, and many famous faces are seen in the aisles. The store carries a full line of caviar, all sizes, all types: Iranian (which the store stopped carrying during the political crisis) and Russian, from the Golden Osetra Malossal of the former Shah of Iran to Beluga Malossol, fourteen ounces for $250. It's kept under lock and key. So are the pâté and the truffles (which

go for $500 per pound). Well, actually, the standard pâtés in the large cans are kept on the open shelf. They retail for about $20. It's only the small sizes (jacket-pocket size) or the expensive pâtés, like those with fresh truffles, that are kept in the little vault. Truffles are a better investment than the dollar these days. A can the diameter of a half-dollar sells for upward of $20, and for bargain hunters, Bloomingdale's may still have a few fourteen-ounce jars that are a "steal" at about $200. Next year, they'll probably cost $500.

Bloomingdale's even has a creative director of foods. Pam Krausman recently developed a new line of fresh-frozen Marcella Hazan pasta and sauces, made in the store's own kitchen according to the noted chef's recipes. In the fall of 1979, the Delicacies department began publishing a newsletter, partly to introduce its customers to new and unusual food items as Bloomingdale's acquires them, and partly to minimize the feeling of intimidation that people sometimes have when encountering unfamiliar foods. The newsletter coincides with Bloomingdale's new focus on developing "couture food," highly specialized items Krausman has created for the store, or imported exclusively by Bloomingdale's. She asked Alain Chapel, one of France's top chefs, where he got the unique raspberry-colored peach preserve served only in his restaurant. He made it, he answered, from peaches that grow between the grapevines in a certain French vineyard. So Bloomingdale's is now the exclusive importer of Pêches de Vigne. Each jar is numbered, and Chapel's mother writes the labels by hand.

Bloomingdale's has developed a line of Marcella Hazan Italian foods that are prepared in Bloomingdale's kitchens.

Not everything in the Delicacies department is packaged. The store features one of the most extensive fresh salad selections in New York, and nothing here is ordinary. Your local deli has shrimp salad? Maybe, but Bloomingdale's has water chestnuts in it. One variety of chicken salad has homemade mayonnaise. Another, called Chicken Madras, includes curry and raisins. There's apple-smoked trout (that means it's smoked over apple wood), and Irish and Scotch and Nova Scotia salmon—all flown in fresh daily.

And then there are the breads. Ah, the breads. It's hard to be sure how many kinds; the store carries, though not all at once, somewhere around 150 varieties.

The bakery has a band of regular customers who come in at predictable times throughout the week. Jed Jaffe, who buys the breads for the store, will deliberately overorder certain items, even at the risk of not selling them, so that there will be some left in the late afternoon or evening for the "late" customers. In case you've wondered, no breads are held over to the next day.

Bloomingdale's refuses to let the department become predictable so they constantly vary the baked goods. Sometimes one type of bread will be discontinued for a while. Then, when it's brought back again, it tends to sell better. (Does absence make the stomach grow fonder?)

The Bakery

Au Chocolat

Apparently, people really are funny about buying food. They'll never buy the last item on the shelf. Bloomingdale's White Plains branch, like all the branches near New York, orders its bread through the main store. They used to order twelve strawberry tarts every Friday. Ten sold; there were always two left. One week, Jaffe got their usual order for a dozen tarts, and he shipped forty-eight instead, just to see what would happen. They sold forty-six; there were two left. The next week, he sent sixty. That time there were a few more left. The next week the store, to counteract Jaffe's creative shipping, took it upon itself to order forty-eight of the tarts. It sold forty-six. So now the normal order of one-dozen strawberry tarts has been raised to a weekly order of four dozen tarts. "You've got to play with the numbers," Jaffe says with a smile. Munch.

If nectar is the food of the gods, Godiva chocolate is nectar to the candy connoisseur, the opiate of educated palates. Like many rare and precious things, Godiva chocolate is hard to find. It's sold in very select stores. It's sold in Au Chocolat,

Bloomingdale's boutique of sweets.

Au Chocolat, on the Fifty-ninth Street side of the main floor, is the ultimate confectionery. It has moments of whimsy; you can find jelly beans and neat little lollipops. Once it even sold candy dinosaur eggs packaged in soft little nests, with instruction booklets for care and hatching.

But essentially, Au Chocolat deals with the serious business of gourmet gorging. Plump candied fruits dipped into darkly bittersweet chocolate. Rich batches of fudge in assorted flavors. Nuts and coconut and other delicacies that lie hidden beneath creamy candy exteriors.

Mostly, Au Chocolat is about chocolate. White chocolate, brown chocolate, dark chocolate, light chocolate, nutted chocolate, silky chocolate, chocolaty chocolate. Chocolate for all seasons.

For Christmas, Au Chocolat even featured chocolate roller skates, chocolate ties (a lot better than eating your shirt), and, for the ultimate in disposable games, a chocolate chess set, compete with a regulation sixty-four square board made of white and brown chocolate. It would seem, at first thought, a bit cannibalistic: As you

Au Gourmet's new packaging is gold and elegant.

capture your opponent's men, you consume them. Then again, it's a great gift for the man who has everything. At the end of the game, he'll need another.

New York has a sweet tooth for more than chocolate, though. Last June, Bloomingdale's found a new way to fill it: open an ice-cream parlor, called The 59th Street Scoop. So they sent Alan Palmer and Lou Giaconelli to Ice-Cream College.

Palmer, under normal circumstances, is the director of menu development and quality control for the restaurants in Bloomingdale's New York store. Giaconelli became the manager of The Scoop. After

Bloomingdale's had decided to open its own ice-cream emporium, the staff of the restaurant and food divisions had a "tasting," sampling different brands of ice cream to find out which tasted best. Swensen's won.

Swensen's is a West Coast–based chain of ice-cream stores that uses its own formula for producing very rich, high-quality confection in a wide variety of flavors. To obtain Swensen's New York franchise, Bloomingdale's had to learn the secret recipes for preparing the frozen goo. The point, you see, is that the ice cream is made right in the store, in small batch freezers, beaten by hand. As hungry customers watch through the front window, a uniformed ice-cream chef folds in the cherries, nuts, and other goodies to create what Bloomingdale's calls "30 indecently delicious flavorites every day."

The 59th Street Scoop doesn't look like an old-fashioned ice-cream parlor. Designed by Naomi Leff, then a member of Barbara D'Arcy's staff, it's a glitter of tile, chrome, and glass, all reflecting the red neon accents. Perhaps most unusual is the shop's self-sufficiency. The ultimate boutique, it is entirely self-contained, with its own entrance (on Fifty-ninth Street, of course) so it can stay open later than the store itself, until 11:00 P.M. daily to serve the nondieting public.

Not all of Bloomingdale's food is the take-out variety. Shopping takes a lot of energy. And, too, shopping in Bloomingdale's is quite often a social activity. So it became imperative for the store to provide restaurants for its hungry customers.

It has created several, each with its own distinct atmosphere and its own distinctive menu. Forty Carrots is a snack bar on the lower level, the Saturday's Generation level, and it's "health food chic," or, as the store puts it, "healthy food." It does carry rich desserts (carrot cake, pecan pie, etc.) filled with sinful sugar, but Bloomingdale's customers do not consider pleasure a sin. And the menu is not vegetarian— Chicken Chutney and Savory Tuna sandwiches are available. (So are quiche of the day, soups, and salads.) But somehow the ambience of the place, which also serves yogurt and carrot juice, is that of a health bar.

If you think that's good, then you're the

consumer Bloomingdale's has directed its message to. (Saturday's Generation buys a lot of jogging shorts and wheat germ.) If you associate health foods with bean sprouts and no salt, this place will come as a decided surprise, because the food here is uniformly good, and usually tinged with surprising flavors.

The Espresso Bar, also on a lower level, became so popular that it was expanded in 1979. It serves snacks and desserts along with coffees, teas, and espresso. While Forty Carrots exudes light woods and sunlight (even though it's below ground level), The Espresso Bar is black and neon, like a Parisian coffeehouse.

For a more traditional restaurant, there's The Green House on the seventh floor, next to the bedspreads. But since this is Bloomingdale's, you wouldn't expect plain coffee and sandwiches. And you don't get them. The foods here have a rather European flair and flavor. There are sandwiches, but they're decidedly more imaginative than the usual fare, such as cream cheese and sliced strawberries served on fruit bread. Individual quiches are available, each served in an earthenware pan-shaped dish. But the soup choice is perhaps the best bet. Hot or cold, a large bowl is accompanied by a small meal: croissant with butter and jam, cheese and fresh fruit, and a glass of chilled juice. Served on a wooden tray, the meal looks very pretty.

Incidentally, all menu descriptions may be nullified by an import fair. When Bloomingdale's turns itself into the American outpost of a specific country, influences of the imported culture permeate every part of the store, including its restaurants. During Bloomingdale's Indian promotion, curries and rice made their way into The Green House. For "Israel the Dream," sandwiches were made with pita instead of Western-style bread. And when China is in residence, chopsticks may take the place of forks.

But Bloomingdale's restaurant of restaurants, the culmination of its epicurian endeavors, is Le Train Bleu. The idea of opening a fine restaurant within the store was first discussed during the original planning for the renovation of the sixth-floor housewares department. Macy's, saluting Bloomingdale's shop boutique concept, had created a flurry of excitement with The Cellar, its own housewares-plus area, and in The Cellar is a West Side branch of an

East Side restaurant. Bloomingdale's, which had planned the expansion of its housewares area considerably before The Cellar opened, retrieved its own thunder with the creation of The Main Course, and could do no less than create a fine restaurant in the vicinity of the marble aisle.

The theory was great. Finding space for a restaurant without taking away any selling space was a bit more difficult. Then someone realized that they could build up and out: construct a flight of stairs, and build the restaurant on the sixth-floor roof of the Third Avenue building. The view was superb: Third Avenue, the East River with Roosevelt Island in the middle of it, and the Queensborough Bridge, with its colorful tram swinging back and forth beside the graceful span.

Marvelous, said all the people, and then they looked at the actual space. It was long and narrow, a peculiar shape for a restaurant. It looks like the dining car of a train, someone said. Let's do an art deco takeoff of the Empire Diner (a "landmark" diner in the Chelsea section of Manhattan that's furnished in glass, silvered mirrors, and candles) and serve good fast foods.

It might have happened that way, except that Marvin Traub made one of his frequent business trips to Europe. Riding the wonderful trains there, he thought to himself: why not reproduce one of these? Let's make it a European dining car.

Fred Palatinus, then busy with the plans for The Main Course, suddenly found himself thinking about trains. He really did. Bloomingdale's priced the cost of buying an actual dining car, and almost bought one until they found it weighed more than the building's roof could support.

All right, said Palatinus, we'll build a restaurant to actual dining car dimensions. Ahem, said Will Hellemeyer, Bloomingdale's food service director. Those things are only about nine feet wide. Let's use the whole roof.

But that will change the proportions, Palatinus argued, and Bloomingdale's executives found themselves mediating between the purist and the pragmatist. Eventually a compromise was struck: They would widen the "car" to fourteen feet, lengthen it to about seventy feet to maintain the correct long, narrow proportion, and make it look like a first-class, turn-of-the-century European dining car.

The finished restaurant, Le Train Bleu, is named after the blue-engined train that ran from Paris to the Riviera. Palatinus re-searched many historic dining cars, decided this was one of the best designed, and reproduced its elegance down to the smallest detail. The mahogany-paneled walls are offset by green velvet, beveled mirrors, wall lamps, velvet upholstered chairs, and brass luggage racks—to hold Bloomingdale's shopping bags, instead of suitcases.

The roof adjacent to Le Train will hold a dining terrace which will feature cocktails and hors d'oeuvres, for customers who want to really get away from the store for a while. If they look to the east, they'll see the bridge and the river. If they look west, they'll see the outside of Le Train Bleu—dark and shining and looking just like a real train.

Le Train Bleu

The restaurant itself has a continental menu, a full-service bar, and formally clad waiters. Customers waiting to be seated stand on the "platform" as a soft voice announces periodically, *"En voiture, attention, passagers pour Lyon, Marseilles, et Monte Carlo,"* the major stops of the original Train Blue. From this vantage point, the "passengers" can look, through a large window to the kitchen, to watch the food being prepared. And, because this is Bloomingdale's, the chefs will mince their vegetables in Cuisinarts, cook them in Air Surge ovens, and use all the other culinary gadgetry for sale in the adjacent Main Course. Le Train is thus, in part, an ongoing demonstration for merchandise available for sale. In fact, many of the things in Le Train are indeed for sale: the gold-bordered plates, the French faceted glassware, the water pitchers and teapots and coffee servers. And, of course, the fine food and wines.

Will Hellemeyer is determined that his restaurants will be a far cry from "normal department store feeding." He uses no outside catering services; all food is freshly prepared in the store, just as it would be in a fine restaurant. His goal is to draw customers to Le Train, as they now go to Forty Carrots—not because they happened to be in the store, but because they specifically wanted to eat at that restaurant. He even dreams that the restaurants will attract new customers for the rest of the store, instead of the normal reverse situation. In most stores, restaurants are seen as a necessary service; you've got to have them so that hungry customers don't go outside to eat and then fail to come back in to shop some more. Hellemeyer wants to make Bloomingdale's restaurants "as self-sufficient, profitable, and high quality as any other department. A restaurant," he says, "is not a stepchild!"

The Model Room

By 1967, Bloomingdale's was the acknowledged leader in the creation of trends in interior design and in furniture itself. It continued to maintain its supremacy in this area while simultaneously it turned its attention toward assuming increased status in fashion.

The store had extended Samuel Bloomingdale's "invention" of the seasonal white sales into established, though artificial, "seasons" for home furnishings. Clothing sells according to actual seasonal changes, and the ready-to-wear industry is completely tied in to the time of year. There was no natural connection between furniture and seasons (with the exception of items such as furniture for garden or patio), so Bloomingdale's *created* two seasons for home furnishings promotions: fall, when children are going back to school, people have just returned from summer vacations, and it feels like the start of a new year; and midspring, generally just after Easter, when people are ready to think about changing their home decor for the summer.

At these two times, Bloomingdale's model rooms and the rest of the furniture floor undergo major changes in design, focus, and color. New merchandise tends to be introduced at these times, so in effect the store presents the new "fashions" in home furnishings.

There are major sales in July and January. At these times, the model rooms are modified, tempered a bit, and the floor is geared to a sale atmosphere. The rooms are less fashion statements than showcases of what the public probably wants to buy. The store may bring in additional stock, and may take existing merchandise and mark it down to sale price. There is a continuity to the furniture lines, though, which is not always obvious but which the store is careful to preserve.

The spring and fall changes entail architectural alterations in the model rooms. Beamed ceilings may be installed, tiled floors laid, and fireplaces added as the rooms are designed to work with specific new themes. Both old and new merchandise are presented in new ways to stimulate customers' ideas about home furnishings, to help them see what they can do with their furniture.

The architecture of the model rooms does not change during the "minor" changes of January and July. Furniture may be rearranged, some items may be added or deleted or moved into different rooms, but the variations are carefully designed to leave the same basic furniture on the floor. An item of furniture is a major purchase. People consider their choices carefully, often returning to the store many times to look at a particular piece or grouping before deciding to buy. Varying the arrangements may provide the necessary spark to convince shoppers that a certain piece will indeed fit in their home or office. But the store deliberately keeps the pieces on the floor, somewhere, to allow shoppers the opportunity to keep coming back until they've made up their minds to buy the merchandise.

The model rooms themselves are intended to inspire customers—not to copy the rooms, but to pick out relevant ideas and incorporate them into their own homes. The rooms are intended for a multitude of purposes: to sell merchandise, to stimulate people, to give ideas, to entertain. Though each set of rooms, and often each room within a single collection, appears radically different from every other room and from rooms that have come before, the furniture itself is carefully selected for continuity. "When we decided we were going to go for broke on a big collection like country French from Henredon, deeply committing ourselves to it, we realized that not everyone would be able to buy everything at once," says Barbara D'Arcy. "People feel more comfortable when they know that they can buy one piece, then come back two years later and buy another piece, and the finishes will match perfectly. A lot of the same furniture in the model rooms is repeated year after year, but with a whole fresh approach."

For some people, however, a particular model room becomes greater than its parts, and they insist on buying the whole room. Since 1958, at least one or two model rooms have been sold, in toto, each season. People even buy the walls.

Barbara D'Arcy

In essence, Bloomingdale's furniture division is divided into two sections. The first is involved in creating and designing the model rooms and the appearance of the furniture floor. Members of this group help create new merchandise or modify existing merchandise. This practice, which began in earnest during the 1950s, is still carried on today and has enabled the store to be the first to introduce certain types of furniture, or specific trends in design, to the United States.

Bloomingdale's presented the first collections of chrome and steel and glass during the early sixties. "When the metal and glass came in," D'Arcy said, "it was so new, it was frightening, even for us. I remember we saw it in Denmark and looked at it for about two years. We thought it was a great look, but not for us; it seemed to be only for hotels, airports, lobbies of airline terminals. But finally we decided that it looked so terrific that we should give it a try."

The store's spirit of adventure was decidedly on the cautious side at first. They brought over one rectangular and one square cocktail table, two lamp tables, and very little stock. But the metal and glass look existed nowhere in the United States except in one of Bloomingdale's model rooms, and it was an enormous success. The small stock was sold out, giving D'Arcy and Carl Levine the confidence to bring over other modern components, to create a total look.

It was during this period that D'Arcy introduced the *étagère* to New York (and

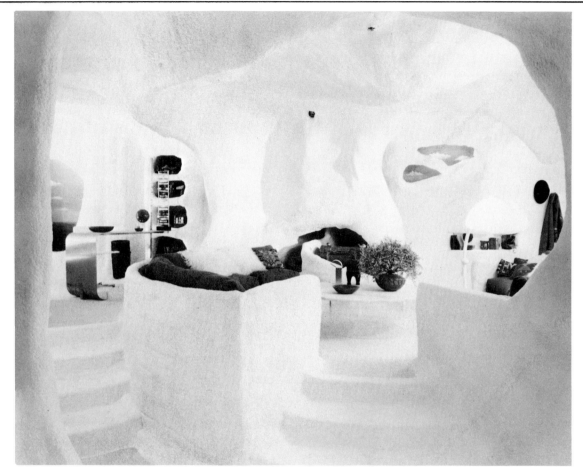

The Cave, Barbara D'Arcy's sculptured "environment" of sprayed urethane, was inspired by the work of Jean Arp.

America) with Levine's dubious assent. "There had never been an item on the American market like the *étagère*," he recalled. "Today it's one of the biggest selling classifications. We did the first *étagère* out of wormy chestnut and iron; I remember Barbara struggling over that. I had great faith in *her*, but I don't know whether I really had faith in that item. Yet since that time, there have been hundreds of thousands of *étagères* sold as American manufacturers picked up that classification."

D'Arcy hit an apex of nationwide impact in 1971 with something everyone dubbed the Cave Room. "This was a unique situation," she recalled, "but I thought it would be simple." It turned out to be anything but. D'Arcy had seen a display of sprayed-on polyurethane and thought it would be fun to use the process to build a model room. Herbert Berman, then in charge of construction for the store, told her she would have to build an armature beneath the polyurethane. "Otherwise we'll never be able to chop the Cave out of Bloomingdale's." So D'Arcy went to work with two carpenters from Berman's crew, to build an enormous framework to shape the room. It took two solid weeks, including Saturdays and Sundays. Once it was finished, screening was attached to the armature frame and they began to spray the whole contraption with urethane.

That created another problem. "We had to wear coveralls and gas masks," D'Arcy remembers ruefully, "and the fumes had to be vented out onto Lexington Avenue. Fortunately, the buildings' windows are about a foot and a half behind the model room space.

"It took us another few days, about a week, to finish the spraying, again working from eight in the morning until about midnight, right through the weekend." The construction of model rooms is carried on in secrecy even under normal conditions. The model room area is closed to the public on a room-by-room basis starting in mid-July until, by the end of the summer, all the rooms are closed. Then they reopen, reset and designed, in mid-September. During all of this work, the customers can hear but not see what is going on.

Some people, of course, try for more than the ear will provide. "We have a bevy of followers," D'Arcy observes, "who try to peek around, when model room time comes, to see what's happening." But the areas are closed off with heavy draping and most peekers don't see much.

What they did see when the Cave Room was unveiled was stunning. The Cave was divided into living room and dining area spaces, on multilevels, with steps leading from the entrance foyers into the main segments. The walls and ceiling were snow white. In the dining area the floor was covered with tiny, quarter-inch-square seg-

ments of mirror. "Not the most practical floor covering in the world, I grant you," D'Arcy admitted. The legs of the dining room table were white plexiglass columns lit from within; reflected in the mirrored floor, they made the entire room glow.

Barbara D'Arcy continued to create the model rooms until September 1972. Then, at the beginning of 1973, Marvin Traub took a rather greater gamble than was usual even for him. Fully aware that Barbara D'Arcy's semiannual model room designs had been largely responsible for bringing the store national and international recognition, Traub made what many thought was a surprising decision: to promote D'Arcy to director of merchandise presentation, and to delegate the design of the much-watched rooms to thirty-five-year-old Richard Knapple, whose tastes and point of view were very different. Traub felt that Bloomingdale's insatiable room-watchers were ready for a change of perspective, and that Knapple, with his more sparsely furnished, subtly colored interiors, would carry room design forward, in Bloomingdale's unending determination to be at the leading end of fashion making.

D'Arcy's new role gave her dominion over the interior design of the whole main store, as well as each of the branches. Traub's imprimature enabled D'Arcy to expand her horizon so that the entire store became one vast model room.

Richard Knapple is a dark-haired man with a neatly trimmed moustache and beard and a vivid imagination. He had come to Bloomingdale's in 1962. When he took over from D'Arcy, there were many who thought that the most creative phase of Bloomingdale's

Fall 1977. The Tutankhamen exhibit was soon to arrive in New York, and Bloomingdale's expected a large interest in Egyptian artifacts. Designer Richard Knapple acquired the statue from Rome's Cinecittà movie studio, where it had been a prop for the film *Cleopatra*.

Spring 1979. This view of Italy is contemporary, with furniture designed by John Saladino. The spareness is modified by wicker and pottery from Sardinia and touches of the Far East.

Spring 1978. Created for India: the Ultimate Fantasy, the storewide import show, this room was inspired by the Lake Palace (now a hotel) in Udaipur.

Spring 1978. A houseboat in Srinagar was the inspiration for this room, which uses brass braziers for heating and a temple swing for its bar.

home furnishing development was over. They were wrong. By whatever mystical process Bloomingdale's picks its creative minds, within a year Knapple was establishing his own reputation in the model rooms.

He began to introduce additional elements. The April 1974 rooms were titled the Artscope collection. Each of the seven rooms contained works of art produced by twenty-two artists representing the New York School of art. The rooms themselves

Fall 1977. This room introduced a line of Korean furniture and a new fabric collection, both of which Bloomingdale's was instrumental in having manufactured.

presaged the store's general move toward modular furniture that spring.

After the steel sculpture and stenciled walls, Knapple turned around the next fall and produced his American rooms, interpretations of various areas of the United States. One room celebrated the northern woodlands, nodding toward the pioneer past with wood beam ceilings and eighteenth-century French-Canadian furnishings. Another had the warm and sandy colors of New Mexico, accented with Indian pottery accessories.

The model room openings had served as a focal point for charity activities at Bloomingdale's, and during the 1970s these parties turned into biannual celebrity events. In the spring of 1974, Knapple's rooms were opened with a benefit for UNICEF chaired by Polly Bergen and attended by, among others, Paul Newman, Arlene Dahl, Betsy von Furstenberg, Joanne Woodward, and author Wyatt Cooper, the late husband of Gloria Vanderbilt.

Sometimes Knapple tied the model rooms in to the subject of the galas which were to open them. The spring 1975 opening was a benefit for the City Center of Music and Drama, the parent organization of the New York City Ballet and New York City Opera. On hand were prima diva Beverly Sills, George Balanchine, Joel Grey, and Mary Lindsay, wife of New York's former mayor, John V. Lindsay. It was the largest event of its type held in the store up until then, and Mrs. Julius Ochs Adler of the *New York Times* family, the development director for City Center, later reported that the event had raised over $17,000 for the arts group.

Knapple's fall 1977 rooms were among his personal favorites because they were basically Egyptian. "I always wanted to do something Egyptian," he said. The handle was "the roots of the past in today's design." He produced an Egyptian table in plexiglass and a pyramid bed, liberally using travertine materials and decorating the rooms with props from the Elizabeth Taylor–Richard Burton film *Cleopatra* and other objects specifically constructed for the rooms. Many of the props were subsequently sold to a West Coast museum, including a pair of sarcophagi which Knapple had especially made from a photograph

Spring 1979. Representing modern Milan, this room has panels of smoked mirror and mirrored plexiglass, and one single amaryllis in each cylinder.

Fall 1978. All the rooms for this show, Overture to the Eighties, followed an operatic theme. This is "Tosca"—more specifically, Scarpia's study. Following Barbara D'Arcy's pattern, Knapple designed most of the furniture and had it made in Europe.

In the spring of 1980, Fred Palatinus presented his first series of model rooms, which he calls "spaces." This space, inspired by Chicago, is part of a two-level living/dining room constructed in charcoal concrete. All of the furniture is black, including the lacquer dining and cocktail tables of Palatinus' own design. Richard Avedon's classic photograph "Dowina with Elephants" has been blown up into a 70' x 90' mural. Floors are set with mica chips, and the steps are made of subway grating.

by a craftsman in Florence. "He did a magnificent job," Knapple recalled.

In the fall of 1979, Richard Knapple announced that he was going into business for himself. He went out with a bang, leaving behind, as his temporary monument, the season's extraordinary model rooms. They depicted several of the world's famous ports, and one room that was quite out of this world. One "terrestrial" room had an inlaid tile floor, another featured huge bunches of fresh bananas that had to be changed once a week. But the most dramatic room was the double-size Spaceport, a vision of the well-dressed spaceship of the future. With curving walls and ceiling, the room looked like a hollow tube, totally black, with ultramodern furniture gleaming softly. The black painted ceiling had been set with tiny lights that winked on and off in response to the sound of voices or of music played on the nearby stereo. One got the impression of multicolored stars winking benignly from a cosmic ceiling.

" 'Safe' is not what it's about here," Knapple commented in retrospect. "Bloomingdale's is concerned with excitement, with titillation." And the model rooms have been one of the principal vehicles through which Bloomingdale's titillates its public. With Knapple's departure, control of their biannual design passed into the hands of Fred Palatinus. Some said it was a reward for his creation of The Main Course and Le Train Bleu. It probably was. In any event, Palatinus assumed his new responsibilities just when Bloomingdale's staff was beginning to engage in a pilgrimage to China, in preparation for the fall 1980 import fair. And so, one week into his new job, Palatinus flew to China to begin seeking the inspiration and the merchandise that culminated in the rooms for the China fair, called Heralding the Dawn of a New Era.

Aside from the model rooms, the importing of new items of furniture, and the development of original or modified designs, Bloomingdale's furniture department has another section, with a separate staff and separate quarters. This is its interior design service, intended to assist customers in furnishing their homes or offices. Richard Ryan has directed the interior design department since 1977, after a dozen years spent working in the home furnishings departments of the main store and several of the branches.

Anyone who wants to avail himself of this service "comes in as a customer and goes out as a client," says Ryan. To effect this transformation, a customer goes to the interior design department and confers with Shirley McChesney, whose role makes her seem more psychologist than receptionist. Through an informal discussion, she elicits the customer's needs (Is he purchasing new furniture to completely redo a particular room, or to add to existing furniture? Does he need help with a studio apartment, an office, a fifteen-room

house?). She also attempts to determine his likes and dislikes, his design preferences (e.g., modern or traditional), and, through all of this, to mesh his personality and predilections with one of the department's sixty-five interior designers.

For the first visit with the designer, the client brings a floor plan of the room(s) to be designed, drawn to scale. After a preliminary meeting, at which the designer tries to get a gestalt of the client's wishes, the client returns for a second visit. Here the designer presents a scale model of the floor plan, with traffic patterns and specific design suggestions. During this early phase, clients occasionally ask for a different designer, sometimes because their points of view are too different and sometimes because the customers have preexisting notions about designers. "Some people want someone who has been here for years," says Ryan, "and others want someone who has just started with us. Then some will want a male, others a female, depending on the feeling they have. In all the years that I have been involved in this, I can only recall one or two cases of reassignment. We try to fill their needs."

If a customer is simply seeking assistance with the purchase of specific furniture, Bloomingdale's will provide advice without charge. For the client seeking a designer's professional counsel about the design of one or more rooms, the store charges only if the purchase is very small; otherwise, in effect the fee is waived. What happens is this: once a client agrees to work with a specific designer, he pays a $250 deposit. This amount is applied to his purchases, and is completely nullified if he buys at least $2,500 worth of merchandise. This fee provides the customer with the designer's assistance in the selection and placing of furniture, and the selection of floor coverings, wall treatments, colors, and accessories. The designer will even have pieces custom-made, if necessary.

Unlike most stores, Bloomingdale's permits its designers to go to outside manufacturers or sources for particular pieces of furniture, draperies, antiques, or carpeting if the store does not carry the necessary items to complete a particular job, but Ryan says this doesn't happen very often, because "our selection here is so tempting." The extensive selection is, of course, one of the main reasons people choose the store as the one place to solve their diverse furnishing needs.

"It is amazing," Ryan notes, "that the Bloomingdale's customer walks in and knows that we will have 'it,' whatever 'it' is. They may not know, we may not know, but through the interview process we throw in adjectives, they throw in adjectives, and somehow it gets done. We talk through the design ideas and then prepare a finished architectural blueprint."

Bloomingdale's storewide import shows invariably have an influence on at least some of the interior design clients. "Rarely do we do an all-India or all-China room," Ryan explains, "but it does influence them, accessory-wise and feeling-wise. You have this wonderful warehouse to pull things from. It's like the best goodie store in the whole world."

Some of the "goodies" are the accessories that Ryan and his staff use to give a room its individuality. "You can make almost anything an accessory," Ryan feels.

"When a spoon is in a drawer, it is a spoon. But when a spoon is laid out on a table, it is an accessory. For instance, Richard Knapple used a swing from a temple in one of his India rooms. It was a swing for a god; he used it minus the god, as a piece on a buffet, and filled it with fruit and things. I made a point of asking some people from India about this, and they thought that it was fine, because it had come through another culture. In other words, we imported it as a piece of art, not as paraphernalia of a religious culture."

Thus, Bloomingdale's brings over quantities of copper cookware, baskets, and earthenware pots, which will mainly be used for decorative purposes. "It's taking the handicraft of another culture and using it in our own way."

Bloomingdale's has a penchant for creating unique merchandise. The home furnishings department, like the ready-to-wear department, has its own fashion coordinators who, along with the chief architect of the model rooms, come up with the concept for an item, a room, or an entire import promotion. The store's buyers then seek out merchandise that fits that theme, or carry sketches, swatches, and drawings to the far corners of the globe to have the items produced to specification.

As a consequence, although the store began upgrading its image by importing heavily from Europe, it now staffs buying offices in India and even more remote places, and its buyers regularly commute to South America, Indonesia, Thailand, Haiti, and the Middle and Far East, as well as to Canada, the British Isles, continental Europe, and, most recently,

The People's Republic of China.

Bloomingdale's continuing development of home furnishings merchandise is well known within the retail industry, and on Monday and Thursday evenings, when the store is open late, buyers from competing stores often mingle with customers, doing "research"—seeing what Bloomingdale's is doing. This is called "shopping the store," and everyone does it. Bloomingdale's buyers, too, check their competition regularly, for no store can afford to be uninformed about what might turn out to be the newest trend in furniture or in prices.

Bloomingdale's is very sensitive to the charge that its merchandise is overpriced. The store carries different grades of furniture and maintains minimum standards of quality for each. Leo Poverman, who was a furniture buyer for Bloomingdale's for more than twenty-five years, explains: "To properly serve our customers we have several grades of excellence. Within the same look, we have something available for the moderate-price customer and the customer who is willing to pay for the best in tailoring and content." Thus, one sofa may feature cushions filled with down and feathers, which would cost considerably more than another filled with foam rubber and Dacron. Yet, superficially, both may look very much alike.

The fact that there are now sixteen Bloomingdale's stores may also affect the price of furniture. Both conventional merchandise and items made specifically for Bloomingdale's are purchased in quantity, which may effect a savings even if it's a very fine, "expensive" item.

Bloomingdale's carries quantities of "standard" items in its warehouse, for rapid delivery. Naturally, customized items take somewhat longer. But some customers simply can't wait, and upon occasion the store has gone out of its way to be obliging.

When Billie Jean King opened an apartment in New York City, her manager went to Bloomingdale's to select some furniture for it. She selected a sofa and asked that it be delivered to Ms. King's apartment within two weeks. The piece happened to be one of the store's better sofas, and the model on display happened to be covered in that season's feature print. To remove the floor sample from a central location meant a possible loss of business.

But Bloomingdale's wanted to make a customer happy. And, too, a number of the sales staff turned out to be tennis enthusiasts. As one of them put it, "Why not help the cause?" So Billie Jean King got her sofa, and Bloomingdale's was the one who had to wait for the replacement to be delivered.

Most people don't shop in Bloomingdale's because they're trying to get bargains, though, or because they expect miraculous service. They may feel that they can get good value (and they can), but mainly they want to be sure that what they buy will be acceptable by their and their friends' standards. They want to be sure to get the Right Look. And while price is relevant for many people, it's not a handicap for a large proportion of Bloomingdale's customers.

Richard Ryan emphasizes that his staff

does an excellent job designing small studio apartments. But Bloomingdale's also lured the American businessman who, suddenly transferred to his firm's Russian office, bought $80,000 worth of Bloomingdale's furniture to take along—to be arranged according to Ryan's floor plan.

Almost 20 percent of the interior design service's clients are foreign nationals setting up large apartments in the United States. "Ambassadors bring their culture with them," Ryan says, and he uses the artifacts and antiques they bring to create a reflection of their own culture. Wealthy business people have a different attitude. "They want this to be their 'American' apartment," Ryan says with a smile, and apparently they're willing to spend lavishly, although the apartment may be used only three or four weeks each year.

The largest interior design assignment Bloomingdale's has done for an individual residence cost $350,000, but some of the smaller jobs have special needs that make them even more challenging to do. Once, the store was asked to completely redecorate a stateroom aboard the Cunard liner *Queen Elizabeth II*—in just four days. The stateroom was to be occupied by a celebrity who was going on a three-month cruise and wanted a special feeling about the room during the trip.

But you can't win them all. The store was once asked to do a major job for the occupant of a large Long Island mansion. The work was being done for cash since the owner did not wish to open a credit account. On the day all of the furnishings were delivered, no one was home. The designer made inquiries at the local police precinct and learned that the owner had fled the country under the dark of night, hotly pursued by federal authorities. Bloomingdale's was left with two vanloads of furnishings, which were eventually sold off through the clearance center stores in New Rochelle and Jericho, New York.

Despite such occasional setbacks, Bloomie's remains one of the major sources of interior design. The store is under contract with a major international banking house and with numerous other corporations to design interior living space for all of their foreign-transferred employees. The store even designs executive office spaces.

For the most part, though, Ryan and his staff design apartments, houses, places for people to live. Some of his clients are even more famous than Bloomingdale's: Bea Arthur, Mrs. Rose Kennedy, Arthur Ashe, Robert Beatty, Gloria Vanderbilt, Ethel Kennedy, Tony Roberts, Angela Lansbury, Ann Bancroft, Eric Leinsdorf, Ed McMahon, Cicely Tyson, Virginia Vestoff, Reggie Jackson, Carmen McRae, Selma Diamond, Robert Redford, Beverly Sills, David Frye, and Leslie Uggams, just to name a few.

eslie Uggams provided one of Rick Ryan's more interesting experiences. "She was doing a show in New York at the time that we were doing her space," said Ryan, "and when I went to speak with her about the job, she was rehearsing the show. She had a home cassette recorder with the show on it, the music and everything. It gave her the cues and whatnot, and we carried on our conversation while she was doing her rehearsal. Sometimes she would be listening to me while she was singing a song.

"As strange as it may seem, she followed everything that was going on and the job went pretty smoothly. She seemed very satisfied with the result."

For the busy client, the one who has neither the time nor the inclination to become deeply involved in the planning and details of decorating an apartment, Bloomingdale's becomes a godsend. "We can do everything down to the last can opener," says Ryan.

With all of its innovation and trend creation, even the Bloomingdale's people are sometimes surprised by what is sold. Ann Bertsch, fashion coordinator of the home furnishings area, remembers: "When we did our big India promotion, we brought back some things that we were sure wouldn't sell. For instance, we bought a bunch of elephants. Big, stuffed elephants, two of them five feet high and about a half-dozen smaller ones. The big ones went for seventeen hundred dollars each at retail. We were really convinced that they wouldn't sell. Well, the first week of the import fair, a man came in and bought all the elephants. He was a jeweler from the Southwest and he wanted to use them for display in his store. The interesting thing was that we had had them made in white, which they don't do in India."

Translation: Bloomingdale's can even sell white elephants.

Show and Tell

"We try hard to sell the sizzle rather than the steak."
—*Joseph Schnee, then senior vice-president for home furnishings and men's wear at Bloomingdale's; quoted in the* New York Times, *September 8, 1974*

Bloomingdale's, now at the level of high chic, has become expert at harnessing all avenues of promotion and publicity. This includes not only catalogs, but day-to-day publicity, shopping bags, special promotions and events, and all aspects of its multimillion-dollar advertising program. It's all designed to sell the image—and, by the way, a staggering amount of merchandise.

The most visible aspect of this highly sophisticated marketing strategy is called "merchandise presentation," which turns the store into high theater. Merchandise presentation entails not only the ways items are displayed for sale, but the creation of displays within the all-important store windows, and the supplementary and complementary designing of walls, departments, and whole sections of the store to create the requisite auras.

When new stores or departments are created, Barbara D'Arcy and her group are called in at a very early stage, to make suggestions on displaying the merchandise. Lately they've been teaching the merchants elements of design and display, to enable them to make the best use of space and to "hang a wall," for even though another department under D'Arcy's supervision displays the merchandise itself (mannequins are *dressed* every ten days to two weeks), Bloomingdale's stock changes so quickly that buyers must sometimes place new items on display when customers, intent on having a particular something, wind up buying the clothes right off the wall—or the mannequin.

In January 1975, Barbara D'Arcy was appointed operating vice-president, one of the very few designers to successfully make the transition to administration. Her influence over Bloomingdale's appearance continues to be extraordinary. As a fellow executive recently said, "Barbara now paints with a very large brush," relying on her staff to carry out the details.

But D'Arcy, a pleasant, cheerful, exceedingly bright woman, is not an artist who fears competition. Operating out of her orange and purple office ("one of my favorite combinations"), often dressed in the same colors, she has gathered a staff of young, talented individuals, has guided them to perform to her own standards of excellence, and knows when to stand back to let their individual inspirations hold sway.

One example among many of the lengths to which Bloomingdale's goes in designing departments or modernizing areas can be seen in the development of The Main Course, the area of the sixth floor devoted to housewares and much, much more.

The impetus for The Main Course began around 1977, when Traub and Schoff created a five-year plan to do major reconstruction of specific areas of the store. The housewares department had had no essential redesign in twenty-five years. Superficially it had changed constantly, of course, with shifting arrays of merchandise, new

wall colors, seasonal displays. But the essential format of the department had been constant. Housewares at Bloomingdale's, as in most other stores, had been an area of open bins, drawers, counters, and cabinets filled with kitchen utensils, cutlery, tableware, dishes, aprons, kitchen timers, pots and pans, and the like.

But in the last decade, there has been a revolution in kitchenware. Convection ovens, food processors, woks, electric ice cream and yogurt makers—these are paraphernalia that reflect a new interest in cooking and entertaining. Suddenly housewares has become big business: not just necessities for a prosaic chore, but articles that transform cooking into a creative activity for sophisticated adults.

Ah, but would it last? That, you see, is the key question for a store. Does this

The neon-lit white marble aisle of the Main Course

Demonstration kitchens beneath the newly created skylight

That's Entertainment

The Real Pros

change betoken a new and relatively permanent change in lifestyle (which thus justifies the store in making a major renovation to accommodate the new merchandise), or is it, if you'll excuse the expression, just a flash in the pan?

Executive vice-president Lester Gribetz persuaded Traub and Schoff that the phenomenal interest in cooking and home entertainment was here to stay, at least for the foreseeable future, and that Bloomingdale's should get behind it.

But allocating floor space in a department store is a rather delicate balancing act. Change the size or location of even one department and you affect several others. So before any changes were made in housewares, the entire sequence of consequences was carefully thought out.

"We didn't simply expand housewares," Traub explains. "First, Jim Schoff and I had made a total plan for what would happen with all facets of home furnishings over a five-year period. We didn't arbitrarily move the linen department from the seventh floor to the sixth floor. It happened because we had made a calculated decision to *ultimately* have much more space for housewares and for linens. As part of our objective we're planning to give less space for furniture, which has the lowest sales per square foot, so we eliminated the furniture department on the eighth floor; and we moved the bath shop from the sixth floor up to the eighth *on a temporary basis* so that, in the long run, we can get the expansion we've planned for."

Traub then held a meeting in his office which included Lester Gribetz, Barbara D'Arcy, and Fred Palatinus, and told them of the portion of the plan that concerned the expansion of the housewares department. Palatinus, as assistant director of merchandise presentation (reporting to D'Arcy), drew the assignment to create a master design to accomplish the expansion. He was also given Traub's personal suggestion: make the new department a "street of shops," carrying still further Traub's conception of Bloomingdale's as a collection of specialized boutiques. (Traub is convinced that people prefer to shop in small, intimate shops rather than big open spaces. "It's a mall that's inside the store.")

Palatinus went back to his office to start incubating some inspiration. He also needed quite a bit of data. Over the next few months, he recalls, "I had intermittent meetings with Lester Gribetz to ask him about the different areas, the different merchandise each would contain, and to determine the functional needs of each area." He also worked very closely with the merchants in charge of each area, asking how much footage they needed to display their merchandise and what special display needs they had. Although the total housewares department was to increase by 25 percent, Palatinus and Gribetz had to do some diplomatic juggling to keep all the merchants relatively happy. As in any such reorganization, everybody insisted his area needed much more space than was available. Some of the space needs were reduced by clever display techniques; Palatinus became familiar with the specific merchandise, and created display and storage facilities that allowed a maximum amount of merchandise to be visible, and yet was flexible enough to be varied to display future items.

Burton Wolf (left), James Beard (center), and Milton Glaser.

Pearla Meyers (right)

James Beard (left) and Carl Sontheimer

Bloomingdale's has a long association with great cooks, who frequently collaborate with the store on culinary ventures. A few years ago several great chefs helped create the Cook's Kitchen, a collection of their personally recommended cooking implements. Naturally, Bloomingdale's held an after-hours party to celebrate.

he final sixth-floor conversion encompassed a 50,000-square-foot area and cost over $2 million. It would have been relatively simple to do what was done had the project been started from scratch. But the entire renovation had to take place while Bloomingdale's was open for business. Herb Berman, who directed the physical construction, said: "Our purpose was to allow the store to function as long as possible in a merchandising capacity." To do this, they broke the total area into 7,000- to 8,000-square-foot segments and kept some open and functioning as they did their construction work on others, under the cover of tarpaulins and panels where possible. To create initial work space, the bath and closet shop were temporarily moved up to the eighth floor, and the outdoor furniture department was temporarily consolidated into a smaller space. Then work crews quickly moved into the vacated areas, to renovate them according to the master plan. As some areas were completed, shops were moved into them and construction was then begun in the vacated spaces. Multiple moves were sometimes necessary to yield the ultimate results of specific shops in specified areas of the floor. Palatinus created an exciting, large, but temporary shop called That's Entertainment, and moved half of the housewares department into it while the construction crew went on to complete the second half of the floor.

In the never-ending attempt to gain more space and take maximum advantage of existing space, Bloomingdale's raised the roof on the Third Avenue side of the building an additional eighteen feet above the existing six floors. The old office area

The Mug Shop

Linens

Something's Brewing

was expanded into a double-decked stock area. The offices themselves were moved up a new flight of stairs to a space which hadn't existed previously.

Barbara D'Arcy, who has an intimate knowledge of the physical structure of the series of buildings that comprises the Fifty-ninth Street store, pointed out that the sixth floor in one particular building was really the top floor, and that building could not support any additional floors. To make an asset of this, she came up with the idea of a skylight. A *huge* skylight. Everyone loved the idea, so Palatinus detailed it, specifying lots of mirror and glass. Then they took the plan to Berman, who brought in special engineers to build it. The resulting skylight is not only leakproof, it's also made of reflective glass, to save energy.

The design plan for the main walkway of this street of shops called for pure white marble. Palatinus saw samples taken from a quarry in Carrera, Italy, and they seemed perfect. But when the actual shipment arrived, it had veins; he had specified un-veined marble. In the midst of ongoing construction, Bloomingdale's executives huddled with marble merchants around fragments of stone, debating the relative merits of various veins and textures. Ultimately, pure white Lasso marble was obtained from a distributor in Queens.

Along the ceiling of the completed Main Course, a green neon strip now leads the customer down the white marble center aisle, past a series of special boutiques housing merchandise by classification.

That's Entertainment, in its final metamorphosis, carries glasses, flatware, serving pieces, and so on. By no coincidence, it's located right next to the Table Linens shop, which carries placemats, tablecloths, napkins, runners, imported damask and the like, so customers can mix and match linens with service.

The Main Course sells everything needed to prepare a Chinese or Japanese dinner. That doesn't only mean it sells woks and chopsticks. It also sells canned water chestnuts, boxes of noodles, and other ingredients for Oriental cooking.

The highlight of The Main Course is, appropriately, underneath the skylight: five demonstration kitchens, designed with the consultation of master chefs James Beard, Burton Wolf, and Milton Glaser. Since the area opened, Bloomingdale's has invited chefs from all over the world to hold forth, generally at the central section, to demonstrate exotic cooking techniques. At the same time, each of the four satellite kitchens features the use of a major cooking implement or technique. The store has held after-hours cooking classes, including one for couples called Saturday Night Flavor, which had people dining and dancing between the aisles of what used to be the place you went when you wanted to buy a potato peeler.

Bloomingdale's is constantly changing its appearance, in the main store and in the branches. It's a gigantic circus, constantly shedding an old tent for a colorful new one, and adding ever more rings and ever more sideshows.

First You Sell the Image...

"*Bessie, it's them—the Bloomingdale couple.*"

Drawing by Koren: © 1973, The New Yorker Magazine. Inc.

Advertising, in all its manifestations, is what draws the customers, either to come to the store in person or to place orders by mail or telephone. We live in an era of sophisticated merchandising, of market analysis, surveys, sampling, and million-dollar ad budgets. Few people question the power of advertising in "moving" (that is, getting people to buy) merchandise. For Bloomingdale's, advertising plays a dual role: it is a device to entice people to purchase a specific product, and it is used to keep the public constantly aware of the store itself. Advertising encompasses the areas of sales promotion, public relations, direct mail, and marketing.

Under Davidson and Schoff's imprimatur, the late Louise Seaman Langdon had directed the store's public relations for nearly a decade, beginning the movement toward lively publicity and active community relations. Ruth Straus headed the advertising department throughout the 50's and the 60's, expanding its focus to encompass Davidson's emphasis on imported and unique merchandise, the decade of import fairs, and the store's switch to higher quality lines. In 1971, when she retired, Marvin Traub decided that it was time to move even further. Bloomingdale's centennial—the hundredth anniversary of its founding—would occur in 1972, and he chose that event as the target date to create a major conceptual change in advertising, publicity, all aspects of the store's image. Lachman gave his approval for changes that would improve and strengthen Bloomingdale's advertising appearance, and with that concordance, Traub broke with the tradition that holds that department store advertising is a specialty unto itself. He went outside the industry and hired Mary Joan Glynn, then vice-president of Doyle Dane Bernbach, one of the country's leading and most avant-garde advertising agencies. Doyle Dane had done the very funny Volkswagen and Orbach's ads of the late 1960s. Compared with them, Bloomingdale's ads were stodgy. Glynn brought with her an irreverence toward advertising and a wittiness that delighted Traub, who liked the idea of portentous Bloomingdale's learning to poke fun at itself. (By the mid-seventies, jokes about itself had become a hallmark of the store.)

Shortly after Glynn arrived to become Bloomingdale's vice-president of communications, she and Traub had lunch together, and he gave her a gestalt of the store. "Saturdays are very busy," he said, and she answered, straight-faced, "They're buying each other." Traub looked at her for a moment, then smiled ruefully. "Well, yes," he agreed, for who could deny that on Saturdays the store becomes a mecca for the city's upwardly mobile singles population? Bloomingdale's picked up the fact, mulled it over for a few years, and the result was the downstairs Espresso Bar, a place to meet, greet, see and be seen, and pause for refreshment before returning to the self-fulfilling chore of Saturday shopping.

But despite Traub's awareness of the importance of Saturdays to the store's business, Glynn found that Bloomingdale's did not advertise in the Saturday newspapers. The prevailing wisdom had been that no one reads ads that day. She shook her head and told Traub: "There's a whole generation who have coffee forever, read the papers, and come over to cruise Bloomingdale's."

See it coming? This was the inspiration for the Saturday's Generation theme. No, not the department; at first, in the early 1970s, it was an advertising concept. Glynn took her idea to vice-president Franklin Simon (now chairman of Bullock's) who gave her the funds to develop it. Bill Berta did the original layout, and Scavullo mocked it up. Then Carl Levine, from his perch atop the forward-thinking home furnishings department, said OK, let's use it and see what happens, and he allowed Glynn to impose her brainchild on an ad for a chair. Thus was produced the first Saturday's Generation advertisement—which ran, naturally, in the Saturday newspapers, and which launched a new era for Bloomingdale's.

Saturday's Generation became a concept the store applied largely to lower-priced goods for young apartment-dwelling careerists. The idea took hold so firmly that the term became symbolic of a certain segment of Bloomingdale's clientele. People who were young at heart (if not in body, though they were often both), not yet affluent (though they were striving to become so), busy with work and play and projects and committees and tennis and the City and the Good Life, and too busy to shop any day but Saturday—these were Saturday's Generation, and they shopped at Bloomingdale's. And contemporary furniture, clean-lined wooden pieces left unfinished or painted with high-gloss lacquers, or molded plastic tables and stacking chairs, or blue jeans (not designer jeans, just well-shaped blue jeans) and brightly colored tops and shiny satiny capes and multistriped woolen mittens and scarves and boots of all heights and shapes and clothes that were *fun*—that was the merchandise of Saturday's Generation. Ultimately, it had to become more than just a concept; in 1974, Bloomingdale's opened a new shop devoted to Saturday's Generation. It was moved around a bit until it established itself in the metro level, where it now plays host to a look, a feeling, a way of life.

By 1972, when Bloomingdale's celebrated its one-hundredth birthday, the gestalt of advertising and publicity had been radically changed. All it lacked was a new look, to cement the transition and make it

Saturday's Generation

as noticeable visually as it was functionally. Glynn, following Traub's cue, used the store's hundredth birthday as the catalyst to implement these visual changes.

She hired the renowned designer Massimo Vignelli to create a new logo typeface for the store. Bloomingdale's had been using varied logos—a curly script signature, an old-fashioned script *B*, all familiar symbols but all reflecting the nineteenth century, when the store was founded. Vignelli designed a streamlined typeface, widely imitated since then but brand-new at the time. All the letters were lower case, clean as chrome, skinny as razors, not bothered by

Saturday's Generation

curlicues or extraneous details. The new type was christened bloomingtype, and re-placed the older script not only in adver-tisements but in every aspect of store dis-play and design: on labels, across the front of T-shirts, even on the outside of the buildings of the main store and the branches. It was a new look, for a new cen-tury, and it made Bloomingdale's seem suddenly *au courant.*

Vignelli then took that same ap-proach to package design, which had been a potpourri of assorted sizes, shapes, colors, and decora-tions. As a result of his redesign, today there are only six box shapes and sizes, all that seems to be needed to con-tain the various types of merchandise. To help the gift wrappers work more rapidly, the boxes are color-coded by size and shape. The coding was deliberate. Of the nine shiny bright colors selected, the store tried to match specific colors to depart-ments that seemed most likely to use cer-tain box shapes and sizes. Yellow and royal blue boxes, for example, are mainly used for children's wear; the more reserved colors, black, gray, and brown, were allot-ted to box shapes primarily used for men's wear; housewares got bright green, be-cause glassware looked particularly good against that color; and red was intended for the main floor and the rest of home fur-nishings. Of course, the wrap desks use boxes according to whatever size is needed, but the formula holds fairly true, and the limited sizes, shapes, and colors have speeded up the flow through what used to be a bottleneck and added so much cheer that the expensive selections of gift wrap paper and ribbons were virtually eliminated. Today, the hallmark of a Bloomingdale's package is a sturdy, solid-color box, sometimes covered with solid-gold paper. Neither box nor paper bears the store's logo. Instead, placed squarely atop each box is Bloomingdale's distinctive gold seal: the simple Bloomingtype letter b.

The new looks were introduced to the public at the inception of Bloomingdale's centennial celebration in the fall of 1972. To epitomize the store's past and future, Bloomingdale's chose as the symbol of the centennial the two-headed Roman god Janus, who simultaneously looks forward to the future and backward to the past. A new escalator connected the two levels of the men's store. A digital "centennial clock" was installed just inside the Third Avenue main entrance, to boost what the store hoped would become a "new tradi-tion"—meeting under the clock. (And four years later, during the bicentennial of the United States, the visiting Queen Elizabeth and Prince Philip did just that.)

For its birthday, the store gave itself "The Party of the Century," held through-out the store on October 3. Though most of Bloomingdale's was open for business as usual that day, the entire eighth floor was closed to customers at 3:00 P.M., when workmen began clearing out all merchan-dise and display counters, removing parti-tions, setting up 130 dinner tables, and transforming the area into a massive ban-quet room in readiness for 1,300 formally attired guests who would attend a sit-down five-course dinner of roast baby pheasant, created by Restaurant Associates. The metamorphosis of the seventh floor into an improvised (and temporary) dance floor took a bit less time, as did the setting up of the bars in the men's store on the lower level, in the fashion department on the third floor, and in the fifth-floor and seventh-floor home furnishings departments, so these areas were open for business as

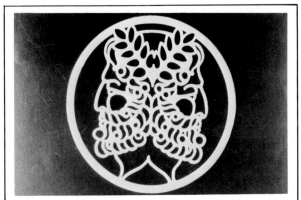

Janus, the symbol for Bloomingdale's 100th anniversary

usual until the store closed at six o'clock. Then, with barely two hours before the first guests were to arrive, Bloomingdale's engineers and staff transformed the store into a display-filled reception hall.

After dinner, the guests applauded the presentation of scrolls to some of Bloomie's favorite people, including advertising monarch Mary Welles Lawrence, consumer advocate Bess Myerson, His Excellency Terence Cardinal Cooke, Judge Henry J. Friendly, and Mayor John V. Lindsay. The store gave a donation of $28,500 to Odyssey House, a drug rehabilitation center, whose choir was there to sing "Impossible Dream."

Bernadine Morris of the *New York Times* called it the "most glittering" of parties. There was something odd about it, though; the store's birthday was actually in April. That was true, Lachman told the *New York Times,* but "the fall is the most

Bloomingdale's "Party of the Century" drew the power elite of New York City. Mary Joan Glynn (left), Mayor John Lindsay (center), His Excellency Terence Cardinal Cooke (right)

exciting part of the year for a department store. And anyhow, when you're one hundred years old, you can take the liberty of celebrating a birthday whenever you choose."

Mary Joan Glynn left Bloomingdale's at the end of 1974 to become president of the Simplicity Pattern Company. She was replaced by a new promotional team. Cathy Cash, formerly the creative director for the fine fragrance division of Revlon, succeeded Joan Glynn in January 1975, shortly after the promotion of Bill Berta to advertising director. And Peggy Healy, who had joined the store in the early seventies, now became the head of public relations and special events.

The store reintroduced drawings as the centerpieces of ads; but this time, they

Bloomingdale's Chairman Lawrence Lachman (left) welcoming former Mayor Robert F. Wagner

Bloomingdale's re-created the umbrellas that had advertised the store in the early years of this century. Now, the slogan reads: "All eyes are on Bloomingdale's."

been senior fashion editor of *Harper's Bazaar* and *Vogue.* Doris Shaw was hired later that year as vice-president for sales promotion.

Which brings us up to today. Quietly controlling Bloomingdale's image empire is a surprisingly soft-spoken, surprisingly young man named Gordon Cooke. After working for Burdines in Miami, another Federated store, Cooke went to Macy's and headed its sales promotion and publicity department before being filched by Bloomingdale's in 1977 to become, at thirty-two, a senior vice-president and a member of the store's administrative and executive boards. Cooke succeeded Doris Shaw, who resigned to become editor in chief of *House Beautiful* magazine.

When Cooke joined Bloomingdale's, the store's current promotional concepts were already largely formed. Bloomingdale's was already perceived as a store catering to the upwardly mobile, to an image-conscious populace concerned with appearance, with being *au courant,* with having immediate access to the newest, the most unusual, the most exciting. The idea was to maintain this hard-won image and augment it, to keep the store constantly in its public's discerning, easily jaded eye.

One of the first things Cooke instituted, just before the 1977 Christmas season, was a continuing series of "conviction ads," in which the store goes out on a proverbial limb and declares, in large print, *"We believe in . . ."* a particular fashion look. The risk is that the store is making prediction; the look in question is for a future fashion item, not a past

were as modern as the new typeface they accompanied. Cathy Cash explained: "Drawings have a big edge in that you don't have to have the product in hand." Then she candidly added: "Besides, I wanted to make a big splash." Three months after she arrived, Bloomingdale's introduced its first Vollbracht drawings.

Cathy Cash resigned and ultimately set up a promotion firm with her new husband (which in 1979 was commissioned to help launch Bloomingdale's new fragrance, bloomie's). She was succeeded in March 1976 by Carrie Donovan, who had or even a present one.

The concept of announcing Bloomingdale's prediction of fashion trends before they become trends originated during the fall 1977 *prêt-à-porter* show. One of the big looks shown in Europe that year was peg pants and the loose, unconstructed jacket. Bloomingdale's buyers and fashion coordinators traveled to the European shows, as did the buyers from many department stores. They looked at what was shown, placed orders for the following spring, and went home.

But Bloomingdale's rarely sits and waits. If anything characterizes its personnel, it is impatience. Being first with the latest is almost an occupational obsession. So, having privately predicted that the peg pants and loose jacket look would sell wildly as soon as it hit New York, Bloomingdale's determined to bring the look to its racks while other stores were still waiting for delivery from Europe.

A contingent of fashion experts contacted a manufacturer in the United States, showed him sketches and specifications of the designs the store wanted, and asked him to manufacture them—fast! Because time was of the essence, they chose a manufacturer of junior clothing because, as Cooke says, "Junior resources don't wait. They act [snap of fingers] like this!"

The merchandise was ready in two weeks, and the day it arrived in the store, Bloomingdale's ran its first conviction ad in the *New York Times,* saying, "We believe in peg trousers and big tops."

Bloomingdale's thus had the new look available for sale months ahead of other stores, and it presented the look not with a simple advertisement, but with a major statement of recommendation backed by the store's knowledgeable fashion expertise. When Bloomingdale's makes that kind of a declaration, its customers, many of whom trust the store's taste to a remarkable degree, are only too ready to concur.

The conviction ads also began a new look in newspaper advertising. The store hired fashion artist Antonio to do the drawings, and deliberately left almost half the available space blank, giving the nearly full-page ad a rich, designed look. Merchandising's prestigious *Tobe Report* reproduced several of the conviction ads as examples of excellence in advertising. So far, in part because the fashion predictions have been correct, the series of conviction ads (which appear only when Bloomingdale's wants to make a major fashion statement) has pulled phenomenally well. The ads themselves are coordinated with displays within the store and in the windows.

"We feel we should be the first to pull a look together," Cooke said in reference to the first conviction ad. "We can sell forward fashion well, and we think we should get it in the store fast and communicate it equally quickly. It means we have to push the manufacturers and push ourselves, but it will help us maintain our trendy image."

It also helps the store's relationship with designers, who are concerned that their concepts be correctly presented to the public. The strength of the store's advertising design and concepts has helped encourage designers and manufacturers to work with Bloomingdale's on new lines because of the store's proven ability to get the message across on new items. And if imitation is the sincerest form of flattery, Bloomingdale's has been complimented by some of its competitors, who have copied its newspaper ad formats down to attempts at imitating the typeface.

Because Bloomingdale's has gained a reputation for its ability to "move" great quantities of widely varied types of merchandise, people seek out members of the store staff in hopes of getting Bloomingdale's to carry whatever they're selling. Usually, news of new products is told to the buyers, those directly responsible for placing an order. But merchandise can have strange, roundabout ways of getting into Bloomingdale's.

Margot Rogoff is Bloomingdale's publicity coordinator. In its simplest sense, this means she is the primary contact between the store and the media: radio, television, magazines, and, primarily, newspapers; and, as Bloomingdale's manages to make news abroad as well as in the United States, she is also the person who provides information to the press in Europe, Asia, and wherever else Bloomingdale's goes to seek new designs, new materials, and new merchandise.

Perhaps because she deals with so many people, Rogoff's name has become known to people who know no one else in the store. And so she gets some rather unusual phone calls. Movie producers call her when they want to shoot a scene in the store. People call her to tell of a new product they have designed/developed/manufactured/discovered which is, they assure her, just *perfect* for Bloomingdale's to carry. She listens, because sometimes they're right. And when they are, Rogoff connects them with the appropriate buyers or executives.

Last summer the annual gift show was held in Los Angeles. One afternoon, Rogoff took some time out to window-shop the elite stores of Beverly Hills. That's where she discovered a "magnificent" bath shop called Jean La Porte, which sells scented soaps, potpourris, sachets, and other delicacies for bath and closet. Rogoff was enchanted, went inside, and spoke to the management. "You've simply *got* to come to Bloomingdale's," she enthused. "Your merchandise would fit *perfectly* into the store."

Perhaps, was the unenthusiastic reply, but a counter in a department store wasn't too thrilling an idea. Jean La Porte originated in Paris; the Beverly Hills shop was their first venture into the United States. When they went to New York, they said with Gallic pride, it would be with their own elegant little store, perhaps on Madison Avenue. . . .

Rogoff, needing more ammunition, rushed back to the gift show and located executive vice-president Lester Gribetz and Julian Tomchin, vice-president and director of fashion for home furnishings and cosmetics. Both were somewhat surprised by her request. They had, after all, come to the West Coast to see the huge merchandising show, and now Rogoff wanted them to leave the convention center to . . . look at a store?

They went, saw, agreed with Rogoff's evaluation, and went inside to explain to the proprietor just what Bloomingdale's happens to be. The result: several months later, Bloomingdale's became the only store on the East Coast to carry the Jean La Porte line.

Antonio's highly distinctive drawings lent greater impact to the conviction ads.

Television advertising came only recently to department stores; Bloomingdale's began using it in the early seventies, and it has become a dominant medium for selling home furnishings. In 1979 the store contracted with Erin Gray, star of "Buck Rogers in the 25th Century," to be Bloomingdale's spokeswoman for a series of home furnishings ads. As part of the deal to get her, Bloomingdale's threw in the ultimate inducement: an employee discount card. And so, long hair swinging provocatively, she led TV viewers to the latest featured merchandise.

Not long afterward, the store recruited Christina Ferrare, the stunning model who is the wife of auto magnate John De Lorean, to do a series of television commercials about ▃▃▃, the remarkable newly redone main floor.

Bloomingdale's recently used a soap opera format instead of the traditional "twin size, just $9.95" for a televised White Sale commercial. Why? Lester Gribetz, executive vice-president of Home Furnishings, says: "We're always different.

Why should we look like every other store? Bloomingdale's has a certain panache that is relevant to its customers. Our customers understand the kind of humor and sophistication in the commercial." Apparently they do; customer traffic increased by one-third over the previous year's White Sale.

The advertising department is responsible for creating the packaging for almost all products carrying Bloomingdale's own label—everything from perfumes to delicacies. And, of course, it creates the everchanging, usually nameless shopping bag. (Never one to slavishly follow even its own trend, in recent years Bloomingdale's has occasionally replaced its name on a particular bag, incorporating it as a design element.)

At any given time, Bloomingdale's may have half a dozen different shopping bags available. The Big Brown Bag (that's what it says on it—no art, no pictures, just the clean, modern type) and its counterpart, The Little Brown Bag, are both available in

The photographs Bloomingdale's uses in its advertisements tend to be as stylish as the clothing they display.

1972–1980

1973–1980

such departments as home furnishings, linens, and men's wear. Both are Joan Glynn's inventions. She dreamed up The Big Brown Bag when Lester Gribetz mentioned that the linen department needed a really big bag to hold pillows. The Little Brown Bag followed naturally a year later, for accessories. The Main Course and ⬛, home of the newly revamped cosmetics area, each have their own shopping bags, as does Au Chocolat, the will-power-shattering confectionary.

But the most famous bag, oddly enough, is one that often has a life of only six or eight weeks. This is the "seasonal bag," primarily used in the women's fashion departments, which is changed about four times a year: in September, at Christmas, in January, and in May. To ensure continuity of style, these bags are usually designed by the artist who is creating the major advertising pieces. Thus Antonio has been called upon to design Bloomingdale's shopping bags during seasons when his artwork was featured in the store's advertisements. If the store happens to be doing a major promotion, like one of its huge import fairs, the seasonal bag will incorporate the promotion's theme, and the resulting design will be coordinated with the rest of the paper goods the store generates: posters, "hang tags" attached to the merchandise, menus in the store's restaurants, and all advertising throughout the time of the promotion.

In January 1977, Bloomingdale's shopping bag created a considerable to-do. The bag featured a sleek, slim, terrific-looking girl, back to the camera, wearing long auburn hair and an exhilarating smile and nothing else. Somehow a rumor reached the gossip columns of *Women's Wear Daily* that the model was none other than Princess Yasmin, the daughter of Rita Hayworth and Ali Khan. Princess Yasmin promptly slapped the store with a $1.1 million damage suit. After two months, meetings among attorneys, and considerable unexpected (and, to a degree, unwelcome) publicity, the matter was smoothed over. Bloomingdale's announced that a settlement had been reached "amicably," and the store issued a public apology which said, in part, "Bloomingdale's wishes to state that the confusion was unintentional and that it is deeply sorry for any inconvenience caused to Princess Yasmin Ali Khan."

The confusion was not only unintentional, it was also understandable. The actual model for the shopping bag photo was Yasmine Sokal, a twenty-two-year-old former New York University student who had recently become a professional model. A striking five feet eleven, Miss Sokal earned $2,500 per day for posing in the nude, as opposed to her normal (dressed) rate of $100 per hour. The Bloomie's bag caper made her an instant minicelebrity, with a feature story in the Sunday *New York Times Magazine.* And the infamous bag naturally became an overnight collector's item.

Bloomingdale's often uses contemporary artists to create its designs, and the shopping bags chronicle some of the major art looks of their eras. In 1976, when the store drifted away from its decade of art-illustrated bags, Arthur Cohen, then vice-president of marketing, hired super photographer Richard Avedon as a design consultant in the catalog area. Avedon was

something of an exception for Bloomingdale's—in many cases, unknown artists have become famous for designing the store's ads, shopping bags, and catalogs. One such artist was Michaele Vollbracht, who was brought in by Cathy Cash. "We launched Michaele Vollbracht into a career in design," Gordon Cooke observed. "He now has his own dress line and a scarf and fabric line." Cooke noted that Vollbracht had had a reputation as a designer when Bloomingdale's retained him, but clearly his relationship with the store has done a great deal to further improve the value of his name, much as it has for others before and since.

After the photo phase (and the "Yasmin" bag), Bloomingdale's returned to art for a couple of years and, except for the India import fair of 1978 and the Israeli fair of 1979, both of which had specially designed bags, Antonio became the basic theme artist, designing, among other things, the first series of conviction ads.

Every design concept, for packaging, shopping bags, catalogs, or whatever, crosses Cooke's desk at some point. Sometimes he and his staff simply go ahead and produce the item, since there is no "formal procedure" for approving designs. Normally, however, they are seen by what Cooke categorizes as "the people who are concerned about the look and the feeling of the store that is being represented through sales promotion." Invariably, this includes Marvin Traub. "He is a promoter himself," Cooke says admiringly, "and so his input is valuable to me."

Traub is more than a promoter, though. He is a connoisseur of talent as well, and, when he discovers very talented individuals, he does not hesitate to recruit them. And when those talented individuals happen to excel in his beloved field of promotion, Traub does not rest until he has them promoting his store. He did that with Gordon Cooke when he "acquired" him from Macy's in 1977. He'd done it in 1971, when he'd lured Mary Joan Glynn from Doyle Dane Bernbach. But Glynn had left Bloomingdale's to head Simplicity Patterns; she'd then moved on from there, and by the summer of 1979 she was senior vice-president of *Esquire* magazine. One day, Traub picked up the newspaper to learn that *Esquire* was in financial trouble. He put down the paper and phoned Glynn. "Joan," said Marvin Traub, "why don't you come home?"

So she did. Now vice-president of marketing and public relations, Glynn is primarily interested in developing new business areas for Bloomingdale's. She has instituted a series of "bridal fairs" at which brides-to-be are invited to attend special presentations, "to establish Bloomingdale's as the authority on style and taste for brides-to-be." Guest speakers from within and outside the store will "educate these women and introduce them to the art of hostessing (entertaining, cooking, decorating)." If this sounds to you like a replay of the 1950s, you haven't been noticing the current trend back to traditional weddings, complete with lace trains and full regalia. Glynn has noticed; Bloomingdale's imported Ann Keating to head its bridal registry as, for years, she headed Tiffany's, and the ongoing presentations will establish Bloomingdale's in the minds of a brand-new generation of consumers as the place to outfit oneself and one's home.

Barbara D'Arcy, creator of the [logo] transformation. To her right are Marvin Traub, chairman; Jack Schultz, executive vice-president; and Lester Gribetz, executive vice-president.

Estée Lauder, her husband, Joe, and Mike Blumenfeld, vice-president of the cosmetics area

"I apologize for the crowding," Traub told the elegantly dressed guests, "but it's good practice for Saturdays." Then he introduced the guest of honor, Robert Joffrey.

Glynn has also begun to explore ways to serve the "new" traveler. When New York City hosted the Metropolitan Transit Authority's convention, Bloomingdale's invited 400 to 500 wives of the delegates for a continental breakfast and a low-key explanation of how the store's personal shopping service could assist them with their every shopping need.

O n November 15, 1979, Bloomingdale's completed , the multimillion-dollar renovation of the cosmetics and accessories section of the main floor. The unveiling obviously deserved a major commemorative event. And so, on the eve of the opening, Bloomingdale's held an after-hours party, the largest such event in its history. To be certain its guests blended well with the art deco decor, invitations requested the 1,500 guests to wear formal attire: black tie for the men, black or white gowns for the women; and when they arrived, the store provided masks for the revelers. The evening was a benefit for the Joffrey Ballet, and host Robert Joffrey presented a retrospective of costumes and makeup the ballet company has worn through the years. It was all a far cry from Bloomingdale's first gala benefit in 1971, held on behalf of the Film Society of Lincoln Center. The store had always held occasional promotional parties or events, but benefits for specific charities have now become seasonal extravaganzas.

Debby Weber, director of special events, has been the key person behind these happenings since 1977. She organized the after-hours parties to accompany the Indian, Israeli, and Chinese import shows, as well as the series of events that go on almost constantly at the store. "She makes miracles happen around here," says Glynn—like arranging to feed 1,500 people at the opening of , for example, and then, perhaps even more remarkably, getting the empty wine glasses removed from the furniture displays, the dirty dishes taken off the tables, the ashtrays fished out from under the racks of clothing, and the whole store cleaned up and put together again before opening for business the next morning.

Often held in conjunction with the fall and spring model room openings, the parties draw about 600 people (events for the major import fairs can draw many more). Some come because they want to support the specific cause; some come because they want to mingle with the inevitable celebrities; and some, including some of those celebrities, come because they want to be among the privileged elite who have been allowed into Bloomingdale's after all the customers and tourists have been ushered out.

Bloomingdale's is constantly generating "special events"—bringing artisans, designers, exhibits, or presentations into the store (or its branches); cosponsoring the Bloomingdale's-Perrier race through Central Park, holding kite-flying or kite-fighting contests or exhibitions, staging "happenings" around the opening of new designer shops. These must be closely coordinated with the advertising department, which itself dreams up ever-new and different ways to promote the store and its merchandise. Because advertising and promotion are both very dear to Marvin Traub, he makes time in his sometimes frantic schedule to discuss promotional ideas and projects, and attends the weekly advertising meetings at which new ads are reviewed and promotions discussed. It's show biz, a constantly shifting montage of sales and circuses, and Traub is the ringmaster.

First Class Mail

Until the mid-seventies, Bloomingdale's paid relatively little attention to mail-order selling. There were seasonal catalogs, of course, that went out to selected charge customers who had ordered by mail in the past; catalogs were also slipped into Sunday newspapers, to reach a larger public. And the home furnishings and linens departments held their traditional biannual sales, celebrated in part with mail-order catalogs. Still, mail and phone sales were a minimal part of the business. Most Bloomingdale's customers preferred to shop in person, so that they could visit their glittering, effervescent, ever-changing mecca of the mercantile.

Joan Glynn took an unusually strong interest in catalogs. She recognized the power of the medium and urged the store to increase its emphasis on selling by mail. Glynn advocated that Bloomingdale's expand the mailing beyond the then-650,000 charge customers, to include potential customers outside of the store's marketing area. But the suggestion was premature; the store wasn't quite ready to act on it.

Glynn had moved Bloomingdale's advertising emphasis from art to photography as part of her effort to make it more exciting. Arthur Cohen, vice-president of marketing, adapted her lead in the catalogs, hiring major photographers to create catalog illustrations that were a cut above the retailing norm of pots, pans, and bathrobes against a white or pastel background.

In 1976, Cohen totally severed ties with tradition. Bloomingdale's startled its followers and detractors alike with a seven-by ten-inch catalog of lingerie, created to commemorate the shift of the lingerie department to its new location on the lower level. The subject, women's undergarments, was normally prosaic. This catalog, titled "Sighs and Whispers," was anything but.

Cohen imported French surrealist photographer Guy Bourdin to do the photography, acceding to his demand for total artistic autonomy. When he arrived in New York, Bourdin invited the city's top sixty-five models to come to the store, took a Polaroid shot of each of them in the nude, then announced imperiously that there was not a beautiful model in Manhattan. To the amazement of Bloomingdale's fairly low-key, highly professional advertising staff, Bourdin declared that none of the professional models would do; instead, he would discover his own subjects.

Bourdin took a full month to find his

Sighs and Whispers

models and complete the catalog shooting, and refused to show Bloomingdale's his work until the day he returned to Paris. Then the store had to decide what to do with the extraordinary photographs he had made. What he had come up with was a group of six snub-nosed, very *young*-looking women, all unknowns, who were then made up to look like . . . well, like what some might call ladies of the night. Bourdin paraded these sloe-eyed Lolitas through a series of scenes showing the young women doing what young women do in the privacy of a house: sitting, three abreast on a sofa, dressed in nothing but sheer bras, panties (in two out of three cases), high-heeled gold shoes, and that come-hither makeup; staring into a mirror to admire their slim bodies, all dressed in lacy red undergarments; sitting on a radia-

tor, in bras and panties, gazing restlessly out the curtainless window into the city that holds the keys to excitement.

The cover shot is the denouement. A slim young woman, wearing more lipstick than clothing, stands shyly beside a chair onto which her bridal attire has been carelessly tossed. Hesitant, eyes demurely lowered, she faces the right side of the picture. And there, at the very edge of the frame, is a man's hand, beckoning. Though we can see no more of him than the hand, he seems to be fully, and formally, dressed: a white shirt cuff and the edge of a black jacket are visible at his wrist. Maybe he's the groom. Maybe he's not.

To be sure, Bourdin had followed Bloomingdale's directive to make the annual lingerie catalog less boring. The photographs were so undeniably provocative, however, that there was no reasonable way to tame them into a conservative sales piece. So the store jumped in with both feet. The photographs were placed on black-bordered pages, and the catalog was designed to look more like an art book than a merchandising tool. When it was released to steam its way to customer's hands, they gasped. Newspapers "reviewed" it, and "Sighs and Whispers" became the season's most risqué collector's item, selling for up to $20 at bookstores after the store's supply was exhausted.

Oh, yes. And Guy Bourdin, monumental ego notwithstanding, was invited back a few years later to perform some more of his idiosyncratic magic.

The store followed this coup by hiring photographers David Hamilton and Richard Avedon to photograph, respectively, the lingerie and apparel catalogs of the next two years, continuing to acquire a powerful response from customers and columnists alike. Critical reviews of merchandising catalogs? Articles in *New York* magazine, the *Los Angeles Times,* and the *Washington Post?* Now, wait a minute, said the powers of Bloomingdale's. We seem to have a very good thing here. . . .

In 1978, Bloomingdale's began a concentrated effort to increase its mail and phone business. The store's reputation was by then so pervasive that even people who have never been to the East Coast know of Bloomingdale's and have a strong sense of what the store is and what types of merchandise it sells. Those who have shopped in it know from firsthand experience. These people all form a core of potential customers who would buy in Bloomingdale's consistently, if only they didn't live so far away from the main store or its branches.

How do you reach customers who can't come in to the store? By direct mail. Who has had the most impressive history of marketing this way? Major credit card companies, who have for several years included mail-order advertisements with their monthly billing statements.

It can be no coincidence, then, that in August 1978 Bloomingdale's hired Doreen McCurley, who had previously been the advertising director of American Express. McCurley set up baseline information, then projected a direction and a goal for the store to utilize direct mail selling to "make a profit without building another store." The existing Bloomingdale's charge list of nearly one million names was segmented to show which customers habitually buy by mail or phone, as opposed to those who buy only through visits to the store. This target group was supplemented by names the store gleaned by renting lists of mail-order buyers who lived outside the stores' trading areas (that is, people who did not live near a Bloomingdale's department store). "We sent Bloomingdale's logo around the country," McCurley says, and the results have been decidedly profitable. Connecting good things, in 1979 Traub and McCurley began negotiations with American Express to enable customers to purchase merchandise from Bloomingdale's and charge the cost to their American Express card. Once discussions were under way, Federated took over the negotiations and eventually signed a contract on behalf of American Express and select Federated stores. Bloomingdale's was the

Bloomingdale's sells Bloomingdale's.

first of those stores to allow its customers to use their American Express card to order merchandise by mail and phone, in July 1979. At the same time, Bloomingdale's put in an "800" number (which Glynn refers to as "the umbilical cord of Bloomingdale's") enabling customers to phone the store free of charge from anywhere in the United States. The combination not only made it easy and comfortable to shop by mail; it also enlarged the scope of the enterprise. Though Bloomingdale's is still physically a regional chain, its sales thrust, within limits, is now national.

What it sells through its catalogs lately is not merely merchandise. Beginning with the Christmas 1978 catalog, the store has offered customers the opportunity to purchase "events." For only $15,000 a couple could enjoy an April-in-Paris weekend. Price seem steep? Not so very; it included a chance to get into the movies (the beautiful couple would be given a part in a film being shot on location in the city), and a new Renault Le Car, "complete with a gift basket of French delicacies."

Sports fans could buy midfield tickets to the Cotton Bowl; music fans could buy a "Lincoln Center Sampler" of performances which, naturally, included opportunities to meet (briefly) and eat with the relevant celebrities.

The concept of selling events was part experiment and part promotional gimmick, but it met with a customer acceptance that surprised the store. Though no one took Bloomingdale's Paris special, substantial numbers subscribed to the more moderately priced ($200–$500) instant happenings. As a result, succeeding catalogs continued to offer activities as well as tangible goods for sale.

In 1979, catalog sales showed an increase of more than 50 percent over the 1978 figures. Judging by this radically increased customer response, the direct-mail innovation has been even more successful than Traub, Cooke, or McCurley expected.

The catalogs themselves continue to experiment with form and design. They're not just lists of items and prices; here, as in the store itself, Bloomingdale's is convinced that one of the avenues to success is through the ephemeral art known to the trade as merchandise presentation.

The Glass Menagerie

One Saturday afternoon in late 1975, Marvin Traub took a day off from the store and went window shopping. Now, window shopping for Traub doesn't mean looking for things to buy, or looking at things one would like to have but doesn't feel like spending money for. For a merchant, window shopping means seeing what other stores are selling, what trends they're featuring, what good promotional or merchandising ideas they've had recently. Bloomingdale's, of all places, does *not* operate in a vacuum, and Traub practices the advice he preaches: get out in the world and see what's happening.

So Traub took a walk around New York City. As usual, he was accompanied by his wife, Lee, who complements his thinking. "Lee Traub is a very good sounding board for me," he muses, referring to her by her whole name, as he usually does. "I bounce ideas off her."

They walked down Fifth Avenue, looking particularly at the windows of stores noted for the most beautiful or most interesting or most unusual displays. It wasn't an idle stroll; Gordon Ryan, the store's display director, was leaving and Traub was thinking of making a change in Bloomingdale's window display, a change in the entire gestalt of the store's most obvious promotional front. Peering, considering, discussing the good ideas and the ones that didn't work, the Traubs came at last to Charles Jourdan, a store that sells expensive shoes and accessories. There in the window of this exclusive shop, the New York branch of a European establishment that caters to women of good taste and filled French purses, was a toilet bowl. Porcelain. Sitting there. In the window of a fine Fifth Avenue emporium. A piece of plumbing. Along with several pairs of French shoes.

A small crowd stood outside, staring at the audacious display. Some people gaped, some grinned, but everyone took notice. Traub looked at the window; he looked at the crowd looking at the window, blocking the sidewalk. "Extraordinary," he said.

"Oh, Jourdan's windows have been great all along," Lee answered.

The next week, the executive personnel department of Bloomingdale's contacted Jourdan's window designer, Candida

Pratts, and invited her to drop by to have a chat. Barbara D'Arcy spoke with her, and told Traub she thought Pratts was extraordinary. Pratts was then interviewed by Brennan, Traub, and Lachman. "I was impressed," Pratts says seriously, "but I was also very happy where I was. It's a nice position to be in."

Indeed. Not quite twenty-five, Candy Pratts was made display director and was given the tremendous responsibility of designing Bloomingdale's interior displays, as well as the ever-changing displays in the main store's thirty-nine windows; she also oversaw all display design in the branch stores. During the four years she remained with Bloomingdale's, she introduced an element of unpredictability to the windows, and radically changed the retail industry's concepts of effective display techniques.

Pratts is dynamic, intense, brilliant, and like most of Bloomingdale's important personnel, tremendously self-confident, even to the point of aggressiveness. She moved display in a new direction. If the windows of the fifties and sixties were theater, her windows were theater of the absurd. "Decorate" is hardly a reasonable term to use for what Candy Pratts does to a store window. For her first fall season, she created a window to display French designer Sonia Rykiel's new line. Startled passers-by looked through the plate glass into what appeared to be the lobby of a 1930s down-at-the-heels hotel, where eight mannequins leaned or sat, bored, waiting for something to happen. One, her shoes tossed carelessly to the side, sprawled on a sofa eating chocolates. Another stood reading a French newspaper. Cigarette butts were strewn about, some in the ashtrays, some in the scraggly potted plants. More than one observer felt the scene had strong lesbian overtones.

The season's Christmas windows included unusual deployment of usual things. One window held several dozen red glass Christmas balls scattered on the floor, all shattered. Dozens of wreaths were plastered on walls with seeming reckless abandon—everywhere but on the doors, their traditional location. Later displays became even more brazen, sometimes touching on the bizarre. To show twelve dresses for the fall 1977 season, Pratts converted six of the Lexington Avenue windows into an exercise in voyeurism. The windows were framed to look like large oval mirrors. Mannequins stood behind "vanity tables" facing the windows, peering into them as if they were really mirrors, combing their hair, fixing their lipstick, adjusting their clothing. The viewer seemed to be looking into a powder room through two-way mirrors as the mannequins did things normally done only in privacy.

Occasionally Pratts went too far, even for risqué Bloomingdale's. One summer the Lexington and Fifty-ninth Street window showed several mannequins apparently trying on bathing suits in a large fitting room. Several of the models had not yet donned the top halves of their two-piece suits. None of the store's top management knew in advance what the window would look like, because Pratts, who reported to D'Arcy, worked with an enormous amount of autonomy. Traub has great respect for his creative staff and prefers to give them their head—but within limits. When he saw the "topless" mannequins, he phoned D'Arcy and quietly asked her opinion of it. It coincided with his (which is unsurprising; perhaps more than anyone else, D'Arcy and Traub visualize the same image for the store), and she quietly took the message to Bloomingdale's enfant terrible. And the steam went out of Lexington and Fifty-ninth Street, until the next time.

But Traub admires Pratts, as do many of Bloomingdale's merchants (and many of the store's competitors). Her philosophy was close to his: "We're not selling a product, we're selling an image first." The image presented by the windows is, of course, paramount. Immediate. It's there twenty-four hours a day; when the store is closed for the night, the windows are the public's only direct relation with the store. "So I try to project an image that will make someone stop. And once they stop, they can't help but see what is in the window. Then we can get them upstairs and they can find out about the button and the zipper and all that other stuff."

Pratts denies that she uses shock for its own sake. Rather, she presents "an illusion." She explained: "It's something that the customer wants, something that she wants to be. Some stores put mannequins in totally ridiculous positions. I never knew anyone who stood like that. If the customer can't believe the position, can't identify with it, how can she identify with the dress on the mannequin? My theory was that we would make the customer associate. In the beginning, of course, there was much theater, that was the claim to fame—the whole theater, the whole scenarios. Those still exist. People say, "Oh, you've changed." No, we haven't changed;

Candy Pratts put Gottex bathing suits into the featured corner window of the store, along with a lot of sand and a few "dead" fish.

How better to spotlight a designer's name than with a giant Rolodex open to his name? The mannequin wears one of Claude Montana's futuristic outfits.

This window juxtaposes images—a man's torso dressed neatly in jacket and shirt, the portrait of a man's head, the folded trousers, even the shoes on the floor: fragmented pieces of a whole, waiting to be assembled.

Yves St. Laurent's bare-backed bathing suits are worn by modest mannequins who cover their faces with fans bearing the designer's name.

During the Indian import fair, Pratts flanked a window with imported Indian elephants, then silhouetted the model in understated elegance.

the public has adjusted, there is not as much shock to it now." (As Pratts said this, several mannequins wearing imported Gottex bathing suits sunned themselves in a window filled with sand—and dead fish.)

She claims that what she mainly tried to do was entertain—"positive and negative. If you're going to make someone interested, you're actually entertaining them. You're actually taking time off their spectrum to investigate it. I'm not trying to push any heavy message. I do not demand, or ask, that you see it [the scene in the window] the way I saw it: it's there, and you read it the way you want to. I just want to make sure it's something you don't pass by. So the windows always have some twist. It may be that the girls are all in fur coats, and all of a sudden one girl is holding a nail in her hand. That would get curiosity. I mean, why does the girl have a nail in her hand? What's the story with the nail? It's open to your own fantasy. I don't believe that you teach; I believe you expose."

Pratts is a conceptualizer, not a technician, and she knows it. As soon as she arrived at Bloomingdale's, she began a search for an assistant. Applicants for the job were, of course, numerous, and competition was rather fierce; the position carried with it the prestige of association with Bloomingdale's famous display department. After interviewing scores of experienced designers, Pratts selected Howard Meadows, a young man already working as a "trimmer" in the store's display department, where he had gained experience exhibiting linens, bath items, table settings, and other home furnishings merchandise.

Their association was symbiotic. Pratts excelled at creating display concepts for

Hats on sculpted busts. Nothing unusual. Except that one of these hats perches atop a shoulder, as Pratts is predictably unpredictable.

apparel ("Fashion is my forte"); she let Meadows design the home furnishings displays. He also assumed responsibility to execute her ideas—or to tell her gently, in his soft southern drawl, that one of her fantasies was not reasonably constructible; they'd then discuss viable alternatives, until they arrived at a means to create an exhibit that conveyed the ambience she was after.

Pratts's fantasies reached her public via a rather circuitous route. She and her staff changed thirty-eight windows every ten days. The window on the corner of Fifty-ninth and Lexington—Pratts's favorite, and the most important in the store—changed every five days. But Candy Pratts herself never stepped into a window and never touched a mannequin, even to make a minute adjustment to a scene. The people who do that are the store's six window trimmers and their staff of assistants.

So the procedure was rather convoluted. The store's fashion coordinators or buyers delivered a steady stream of merchandise to Pratts's office: key items of apparel or home furnishings, things they wanted her to feature. She studied it all, gathered accessories, conceptualized the scenarios ("I see slide shows in my head") and then told her ideas directly to Meadows and the trimmers. She never sketched her ideas and went to great lengths to avoid writing memos. Instead, she presented the merchandise itself, described the window presentation she visualized, and sometimes acted out the scenes. "After three years, there was a much better relationship with the trimmers, and a much better understanding. Some trimmers understood the style, they contributed. I would correct it or add to it, make sure that it's still kept in the signature." And after the trimmers absorbed her gestalt and left with the merchandise, Pratts moved on to planning the next scenarios. She claims she rarely looked at the finished windows. "I've already seen them, in my head."

When asked how she determined the style for each season's windows, she answered unabashedly: "The style was Candy Pratts!" But for all her apparent ego Pratts has respect for clothing designers and tried to present their designs in accordance with their apparent points of view. Kalman Ruttenstein, vice-president of fashion direction, often asked her to accompany him to the European shows, to see how the designers present their own clothes. "I don't duplicate what I saw on the runway," Pratts explains unnecessarily, "but I respect a designer. I mean, Yves Saint Laurent I do not correct. I present his clothing the way he presented it. As an artist, I wouldn't want anyone to come over to me to redo my art." No one would dare.

In addition to store windows, Pratts handled merchandise display within the store: mannequins, cases, shops, walls, and so on—or, as Pratts put it, "Everything other than bathrooms." Her concepts here, too, were uncommon. In 1976 she spent $5,000 for a lifelike talking robot which acted as a zookeeper for the toy department during the Christmas season. It introduced fascinated children to the stuffed animals with the W. C. Fieldsian pitch: spiel, "Here comes the grizzly bear. He eats honey and sweets. He likes kids, too. Generally for breakfast."

One of Bloomingdale's most radical display departures concerns the "normal," nonspeaking mannequins, which have long been a central facet of clothing display in department and apparel stores. Pratts, like many customers themselves, impatiently rejected the artificial poses and gestures that have been traditionally imposed on the mannequins. She began placing them in realistic positions and groupings throughout the store. A group of three mannequins might be found standing near one another, in apparent conversation. One might be brushing a piece of lint off another's skirt. Sometimes the mannequins were seated on quite ordinary chairs or lounges placed on the selling floor. Foot-weary customers occasionally took advantage of an extra bit of space on the lounge and squeezed in to take a seat beside the frozen models, whose positions were so realistic that the unwary shopper might be taken unawares. All too many people rounding a clothes rack came upon a mannequin or two who looked precisely like other customers; the real people instinctively nodded hello, moved off to consider a row of skirts or dresses, then glanced back, suddenly unsure, and sheepishly realized they'd greeted a wooden dummy.

Pratts did not restrict her mannequins to formal behavior, of course. In the let-your-hair-down atmosphere of the lower level's Saturday's Generation, a jumpsuited mannequin once lounged on a low platform, casually listening to the disco music piped in.

The mannequin business itself is a tight little industry which supplies the figures to stores throughout the world. Each mannequin is actually modeled after a real person, and the resulting line of mannequins is often called by the real woman's first name, so there might be the Suzie line, and the Bernice line, and so on.

In 1978, Candy Pratts commissioned Adele Roothstein in London, probably the

A shoe is a shoe is a shoe. But when Pratts suspends two of them on a pile of black disks, and litters the floor with . . . what? Marbles? Large beads? It catches the eye of the passerby—and that's what it's all about.

Pratts' unconventional approach allowed her to place these mannequins with their backs to the window. Their faces, and their cleavage, are visible only in the overhead mirror.

finest and largest of the mannequin manufacturing companies, to create a black mannequin. Not just a standard mannequin that had been painted to have a dark complexion, but a new mannequin based on a real, and smashingly attractive, black woman. Pratts chose Toukie Smith, sister of fashion designer Willie Smith, to model for the face and body, then asked Roothstein to create the mannequin in six different poses. (The use of interchangeable parts allow each mannequin a degree of flexibility. Hands may be open or closed, arms or torso may be straight or bent.)

Since Bloomingdale's had designed the new model, Roothstein gave it a three-month exclusive during which the mannequin was not sold to other stores. Afterward, the manufacturer lightened the complexion and released it for sale to other merchants. At the same time, Bloomingdale's, which had been using the model only in its main store, sent Toukie mannequins to all of the branch stores. And now that everyone else had the design, Pratts, who never even copies herself, proceeded to inaugurate the next trend in mannequins: the "bisque" complexion, designed to simulate the skin tones of Latin women. "She became a cultural form," Pratts says. "Women are concerned with skin," presumably as much as with cosmetics and clothing.

Bloomingdale's owns about one hundred "girls," and they're handled with considerable care. Each mannequin costs at least $550, and the store buys two new "collections" every year. Because Bloomingdale's buys so many and showcases them so well, the store usually has "first view" of new models. Once purchased, each mannequin must be maintained and her appearance kept current. Cosmetics, hairdo, even positions must be in the vanguard of new, distinguished fashion, in keeping with the trend-setting clothes that will be modeled. Pratts often used a standard mannequin but changed its pose, so that even though other stores might own the same basic figure, they wouldn't be able to display it in precisely the same way.

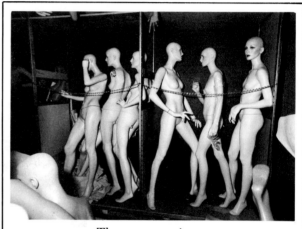

The mannequin room

There is a special refurbishing budget for the mannequins. They must be carefully sandblasted to remove old "makeup" or to change or even their "complexion." The facial paint is redone every two months with specially blended colors, and is applied by "makeup specialists" flown in from London. Eyebrows can be made heavy or thin, lipstick pale or deep. Even the eyes can be changed, both in color and direction, to help convey the appropriate fashion message.

In addition to the standard, highly realistic mannequins, Bloomingdale's commissions Siegfried Liebmann to create special heads and hands, which are used to display such things as hats, gloves and jewelry.

Liebmann's mannequins are highly stylized; sleek modern faceless creatures with Modiglianian long necks and thin, tapering fingers. One resides in the Museum of Modern Art. In Bloomingdale's, they represent high style, and demonstrate the store's use of elements of merchandise display to set the tone and mood for selling merchandise.

Merchandising presentation concerns itself with displaying whatever the store wants to sell. The display department, working in close coordination with Bloomingdale's buyers and fashion coordinators, spotlights merchandise that is being featured in each selling department. This usually leads to different themes in different areas. But now that the store has resumed its mammoth import fairs ("Not necessarily annually," Marvin Traub cautions, "but whenever the appropriate ideas and opportunities exist"), Pratts, Meadows, and staff have gotten involved in major displays that incorporate the entire store. In the spring of 1978, Bloomingdale's had reinstituted the storewide Import Fairs it featured throughout the 1960s. The first of the current series was an eight-week promotion called "India: The Ultimate Fantasy." The extravaganza, which took place in each of the branch stores as well as the main store, entailed much more than just merchandise. Indian arts, handicrafts and cultural activities were also featured, both in the stores themselves and through cooperative events in concert halls and art galleries. India so invaded the public's consciousness that the merchandising venture ultimately affected United States import-export relations with the subcontinent, and the entire affair was

Bloomingdale's and Air India jointly sponsored a poster competition, seeking a design for the import fair the store called India: the Ultimate Fantasy. The prize went to Anand Zaveri, and his winged elephant appeared virtually everywhere in the store, as well as on the spring 1978 shopping bag.

raised to the level of international diplomacy.

The event began with a festival to benefit the Smithsonian Institution, hosted by Bloomingdale's and the Indian Ambassador, Nani Arheshir Palkhivala. The store's boutiques went tongue-in-cheek eastern, with names designed to catch as much fantasy as their merchandise. The in-store displays cost $100,000 and included a life-size, sequin-covered canvas camel, a real bullock cart drawn by life-size fabric bulls wearing Indian ceremonial dress, carved

Bloomingdale's boutiques went tongue-in-cheek Eastern. The shops were designed to present the Indian, or Indian-inspired, merchandise in settings at least as exotic as anything the customer might imagine the real India to be.

Indian performers brought their culture to the Bloomingdale's chain. Here, Mallika Sarabhai performs a traditional Bharat Natyam dance of India's southeastern coast.

wooden columns and panels, and the entire façade of a building, taken apart and shipped in pieces, then reconstructed in the store. As Carl Levine noted, the promotion was intended to "bring *spectacle* to the store." By the end of May, it had made such an impression, on India as well as on the Bloomingdale's customer, that it was held over for two more weeks to allow Prime Minister Morarji Desai to see it during his state visit the next month. And so, on June 12, 1978, the ruling head of state of India came to Bloomingdale's to see the largest display of Indian merchandise outside his own country, "India: The Ultimate Fantasy."

The India fantasmagoria was Candy Pratts's first promotion of a country, and Barbara D'Arcy went along to be guide and mentor. By the end of that exposition, D'Arcy was engrossed in the renovations of the main floor, the branch stores, and myriad other things, so Pratts was sent off to do the Israeli fair pretty much on her own.

"I was in charge of producing the event," Pratts said. "India was easier, in a

The import fair had spin-offs throughout the several cities in which it was held. In New York's Central Park, a kite-flying contest was held, with "human fly" George Willig as one of the judges.

way, because I bought the whole country. It was very easy to buy palaces and tell people to knock down ceilings, buy columns. . . . You could actually come back with architectural fragments and materials to work with."

But Israel was a very different situation indeed. First of all, it seems to have mattered in a different way to Bloomingdale's leaders. Perhaps it was philosophical, perhaps philanthropic, but certainly the Israeli promotion was not purely a business matter. Oh, to be sure, the store went into it to make money. That's the name of the game. But there was an element in this event that transcended the mercenary, and resulted in a startling reversal of the historical development of museum-into-store. In the spring of 1979, portions of Bloomingdale's were turned into a museum.

It had started the previous May when Zvi Dinstein, Israeli economic ambassador to North America, approached Traub to suggest that Bloomingdale's do an Israeli import fair. Plans had already been made to feature Italian merchandise in the Home Furnishings department and in the model rooms for the spring 1979 season, but furniture is not one of Israel's manufacturing strengths anyway. Look at what else we have, Dinstein urged. So Bloomingdale's, which had been buying select merchandise from Israel for years, sent a scouting party of buyers to explore the marketplace as a whole.

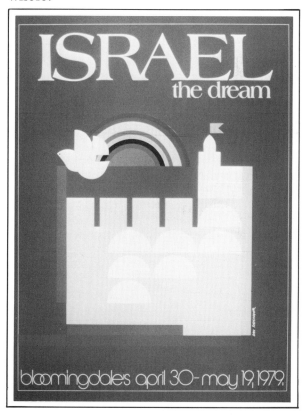

By the end of the summer, the data was in. All right, said Bloomingdale's, we'll do it. And then Israel, like several countries before it, began to receive its crash course in Bloomingdale's concept of appropriate merchandise—always politely, and extremely selectively. Some items were dubbed quite marketable "as is"; the store just placed orders for quantities. But

Bloomingdale's has a penchant for getting involved in the creation of the merchandise it buys; it is the ultimate store-as-creator.

How does it work? Here's one example among many. Riki Ben Ari is a talented young Israeli fashion designer, who, with her husband, owns a small factory that manufactures the clothing she designs. Bloomingdale's fashion scouts "discovered" her and decided to do a feature with her apparel. Kal Ruttenstein invited her to come to New York for a month. He assigned a fashion coordinator to walk her through the store, to help get the feel of its merchandise and its ambiance. They introduced her to new fabrics, suggested styling ideas, and gave her a bit of Bloomingdale's perspective on what its customers might be interested in wearing come the warm days of 1979.

The following spring, Riki Ben Ari's collection, designed exclusively for Bloomingdale's, arrived in New York and was to be given a feature position in a shop called the Jaffa Gate, near the third-floor escalator. The store took out a full-page ad in the *New York Times,* picturing several of Ben Ari's polished-cotton outfits and announcing that the designer would be on hand from noon to 3:00 P.M. to greet customers as her collection was informally modeled.

It didn't come off quite as planned. The ad appeared in the morning paper, and Ben Ari arrived at Bloomingdale's shortly after noon, just in time to see two customers not-so-politely fighting over the privilege of buying the last skirt on the racks. The collection was completely sold out, even the items that were to have been

Exhibition of miniature synagogues

Artifacts from the Israel Museum in Jerusalem

modeled. The buyer rushed over to Ben Ari as she walked through the Jaffa Gate, took her by the arm and steered her hurriedly to an inner office to phone her husband at their factory in Israel and instruct him to ship any and all available garments to New York at once, and put the factory into high gear to complete and ship more goods as quickly as possible. Ben Ari made the call, then wandered out to the selling floor again and just stood there for a while, looking a bit dazed.

Not all the Israeli designers or firms were new, of course, either to Bloomingdale's or to the United States. Beged-Or, the house of leather and suede, sent its fall line of coats and suits, which sold despite

Ancient costumes and jewelry were protected by transparent display cases.

event, which was the largest promotion of Israeli merchandise ever held outside that country.

As with the Indian promotion, however, Bloomingdale's wanted to present a picture of the culture, not only a display of consumer goods. And that's where this event differed from its predecessors. Everything brought over for the Indian event—wall hangings, architectural fragments, items used to decorate the store—was all for sale (and virtually all were sold). For "Israel the Dream," thousands of square feet of floor space were used to house displays that were not for sale. They were exhibits, attracting browsers as if to a museum. A sacred tenet of merchandising says: Use every available bit of space to *sell.* Bloomingdale's broke the rule, flagrantly.

Candy Pratts had selected exhibits from Israel's museums, universities and institutions: an archeological display, including centuries-old clay sarcophagi; ethnic costumes and jewelry; a collection of minia-

the warm spring weather. A group of Gottex bathing suits was featured, several different styles using the same two colors (an idea that Bloomingdale's had suggested to the manufacturer, with whom, like Beged-Or, it has done business for years). In all, Bloomingdale's retailed about $5 million worth of merchandise from Israel for the

Israeli Head of State Ephraim Katzir with Bloomingdale's Chairman Traub and President Schoff at the store's party celebrating the import fair

Guest of honor Zubin Mehta and his wife, Nancy

ture synagogues; a computerized program that displayed information, on request, about life in the Diaspora; a prismatic multimedia display called the "Crystal Mountain," which projected the varied dimensions of the Weizmann Institute of Science. Traub met with everyone, from Prime Minister Menachem Begin to the curators of Israel's museums, to gain Israel's cooperation and permission to allow some of the art objects out of the country. The resulting promotion was reviewed in the entertainment section of the *New York Times*. Richard Shepard wrote: "Thanks to Israel, Bloomingdale's is a nonshopper's paradise. Throughout Bloomingdale's seven shopping floors is scattered a large exhibit, 'Israel the Dream' . . . [which] turns corners of the store into tourist spots."

And the tourists came, by the busload, some with guides and others calling the store to request that Bloomingdale's provide guides to show them through the exhibits. The promotion resulted in a sales gain, throughout the entire Bloomingdale's chain, of about 15 percent during the month of the import fair. The sales increase was 50 percent higher than had been expected for that period, and the store's buyers began making return trips to Israel almost as soon as the promotion ended.

In late summer of 1979, Candy Pratts left Bloomingdale's to go into business with Peggy Healy. This time there was no need for Traub to scout the city seeking a replacement. The obvious choice, Howard Meadows, was readily at hand. But was he really up to the job? asked the skeptics. Certainly he could do the job, but could he

do it spectacularly, in the manner to which Bloomingdale's had become accustomed?

Actually, he'd had more direct experience doing just that than most people realized. And when Pratts left suddenly, Meadows found himself able to call the shots. He began softly, but not noticeably, rejecting blatant imagery in favor of a subtlety that requires an occasional double take. Meadows uses common, everyday objects "to help people see." One of his first windows featured a single mannequin in a pink knitted Dorothy Bis dress. On a shelf behind her was a row of containers of baby powder. Meadows had superimposed on a sophisticated outfit his realization that it happened to be in a baby pink color. Noteworthy? It doesn't seem so, until one learns that for the next two weeks, the woman who handles Bloomingdale's information desk became accustomed to hearing customers ask where to find "the knitted

Howard Meadows

Betsey Johnson's playful clothes are presented beside trick "paint cans" from Pop/Eye Productions. This is an instance in which one of Bloomingdale's window designs could later be seen, in respectful imitation, throughout the city.

This window featured the "launch" of Mary MacFadden's first linen collection. Colored water, an emerald mirror, and a shimmering blue curtain paralleled the pastel opalescence of the sheets and pillow cases.

These carefully crafted silk flowers are one of the store's perennial best sellers. But how many times can you display flowers without the very topic beginning to pall? So Meadows put them into a naturalistic setting: sacks of peat moss.

To call attention to these hand-painted silk dresses, Meadows provided one hundred paintbrushes, dipped in the same colors as the designs on the dresses.

dresses in baby colors." The bottom line for window display is, after all, getting customers to come in off the street.

Meadows has some strong feelings about how to accomplish that. "Windows are silent salesmen," he feels, and Pratts knew that too. But which windows? Pratts focused her energies on Lexington Avenue. Meadows says he wants to spotlight Third Avenue, in part because Bloomingdale's address, after all, is One Thousand Third Avenue.

By the end of October, Meadows had come into his own. The Lexington Avenue windows, always the major showcases, bore a totally different stamp and reflected a different conceptual base. Meadows created something of an in-store revolution by reversing the traditional roles of the two corner windows. For as long as anyone could remember, the Sixtieth Street corner had featured a home furnishings display (which, under Candy Pratts's reign, he had designed and executed). And the Fifty-ninth Street corner had spotlighted women's fashions—had, in fact, been the location in which Bloomingdale's made its most important fashion statement, featuring a major designer's noteworthy new collection, revealing a new designer fragrance (or Bloomie's own), or heralding a major fashion trend.

Meadows transposed the two windows. Heresy! Customers looking for designer clothing in the Fifty-ninth Street window found a bedroom scene instead, cheerfully draped with Mary McFadden's newest venture into designing sheets and linens. And the Sixtieth Street corner held a collection of designer lingerie instead of the usual home furnishings scene.

Meadows hung Kenzo's line of "active sportswear" in a locker-room setting.

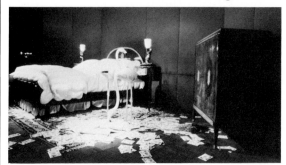

The linens themselves carry a morning-glory theme, so Meadows carried the idea to a whimsical conclusion. First, he strewed the floor with packets of morning-glory seeds. Then, following the idea to an extreme, he added flamingos to munch on the seeds.

The understated obvious: men's clothing, neatly placed on an architect's board and chair. The message is simple and obvious: these are the clothes of a professional, of a creative person, of a man who thinks for himself.

Why? Just for the sake of being different? In part, Meadows agreed, and wondered aloud whether total predictability was good for business. (Come to think of it, it certainly doesn't seem to be in keeping with Bloomingdale's merchandising philosophy.) "Just think about Third Avenue," Meadows mused, his blue eyes softening as he visualized it himself. "Across the street are those four movie theaters, and every night there are lines of people waiting to get in. That's a command audience, not to mention the great numbers of people who walk along Third Avenue instead of Lexington. Yet the Third Avenue windows have always held our least-inspired displays."

In defense of the past, there is some reason for this. The windows on Third Avenue have rather shallow display cases behind them, precluding the possibility of the complex three-dimensional exhibits that can fit into the deeper Lexington Avenue window cases. But Meadows has a point; use of conventional or predictable displays is not what Bloomingdale's is all about. It's also not good merchandising, and new though he is to the position of display director, Meadows reveals a surprisingly astute, and largely intuitive, grasp of some of the same marketing display principles that motivate Traub and D'Arcy.

"What I'd really like to do is make all the windows unpredictable. Move the major display from one location to another, from time to time, so that the customers won't only go to look at one particular window and ignore all the others. This way, they'll look at many windows, seeking the major display, and in the process they'll notice a lot more of the merchandise."

Celebrities like these seem to hang out at Bloomingdale's. Some came to shop. Some came to participate in special promotions. Some came to the extravaganzas the store throws to support favored charities. Some came to watch the other celebrities.

Polly Bergen and Henry Fonda

Calvin Klein (left) and Diana Vreeland

Hermione Gingold

Ethel Merman

Marisa Berenson
and Tony Roberts

Diane Von Furstenberg

Ralph and Ricki Lauren

Richard Parks (left) and Pierre Cardin

Mary Joan Glynn and Ismail Merchant

Cheray (left) and Peter Duchin
and Mrs. Audrey Zauderer

Ben Vereen

Givenchy and Regine

Pauline Trigere (left),
Mrs. and Mr. Paul Woolard

Dame Margot Fonteyne

Carroll O'Connor
and Polly Bergen

Adolph Green

Calvin Klein

Andy Warhol

Alexandra and Arthur Schlesinger
and Stephen Smith (right)

Princess Benedikte
of Denmark

Lord Churchill

Bette Davis

Kenzo and Grace Jones

Governor Hugh Carey,
Estée and Joe Lauder

Oliver Smith (left), company director
of the American Ballet Theater, with
Jacqueline Kennedy Onassis and Marvin
Traub

Tammy Grimes

Rosie Grier

Duke Ellington

Norris Church, Norman Mailer,
and Alexandra Schlesinger

Eunice Shriver, Jean Smith,
and Pat Lawford

Hollywood Goes Bloomingdale's

Bloomingdale's has long been a media favorite, and the store has been discussed on radio and television and has even been mentioned, en passant, in films. But in 1979 Hollywood decided to give Bloomingdale's the chance most actors yearn for: a feature part in a major motion picture. The store was given a juicy role in Paramount Pictures' romantic comedy *Starting Over*, starring Burt Reynolds, Candice Bergen, and Jill Clayburgh.

Clayburgh seems to have an ongoing cinematic relationship with Bloomingdale's. In her starring role in *An Unmarried Woman*, she plays the part of a woman who is contentedly married until her husband suddenly announces that he's leaving her; it seems he met another woman while he was at the shirt counter in . . . guess where?

The coincidence goes even further. Michael Murphy, the actor who plays the errant husband in *An Unmarried Woman,* also plays a role in Woody Allen's film *Manhattan,* in which, once again, he meets his inamorata at Bloomingdale's. This time the scene, between Murphy and Diane Keaton, actually appears on the screen. The major dialogue portions of the scene were filmed right after the store closed one evening, in front of one of the cosmetic counters on the main floor. Traub came down to say hello, and Mike Blumenfeld, vice-president of the cosmetics division, wandered over to watch. Allen told publicity liaison Margot Rogoff that he loves the store: "I'm there every Saturday. But I haven't been picked up yet."

He directs quietly, calmly, and his small crew did its work silently and with remarkable swiftness, wrapping it up in only four and a half hours. But Woody had wanted some "live" footage, too, shot while the store was open and the normal crowds of customers milled about. He promised that the filming would not disrupt the normal store activities, that "no one will notice" the presence of Woody Allen, Michael Murphy, Diane Keaton, a crew of staff and technicians, and the paraphernalia of a cinematic production. Amazingly, he seems to have been right. At three o'clock that afternoon Allen moved a small film crew onto the main floor, where they set up their camera near the information booth, under the sheltering angle of an escalator. There they took a long shot of the daytime crowd, and managed to do it so unobtrusively that most customers weren't even aware of the touch of Hollywood in their New York store.

Twentieth Century-Fox also shot a brief scene in Bloomingdale's in the spring of 1979. The film was *Willie and Phil,* directed by Paul Mazursky and starring Margot Kidder as a character who worked in the cosmetic department, demonstrating nail polish at the Elizabeth Arden counter.

References to Bloomingdale's are continuously found in films today. In *California Suite,* Alan Alda defends his choice of clothes by stating that they were bought in Bloomingdale's and in *The Electric Horseman,* Robert Redford teases Jane Fonda about her "Bloomingburg" boots.

But in *Starting Over,* Paramount wanted to do much more than mention the store or show it briefly. This time, the department store scenes form an integral part of the plot. In the film, Candice Bergen becomes an intellectually liberated woman and decides to carry the spirit through to her personal life, so she leaves husband Burt Reynolds. Lonely and bewildered for a while, he finally meets Jill Clayburgh. She falls in love with him, and in time they move in together.

They need a sofa to complete their shared apartment, so they go to a department store to look at the furniture in the model rooms. But Reynolds has an anxiety attack there; he is unable to make this final, absolute break from his former wife. So Reynolds and Clayburgh leave the store sans the couch, and soon stop seeing each other.

Ultimately Reynolds realizes that he's made a mistake. He wants to live with Clayburgh, wants to marry her—but how can he regain her trust? His solution: he buys the sofa they had seen, and presents it to Clayburgh as the symbol of his commitment to their relationship.

The film was being made in New York City and in Boston, the actual locales of the story, and the department store scene takes place in Boston. But the production crew couldn't find a Boston store to fit their needs, so they fanned outward, looking at other possible locations. At one point they zeroed in on the White Plains, New York, branch of Bloomingdale's because it had the right ambience inside, and outside "it looked like Boston." Paramount said maybe, but couldn't they find something closer to one of the shooting sites? At that point the producers contacted Mildred Collins, whose firm develops promotional tie-ins for Paramount, and asked her to make some suggestions.

Collins had worked with Bloomingdale's flagship store in the past and sensed that it would be ideal for the film. The factor of the model room, of course, made Bloomingdale's come immediately to mind; Barbara D'Arcy had made the very concept of model rooms inextricably related to Bloomingdale's. Moreover, Collins knew some of the complexities the in-store filming would entail, and realized that many stores simply lacked the ability—and the flexibility—to accommodate the needs of a film production. She suspected that Bloomingdale's would be willing to do it, and she knew, too, the interior of the main store would be appropriate for the shots of Reynolds and Clayburgh in the furniture department. But the freneticism of Fifty-ninth Street and Lexington Avenue doesn't look much like the quiet elegance of Boston, where the scene was supposed to take place. So Collins phoned Bloomingdale's and asked for their opinion and suggestions.

Bloomingdale's was delighted with the idea, and suggested a solution to the problem of the indoor-outdoor shots: film the interior scenes in the New York store (which was most able to adapt itself to the production needs) and the exterior scenes outside of Bloomingdale's furniture store in Chestnut Hill, right outside of Boston. That way, the ambiance of the location would be correct, and Bloomingdale's would make sure that it had two identical sofas on hand: one in each store.

For Paramount, the suggestion was ideal. It would be no problem whatsoever to make the two locations look like different parts of the same store. Film is perfect for such sleight-of-fact; the medium specializes in making one thing look like another. (You didn't really believe that Superman could fly?)

But it created some unique problems for Bloomingdale's. They had to work with time considerations, logistics, and the needs of both the film script and the production budget.

First, there were the needs of the script. Paramount needed a model room design that would be appropriate for the character played by Burt Reynolds. Production designer George Jenkins felt that the model room should be designed by Bloomingdale's, to fit the script's need and to simultaneously reflect the store's image. So Jenkins met with Richard Knapple, then the designer of the store's model rooms, and outlined the basic storyline and plot needs. Knapple then created an ultramodern design, with chrome walls and ceiling trim,

Jill Clayburgh and Burt Reynolds in *Starting Over*

spare, clean-lined furniture, and dramatic plants and fixtures. To his amazement, the design was rejected, and the studio apologetically realized that in their own assumption that Bloomingdale's interior design settings were infallible, they'd neglected to provide Knapple with sufficient information about the Reynolds character's taste and budget. The omission was hastily rectified: it seems that Reynolds would have felt comfortable in a more traditional setting. So Knapple good-naturedly went back to his drawing board and created a second design, replacing the metal molding with wood and softening the cold, pure lines with traditional furniture and a fireplace.

That fireplace came in rather handy.

Paramount had originally intended to shoot the scene with two model rooms: a living room and a bedroom. But they revised the script during the course of production and decided to omit the bedroom. So Knapple revised his design yet again, incorporating the bedroom portion as an extension of the living room.

This revealed yet another problem: Where would the cameras stand? For certain shots, the filming now required the model room to have movable walls. Solution: Knapple gave the fireplace mobility. When it's visible as a background in certain shots, it sits sedately in place, as traditional fireplaces are wont to do. But when a camera must come in for a particular tight shot and the fireplace is not visible in the scene, it's simply moved aside to give the camera a better vantage place. Knapple's choice of unusual upholstery fabrics never made it to the filming stage either. The filming schedule was simply too tight to wait for them, so available fabrics were used to expedite the production.

When the final designs and planning were completed, they were shown to producer/director Alan Pakula, who approved them immediately. The next step was to get it all done in time for the shooting date.

The segment concerning the Boston Bloomingdale's showed Reynolds and actor Austin Pendleton emerging from the store with the sofa. But the film's story was supposed to take place during Christmas—and this was mid-January. Paramount had requested that Bloomingdale's retain its Christmas decorations, and the store had agreed, but surely not even a movie studio could expect it to keep the decorations in place. In January? Christmas decorations? In a store that prides itself on its timely, ever-changing displays? Impossible.

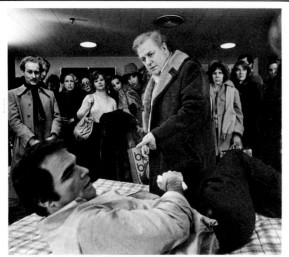

As a crowd of pseudoshoppers watches (notice the Big Brown Bags), actor Charles Durning comforts a distraught Burt Reynolds.

So it didn't. And when Paramount finished filming the rest of the film and called to say they were ready to shoot the Bloomingdale's exterior shots, the Boston store's display department simply got out the carefully preserved Christmas decorations and put them back into those windows that would appear in the scene. While staid Bostonians may have sniffed that Bloomingdale's was jumping the Christmas season by eleven months, the outdoor filming began.

Several weeks later, it was finished. Cast and crew were ready to film the much more complex New York segment.

Film personnel started walking in and out of the New York store all day Monday and Tuesday, February 5 and 6, planning routes, determining what electrical and other equipment was already available and what they'd have to bring in, roughly plotting shots and locations and logistics. At 5:00 P.M. on Tuesday evening, they started bringing in the cumbersome equipment, driving their huge vans down East Sixtieth Street to Bloomingdale's loading bay and hauling it in along the path usually reserved for incoming fashions and other merchandise. Trailers and portable dressing rooms for the stars and cast drove up and parked all along the street, oblivious to the curious glances of homeward-rushing New Yorkers. Even as the last customers were leaving the store, the film crew, in conjunction with some of Bloomingdale's own in-house construction personnel (by now well used to setting up nighttime spectaculars that would disappear before the store opened the next morning) were at work converting the fifth floor into a film set.

The shooting began at 7:00 P.M., and after watching for a few moments, some members of the public relations department rode down to the first floor and through the employee's door—right into a waiting throng of people. Because the *New York Times* had published a story the previous week, telling all about the movie to be made at Bloomingdale's, the publicists assumed that they were facing a mob of cinema fans eagerly awaiting a sight of their favorite movie stars. But the ways of Hollywood are far more subtle. The hundreds of people were all production extras, patiently waiting to be summoned to the fifth floor. And as soon as the real customers, designers, and members of the Bloomingdale's sales force had left the store, this horde of replicas was ushered upstairs, to take their places as customers, designers, and members of the Bloomingdale's sales force.

They worked until shortly past 2:00 A.M. that first night, then returned at 6:00 P.M. on Wednesday and filmed until 5:00 A.M. the following morning, and it was all over but the editing. Now it would be up to the critics to determine whether Bloomingdale's would make it as a film star.

The Men at the Top

Business establishments, like nations, go through different eras. There are eras of prosperity, eras of expansionism, eras of confusion and indecisiveness, eras of aggressive growth. The times have much to do with this, outside factors can have greater or lesser degrees of influence, but the major ingredient in determining the condition of a business, or a country, is its leadership.

From 1947 through 1980, Bloomingdale's went through four eras. Throughout them, the store's prosperity increased, but the executive teams who headed the store from 1947 to 1963, from 1963 to 1969, and from 1969 to 1978, and the leadership that has governed the corporation since then, have done what is virtually unique in retailing history. They have totally changed the format of Bloomingdale's, from what it was to what it is today.

Lyman Bloomingdale had established a neighborhood store geared to high promotion, low prices, and fast turnover of goods. His son Samuel carried on the tradition, making the store bigger but just more of the same. Michael Schaap, the first nonfamily head of the store, kept it financially healthy through the Depression but did little to change

what the founders had begun. The big change, the one that altered the store's very personality, its perception of itself, and the perception in which everyone else holds it, began with the 1947 change in management.

James Schoff had assumed the presidency of the store in 1944, and had brought in J. Edward Davidson to be chairman of the board. While Davidson built the merchandising area, raising the levels of taste and quality, emphasizing imported goods and unique items tailored specifically for Bloomingdale's, Schoff concentrated on developing an executive staff equal to the aggressive, rapidly growing business. By 1960, when Schoff was sixty and Davidson fifty-nine, it was obvious that Bloomingdale's needed a clear line of succession for the day when they would step down from their leadership of the now virtually transformed store and its growing line of suburban branches. Following their policy of promoting people from within, Schoff and Davidson chose as their successors two men who had each spent more than a decade with the store: Lawrence Lachman and Marvin Traub.

Lachman had joined the store in 1947 as treasurer, become vice-president of per-

Michael Schaap

James S. Schoff, Sr.

J. Edward Davidson

Harold Krensky

Lawrence Lachman

Marvin S. Traub

James S. Schoff, Jr.

sonnel and operations in 1953, and been promoted to executive vice-president in 1958. Federated had great respect for his financial abilities, and he was an executive who could inspire and motivate his staff.

In June 1962, Davidson relinquished his day-to-day responsibilities as chairman of the board, devoting all of his time to further developing Bloomingdale's import business. He formally retired in 1963 (though he remained a consultant to the store). Schoff, then sixty-three, moved up to the position of chairman, still retaining the title of chief executive officer. The following February, Lawrence Lachman, at forty-seven, became president of Bloomingdale's—and note: there were now two operations men running the store.

But there was no merchandising head! So, in 1962, the thirty-seven-year-old Marvin Traub was promoted from his position as vice-president for home furnishings to executive vice-president of the store. Significantly, he was also appointed *general merchandising manager,* a title formerly held by Jed Davidson throughout his tenure as chairman. Traub, without benefit of the highest office, was in fact the store's merchandising head. No retailing establishment could operate without one.

In December 1965, Schoff retired as chief executive officer of the store, but remained as chairman of the board. Officially, it was announced that he had "retired from active management," and Lachman became the chief executive officer. Obviously, though, Schoff still retained the imprimatur of control. The following November, Schoff stepped down all the way. Under his and Davidson's joint leadership, Bloomingdale's had opened four suburban branches in New York, New Jersey, and Connecticut, and helped the sales of the Manhattan store grow at the greatest rate in Bloomingdale's then ninety-one-year history.

The careful withdrawal-in-stages, coupled with nurturing, support, and encouragement of the next generation of leadership, was obviously intended to "ensure increased depth and continuity of management," as Ralph Lazarus, then president of Federated, put it. But while Federated's directors were comfortable with Lachman as chairman, they were concerned that Traub, despite his obvious abilities, was still too young to become president of the store that was, after all, their golden goose. So Harold Krensky was brought back to Bloomingdale's to head the critical merchandising end of the business. Krensky (the senior vice-president of merchandising and publicity at Bloomingdale's until 1959) had been transferred to Filene's, Federated's Boston store, where in six years he'd moved from executive vice-president to chairman of the board. Now, at fifty-four, he was brought back to Bloomingdale's and given the interesting dual title of chairman of the board and *managing director.* He stayed for a couple of years; by then he knew, as he remarked later, that there had really been no need for him to come back. So Krensky left Bloomingdale's and went into the management of the parent corporation itself, becoming a group president of Federated in 1969 and president of the entire organization in 1973.

Even as he and Lachman held titular sway over Bloomingdale's, however, and even though Krensky was a merchandising man, it was open knowledge that Marvin Traub was working very closely with them. Isadore Barmash, the erudite financial columnist of the *New York Times,* stated what the industry believed: that Traub, "as the No. 3 man and as general merchandising manager, has worked closely with them on formulating both merchandising and operating policy."

And finally, in 1969, when the conjunction of the stars seemed auspicious, Bloomingdale's gained the well-honed top management team that controlled its course for the next decade. Lawrence Lachman, then fifty-three, was moved up to Davidson's old position as chairman of the board, and the forty-four-year-old Marvin Traub was made president, Schoff's old role. Bloomingdale's again had two top executives at the helm, one an operations expert and one an innovator in merchandising.

The nine years of the Lachman-Traub partnership were a very profitable time for the business, which grew from one central store with five branches into a fifteen-store chain, extending from Boston to Washington, which then accounted for more than $400 million of Federated Department Stores' annual sales. During this time, Bloomingdale's refined the broad goals set down by Davidson and Schoff.

In the spring of 1978, Larry Lachman resigned at the age of sixty-two to become a private business consultant. "I've always felt that if possible one should always have something to look forward to," he told the

Times at the announcement of his early retirement. "As I neared the formal retirement age, I decided that the combination of my corporate and community activities had given me an unusual insight into all kinds of complex problems that could help different kinds of companies. So I decided to become a consultant."

Upon Lachman's departure, Traub ascended to the role of chairman of the board and chief executive officer of Bloomingdale's. The presidential office was filled by James S. Schoff, Jr. The younger Schoff had joined Bloomingdale's furniture division in 1960, become a divisional merchandise manager for home furnishings three years later, and then in 1968, as a merchandise vice-president, had taken charge of Bloomingdale's plans to build a chain of home furnishings outlets in various markets in the Northeast, when Bloomingdale's first began to test its reception in suburban areas. After a few more promotions, he'd been named executive vice-president in 1977.

Since they've known one another and worked together for years, Traub and Schoff, Jr., immediately established a very close partnership. They share perceptions and goals, because they've come up through the same route, both products of Bloomingdale's system of honing executive talent to a sharp edge. They are the embodiment of Schoff, Sr., and Davidson's concept: an ongoing executive staff that would provide a "continuity of thought" from one era to the next.

Bloomingdale's will continue to follow its well-established merchandising philosophy under its new leadership, because at the moment there's no real need to change. The annual import fairs of the sixties have been reestablished as multi-million-dollar ventures, the store has modified its statement about interior design, and its fashion apparel division has mushroomed. Underlying all of this is Bloomingdale's personal conception of "merchandising presentation"—the store as theater, as museum, as a center for entertainment, or even, as *Time* called it, as "an adult Disneyland."

And the public buys the formula, buys it big. According to Traub, in 1979 the Bloomingdale's chain took in over $518 million.

That's entertainment!

佈明代

In the fall of 1980, Bloomingdale's brought China to the United States. It was the store's largest, most ambitious import fair, and the largest Chinese exhibition in the nation. For it, Bloomingdale's had imported or created merchandise with a retail value in excess of $10 million. In its inimitably exuberant fashion, this was Bloomingdale's way of ushering itself into a new decade.

The name of the fair was highly symbolic. First, a pictograph of the store's name was created. Phoneticized into Chinese, "Bloomingdale's" becomes *Boo Ming Dai.* And that, translated as Heralding the Dawn of a New Era, became the name of the import fair, with all that it symbolizes for China, for Bloomingdale's and for the new decade.

Chinese merchandise wasn't new to the store, which had imported it until China's revolution in 1949 effectively closed the country to trade with the West. In 1971, the United Nations voted to "recognize" the People's Republic of China. Chinese diplomats were present at the UN headquarters in New York as the final vote was taken. After more than twenty years, their country had at last received the world's acknowledgment. It was a momentous occasion.

That very day, Bloomingdale's opened its newest boutique. It was called China Passage, and it didn't have a tremendous diversity of items: bamboo backscratchers, $650 fish tanks, umbrellas, twenty-five-inch-diameter "coolie hats," blue cotton workers' jackets and pants. But it was the first store in the United States to carry merchandise from the People's Republic of China.

Though the UN recognition led to the lifting of the trade embargo, no one, not even Bloomingdale's, could import goods, have them delivered, and set up a brand-new shop in the course of a single day. What had happened was an evaluation of probabilities. While China had sought UN recognition for years, this time it seemed extremely likely that the vote would go through. Bloomingdale's had gambled on that likelihood and had contacted François Dautresme, owner of the Compagnie Française de l'Orient et de la Chine shops. Dautresme, who had been buying from mainland China for ten years, was then expecting a shipment of Chinese goods to be delivered by freighter. Bloomingdale's buyers saw the shipment, bought it in toto, had it shipped to New York immediately, and set up the new shop so that it could open the very day China received its formal recognition.

The next year the store featured Chinese baskets, also imported through France. Then Richard Nixon made a much-heralded trip to China, the United States and China resumed trade relations, and China announced that it would permit Americans to attend the Canton Fair, a semiannual showing of wares to foreign businessmen.

From that time to the present, Bloomingdale's has sent representatives to every Canton Fair. Carl Levine went over every year, probably more than any other store executive, and became Bloomingdale's resident China expert.

In 1972, Levine saw a bamboo chair sitting by the edge of a pool in The Forbidden City. Later, he met with the head of the rattan furniture department of the Canton Arts and Crafts Corporation and asked him to drive to the pool to look at the chair, to see if he could reproduce it. The man couldn't imagine why Levine would want such a thing, but he graciously complied. Afterward, they exchanged business cards so the official could arrange to ship him the reproduction.

Bloomingdale's staff carry reversible cards to China; they are printed in English on one side and in Chinese characters on the reverse. (The Chinese's business cards are the same.) In Chinese characters, the name Levine becomes Lee Wing. The trade minister looked at that side of the card and said that his own name was Lee Wing, too. "We seem to be connected by more than a bond of rattan," he said, his almond-shaped black eyes looking solemnly into Levine's round blue ones. "Maybe we're related."

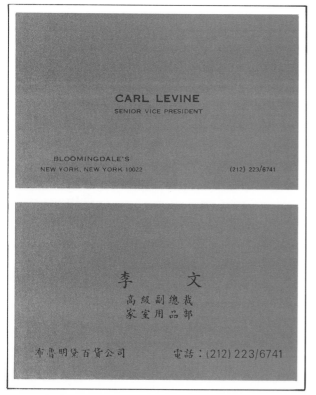

The first few years, buyers explored the availability of existing Chinese merchandise: rattan furniture, bamboo items, ceramic and jade figures, semiprecious jewelry. Gradually, China and Bloomingdale's grew used to one another. In 1975, Levine and his group were permitted, for the first time, to see a bit more of the country. They visited not only Canton, but Shanghai, Peking (now spelled Beijing), and Tientsin.

"When we came out of China," reported Levine at the time, "we were very pleased because we're finally able to have our own designs reproduced there now." It wasn't done on a large scale, but the store was beginning to do in China what Levine and D'Arcy had first done in Italy in the late fifties: develop new merchandise that was specifically tailored for the Bloomingdale's customer.

The end of the seventies saw a major political change in China, and the new administration was much more amenable to contact with the West. Marvin Traub, Jim Schoff, and Carl Levine began talking about the possibility of making a major purchase of Chinese goods, and even, if it could be arranged, holding a Chinese import fair. Traub invited Chinese officials to be his guests during Bloomingdale's Indian promotion in 1977, and again the next year, when the store featured Israel. But the Chinese, swamped with invitations, declined to make an official visit (although their familiarity with these events, and with the store in general, indicated that they had visited Bloomingdale's unofficially on numerous occasions). They made no real indication that China intended to pay more attention to Bloomingdale's than they paid to other American stores.

Then in the spring of 1978, Federated chairman Ralph Lazarus visited China and raised the idea of a possible Bloomingdale's import fair. To his amazement, he found the Chinese totally aware of the store's interest in their country—and they acknowledged that they, in turn, might be interested in Bloomingdale's.

Traub began formal correspondence with the Chinese Embassy, and in a letter to the ambassador, he proposed that Bloomingdale's hold a major Chinese import fair. In the fall of 1978 he, Levine, and Jack Schultz made a trip to Washington, to ask for a specific embassy liaison with whom they could develop the complex project. And, because foreigners may not travel in China without a "host," they asked for one. Chinatex, the Chinese Textile Corporation, which controls the export of all fabrics and garments, became Bloomingdale's "host corporation," their entrée to the intricacies of doing business under the constraints of the People's Republic.

Now that the door had been opened, Bloomingdale's had to make sure it wanted to step inside. So it began sending groups of its personnel to China—executives, buyers, and fashion coordinators—to explore Chinese resources in depth. Their mission was twofold: to see what merchandise was already available, and to find out what original items the Chinese manufacturers would be willing and able to produce for the store.

The pivotal trip occurred in February 1979 when a group of eleven Bloomingdaler's went to make the crucial assessment. With Carl Levine in charge, the group also included Julian Tomchin, Bloomingdale's brand new director of home furnishing's fashion. Tomchin, a textile and industrial designer who had been closely associated with the store for more than ten years (he designed the 1972 shopping bag that celebrated the creation of bloomingtype), was hired the day after Christmas 1978, to centralize the fashion coordination of all facets of the home furnishings department. Over the next five weeks, on the store's behalf, he made two trips to Paris (one for just a weekend) and one to California, and in February he found himself in China.

The group flew to Hong Kong, took a train to the edge of the New Territories, walked over a bridge and into a huge official building (wondering anxiously what was being done with their luggage), and emerged on the other side in Sumchin, across the border—in mainland China. That's when the fun began.

As the Chinese tried, in their extraordinarily courteous way, to entertain their guests, the Bloomingdale's troop tried, without hurting anyone's feelings, to explain that they were there to *work,* not just sightsee. Everywhere they went, the streets were crowded with people. ("Every corner looked like Fifty-ninth and Lexington.") These people stared at the visitors with open and unabashed curiosity. In our culture it's rude to point. In China, such curiosity is part of social convention. The Bloomingdale's group became accustomed to Chinese strangers walking right up to them, peering into their faces, and smiling. Individuals would stop them in the streets, so they could practice their English. Equipped as they were with guides and

Julian Tomchin spotted these wooden buckets in Guilin, but it took months to find out where they were made. He thought they'd make nice planters; the Chinese use them for manure.

Carved wooden doors in Shanghai's Antiques Warehouse. Marvin Traub liked them for their decorative value, and Bloomingdale's will try to import them.

translators, Tomchin nonetheless says, "There's no point of reference in China to anything we're familiar with. You have to start from scratch. It's like going to Mars." Americans used to all-night restaurants quickly learned to eat as much as they could at the three daily meals, because no between-meal or after-dinner snacks were available. And although the food was generally excellent, it was also . . . unusual. Levine remembers having a marvelous dinner in Canton. Afterward, he asked the government guide the name of the excellent chicken dish they had eaten. The guide looked puzzled as Levine explained just which dish he meant. "Oh," said the guide. "That was dog."

In Canton, Tomchin and buyer Ron Klein found stacks of small baskets nested within one another. In true Bloomingdale's fashion, the two decided there was a much better way to use them: turn them over, still stacked, wire the inverted pile, and turn the whole into a lamp base. A Chinese standing nearby overheard their conversa-

tion, and interrupted them. He knew English and could understand their words, but the concept was incomprehensible: What did baskets have to do with lamp bases? Tomchin explained, demonstrated, and explained some more. Finally, light dawned in the man's eyes.

A few days later, Mr. Liu, head of the Canton branch of the National Arts and Crafts Export Corporation (which includes both baskets and lamps under its domain), approached Tomchin and Klein and asked them to give his members a lecture on lamps. So they did.

Under normal (for us) circumstances, one can sympathize with the difficulty the Chinese had in visualizing a bunch of upside-down baskets as a lamp base. From their point of view, the situation was even more outlandish. The country's internal problems during the 1940s effectively cut

Vases in the Shanghai Antiques Warehouse

A vase in Guangzhou (Canton). Bloomingdale's hopes to import them as lamp bases.

them off from the Western world, so that they stopped getting design input from the West in the thirties. Since that time, they have continued to produce merchandise, especially for export, in their version of 1930s art deco. Although Central Europe has been dealing with China since the fifties, Bloomingdale's provided among the first really new design ideas they had had in forty years.

Tomchin found much Chinese merchandise to be adequate, but *familiar*. There were no surprises. "We can sell six times more of the familiar as long as we also provide merchandise that is *new*. Our customer expects it from us!"

So the group set about trying to create new items. They also sought very old items—antiques. And one day, Carl Levine arranged for a trip to see some antique brass and pottery. Everyone was invited to come along, but Amy Wall didn't want to go.

Amy Wall, the junior member of the entourage, is the group manager of certain bedding areas (things like decorative pillows and bedspreads). No one was paying too much attention to bedding; they all wanted to see things like jade and Ming vases and dragons. (In truth, each was seeking merchandise for his or her own area.) So Amy Wall talked to one of the guides and got herself and the group invited to a down (feather) factory. For some unaccountable reason, the rest of the group chose to look at the antiques, so she was left to visit the factory alone.

Now, Amy Wall is a statuesque five feet eight, with blond hair and blue eyes, and is in her mid-twenties. When she was first introduced to Mr. Wu, Bloomingdale's chief liaison, he had affectionately dubbed her "The Great Wall." Dressed in her black coat and red cowboy boots, she and the inevitable interpreter went to see a down factory just outside the city. When they arrived, they were handed white robes to put over their clothing. The Chinese are, as a rule, of small stature. Wall's smock came to her knees; beneath it protruded her bright red boots. Further armed with a shower cap and surgical mask, she and the interpreter were led into the unheated factory—where workers turned, stared, rushed up to look at her, then bent low to peer at her boots.

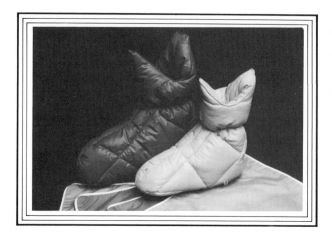

Wall tried to explain some ideas for merchandise she was interested in. It turned out that her interpreter could only understand her if she spoke very, very slowly. "I had to put myself on thirty-three instead of seventy-eight," she chatters in her normal machine-gun speech. She took a look at the factory's merchandise catalog, then carefully explained that she wanted them to modify one of their items: booties. Down-filled, warm-as-toast booties.

"The ones they had looked like Neil Armstrong's space boots," she lamented, and what she wanted were cute, funny, happy booties. And the colors. "They showed me light blue, light pink, and white." She wanted "hot" colors, and eventually found a bright blue, red, and yellow, which the factory normally used for its sleeping bags. Now all she needed was a pattern, and she had to supply it. So she took out a pencil and sketched a pattern. Then she traced her own foot to establish a size, handed pattern and footprint to the factory's foreman, and went back to the hotel, wondering what, if anything, would come of the whole venture.

The next day, the representative of the Animal Byproducts Corporation (who else would be in charge of down?) contacted Wall: a sample pair of booties was ready. She took a look. The practical Chinese had created a rugged little boot, complete with a sole. No, not quite what she had in mind. So they tried again—and that time, they got it. The final bootie was adorable, and warm enough to insulate the coldest foot, even against Shanghai's chill. Now Wall would need a full set of samples: three pairs, one in each color, one in each size—small, medium and large—to take back to New York. How do you indicate American sizes to a factory in Shanghai? You go back to the Bloomingdale's group and measure everybody's feet, that's how, and after you've found people with what seem to be representative foot sizes, you draw three pairs of footprints: small, medium, and large. The people at the factory thought the penciled outlines were a fine guide to produce the rest of the samples.

The Bloomingdale's scouting party returned to New York a few weeks later, optimistic that there was a large base of viable merchandise to import, and that the Chinese would try very hard to develop new merchandise in conjunction with the store. And so, in March 1979, Traub and

Schoff made the final decision: Bloomingdale's would do a China import fair in the fall of 1980.

Over the next year and a half, the store's fashion coordinators and buyers kept up a constant shuttle between New York and China. As they ordered merchandise (or had it made), it would be shipped, arriving intermittently in New York. When two pairs of Wall's bootie samples arrived, the advertising department fell in love with them and decided to begin to market them before the actual promotion began. They would appear in the 1979 Christmas catalog. There was only one problem; only a red pair and a yellow pair had arrived in New York. There was no sample of the blue pair. Dozens of Telexes flew back and forth; no blue booties. Finally the Shanghai factory found what seemed to it to be a solution to the problem. There was another Bloomingdale's group in China; they would give the sample to them.

In Beijing, Traub meets with Mr. Chia Shih, vice-minister of foreign trade. To explain what Bloomingdale's means by an import fair, Traub carried albums of the India and Israel promotions and showed them to officials throughout China.

So Amy Wall received a final Telex from Shanghai: "Gave sample to M. Traub." And Marvin Traub wound up carrying the blue booties back to New York. The cozy creations were the hit of the Christmas season; in fact, the first shipment of 500 pairs sold out within one week of their arrival.

In July 1979, Marvin Traub made his first trip to China, accompanied by his wife, Lee. Traub had already drafted a six-page agreement that spelled out precisely what Bloomingdale's and China would do for each other. He had it translated in Hong Kong, then went on to Beijing (Peking) where he met with the vice-minister of trade. On July 4, representatives of the ministry met with Traub to go over the document line by line. They signed it the next evening at a formal banquet, but the agreement is symbolically dated July 4. (It is interesting to note that the United States did not sign a trade agreement with China until two days after the Bloomingdale's-China pact.)

Traub met with Leonard Woodcock, the U.S. ambassador to China, who was very pleased with the whole situation. Traub also invited Fox Butterfield to the celebratory banquet. Butterfield is chief of the *New York Times* bureau in Beijing, and he was staying at the same hotel as Marvin and Lee Traub, but it took two days to find that out, because his name was listed under the letter *F* on the hotel directory. (The Chinese place the family name first and the given name afterward.)

Because he likes to know the customs of each country he visits, Traub had done extensive reading about China before his trip. But it isn't easy to remember cultural differences. He was all right during that first dinner in Beijing, but a few evenings later, at a dinner in Canton, he got involved in a conversation and forgot one of the local customs. "If you are a guest of honor at dinner," he explained, "no one will eat until you do. I wondered why no one was eating, until I realized it was my fault."

Spools of silk yarn in Hangzhou

Besides getting the agreement signed, Traub was in China to feel it out, to get a gestalt of the people, the merchandise, the place, the possibilities for promotion and display. He rarely buys merchandise himself, but is forever considering new ideas. He and Lee were accompanied by Julian Tomchin (who was by then making his third China trip in five months) and by Dennis Wong, head of Bloomingdale's Hong Kong office, and his wife.

In Soochow, about an hour by train from Shanghai, they visited the factory that does the embroidery on silk fabric for the Beijing Opera. After the group admired the handiwork, the time came to go. But the head of the factory was eager to have them place an order. "What can we make for you?" she asked. "Show us what you need."

Tomchin pulled out his ever-present sketch pad (he recorded all of his trips in sketches and snapshots) and roughed out some ideas for decorative pillows. Traub was fascinated. (As Tomchin recalled, "After days of me watching him, he was finally watching *me* work.") Six weeks later, Tomchin returned to Shanghai and asked someone to contact the factory in Soochow to see what was happening with the embroidery. An official smiled and presented a whole line of samples, ready and waiting.

Tomchin carried them back and showed them to Traub. "I'll never forget the expression of fatherdom on Traub's face when he saw them," Tomchin recalls. Well, that may be just a bit exaggerated, but certainly many of Bloomingdale's executives get a great kick out of seeing the items they create become realities. And they originated widely divergent types of merchandise in China.

Bloomingdale's created a pattern for a fine porcelain dinner set, based on an eighteenth-century design. They explored the possibilities of Cinnabar, the technique of carving heavily lacquered objects. Most of the carvings were beautiful but much too fussy. Finally, Tomchin found one simple carved box; then the store worked for months to provide detailed sketches so that the Chinese could develop a whole desk collection—everything from picture frames to pen holders—in that pattern. They located a source for the cooking equipment actually used in China, as opposed to the much less interesting items normally exported. They selected artifacts from the Imperial Palace

Bloomingdale's held a contest for the best poster design. Since Chinese newspapers carry only official news stories, the contest was announced by notices posted on an "information wall," a public bulletin board. The winning poster was designed by a Shanghai artist.

and asked to have them reproduced.

There would be two major furniture collections. Rattan items would come from China itself. But the store also invited Baker to make a major hardwood collection, and they agreed to produce, in dark ash, copies of sixteenth- and seventeenth-century Chinese designs.

At a gift shop in the Imperial City in Beijing, Traub examines a piece of art. Beside him is his translator, Mr. Tsung, and at the extreme right is Dennis Wong, Bloomingdale's Hong Kong representative.

Bloomingdale's also imported one-of-a-kind pieces of antique furniture, scrolls, embroidered silk, jewelry, and a great deal of art.

"We think China will be important in the future," Traub says, "an important source of merchandise for Bloomingdale's. We are establishing it as a base." As with all the other countries that have starred in a Bloomingdale's presentation, the store intends to maintain an ongoing interest. The huge import fair is in part to introduce the store's customers to this new merchandise, and partly to urge China to gear up to a high level of production.

And after the fair is over, the buyers and fashion coordinators will go back, to continue developing and importing Chinese merchandise.

One day, right in the midst of the planning and preparations for the Chinese promotion, the head of the African Trade Mission approached Glynn to discuss the possibility of Bloomingdale's staging an African import fair sometime in the near future. The two spoke cordially for a while, then the dignitary left. Glynn returned to her desk.

A few moments later, Mary Liska, her longtime secretary, walked into the office and found Glynn staring into space.

"What's the matter?" Mary asked.

And Glynn—Mary Joan Glynn, who deals with popes, queens, and Marvin Traub with imperturbable equanimity—shook her head wonderingly.

"We no longer deal in countries," she said softly. "Bloomingdale's now deals in continents."

Illustration Credits

The Bloomingdale family graciously made available to me its personal archives, for illustrations of the early years of the business. Bloomingdale's itself most kindly allowed me to use many pictures of the store and its advertisements and displays.

The Bloomingdale Family: all pictures in Part 1; page 65; second color section, page 1, left.

Bloomingdale's: 69; 73, top left; 75, left; 77, left; 92, bottom middle; 99; 104, top left; 106; 114; 115; 116, right; 117; 118; 126, top left; 133; 135; 146; 148; 164; 182, bottom; second color section, page 1, right, pages 2, 3, 4; 216, top left, bottom, first two pictures; 218; 220; 227.

I am also grateful to the following individuals and businesses for permission to use their designs, photographs, or illustrations.

Clayton Adams: 224.

Antonio: 121; 122; 180; second color section, page 4, top left and center, bottom center.

Allen Arpadi: 116, left; 137, top; 138; 166, top.

Brian Burdine: second color section, page 4, bottom left, bottom right.

Guy Bourdin: 187.

Fabian Bachrach: 216, top middle and right.

Edgar de Evia: 155; 156; 157; 158; first color section, page 2, bottom, page 3.

Willo Font: 194; 195; 197; 198; 204; 205; 206; first color section, page 4.

Alexandre Georges: 97.

Lois Kiener: 102

Jonah Kinigstein: second color section, page 2, top center and right.

Bruce Laurance: 181; second color section, page 3, top right.

Siegfried Liebmann: 91, top and bottom left, bottom right.

Merchandise Display News: 92, top right.

Richard Martino: second color section, page 2, middle left.

Pach Brothers: 216, bottom right, two pictures.

Paramount Pictures: 213; 214.

Pernold Photography: 101.

Leonard Restivo: second color section, page 2, bottom left.

Dan Reisinger: second color section, page 4, middle center, middle right; 201, right.

Pierre Scherman: 9; 10; 11; 12; 126, top right, middle, bottom; 136; 137, bottom; 141, top; 144; 149; 152; 165; 166, bottom; 168; 169; 170; 174; 176; 177; 184; 189, top left; 190, top right; 200; 201, left; 202; 203; 207; 208; 209; 210.

Ron Schwerin: 141, right; 145, top right, bottom right.

Richard Averill Smith: 71; 72; 73, bottom left, bottom right, top right, middle right; 75, right; 76; 77, top right, bottom right; 78; 80; 81; 82; 84; 85; 86; first color section, page 1, page 2, top and middle; 153.

Lawrence Stein: 139; 143; 145, left; 189, top right, middle, bottom; 190, top left, middle, bottom.

Retail Reporting Bureau: 89; 91, top right, middle right; 92, bottom left, bottom right; 94.

Virginia Roehl: 67; 92, top left.

Roedel Photography: 100; 103; 104, bottom left, top right.

Julian Tomchin: 182, top; 219; 222; 223; 225; 226; 228.

Michaele Vollbracht: second color section, page 2, bottom center, bottom right, page 3, top left.

Arnand Zaveri: second color section, page 4, top right; 199.

The following models appear in illustrations in the book: Lisa Cooper, Ford Models, Inc., 181, bottom (woman at left); Debbie Dickinson, Elite Model Management Corp., 187; Janice Dickinson, Elite Model Management Corp., 181, bottom (woman in center); Patti Hansen, Wilhelmina Model Agency, 181, top; Yasmine, Elite Model Management Corp., second color section, page 3, top right.